# CRIME HAS ITS HEROES

## Books by H. Montgomery Hyde

The Central Criminal Court (The Old Bailey)
From a photograph taken about 1930

# CRIME HAS ITS HEROES

## H. Montgomery Hyde

Constable London

First published in Great Britain 1976
by Constable and Company Ltd
10 Orange Street London WC2H 7EG
Copyright © 1976 by Harford Productions Ltd

ISBN 0 09 461550 0

Set in Monotype Imprint 11pt.
Printed in Great Britain
by Ebenezer Baylis and Son Ltd
The Trinity Press, Worcester, and London

Le crime a ses héros; l'erreur a ses martyrs:
Du vrai zèle et du faux vains juges que nous sommes!

Voltaire *Henriade* (1723)

# Contents

# Illustrations

There are 61 illustrations, which appear between pages 116 and 117 and depict various scenes and characters from the cases described.

# Preface

The twenty criminal trials described here span roughly the last quarter of the nineteenth century and the first half of the present century. Some are better known than others, just as some resulted in conviction and others in acquittal. Twelve are concerned with murder; the remainder with a variety of offences including fraud, perjury, forgery, bribery and corruption, espionage and sabotage, annoying women in a public place, and disclosing confidential information in breach of the Official Secrets Act. Ten of the cases were tried in British courts, eight in America, one in France, and one in Holland. The murders, which form rather more than half the total of the cases tried, were carried out by a variety of means, including shooting, poisoning, knifing, battering, burning, and drowning. The cases have been specially chosen for their human interest, legal implications, and, particularly as regards the better known trials, for the fresh details which have subsequently come to light. Two of the trials took place largely or wholly *in camera*, and it is only recently that most of what transpired in the court room under cover of secrecy has become available. All the trials command attention for one reason or another.

Some of the accounts have previously appeared in part-work form and I am grateful to the publishers of *Crimes and Punishment*, Phoebus Publishing Co. and BPC Publishing Ltd., for their permission to include them in this book together with the illustrations.

H.M.H.

# Butcher or Baronet?

In England there used to be a special form of proceeding for criminal trials of exceptional importance. It was known as a trial at bar, and took place with two or more judges presiding, with a special jury possessing a property qualification as householders. Such a trial opened in Westminster Hall on 23 April 1873 before the Lord Chief Justice of England Sir Alexander Cockburn, Mr Justice Mellor and Mr Justice Lush, when thirty-nine-year-old Arthur Orton, alias Thomas Castro, alias Sir Roger Tichborne, was prosecuted for perjury in respect of allegedly false evidence he had given in an earlier civil action. In a trial at bar there was no dock and the accused was accommodated at a table in the well of the court. On this occasion he was a man of considerable bulk, weighing over 330 pounds, with a large round face and an abundance of fair and rather wavy hair. He rose and bowed to the judges in their dark blue robes, salmon-coloured silk sleeves and round fur tippets as they took their places on the bench, but they did not return his salutation. Close by him sat his leading counsel Dr Edward Kenealy, a rumbustious Irishman, who since he was a Queen's Counsel had to obtain a special dispensation from Queen Victoria to appear for the defence. The prosecuting team was led by Henry Hawkins, QC, an excellent criminal lawyer, later Lord Brampton and nicknamed somewhat unjustly 'Hanging Hawkins' when he was on the bench.

The prosecutor's opening speech to the jury, in which he recounted at length the story of the accused and his crimes, which Hawkins described as being 'as black and foul as Justice ever raised her sword to strike', occupied five-and-a-half days and was a fitting prelude to the longest criminal trial in English history, lasting as it did for 188 days in all and not finishing until 28 February 1874. The costs of this extraordinary trial were enormous, those of the defence being largely met by public subscription, since the accused, who claimed to be Sir Roger Doughty-Tichborne, twelfth baronet, had many sympathisers. Indeed public opinion was largely divided on the question whether the Tichborne claimant, as he was generally known, was the twelfth baronet or simply an impostor.

The accused was not the man he claimed to be, said Hawkins, but an adventurer named Arthur Orton, who came from Wapping in London's East End docks where his father was a butcher. On the other hand, the Doughty-Tichbornes were an old Roman Catholic family of considerable wealth, whose seat was at Tichborne Park, Alresford, in Hampshire. The real Roger Charles Doughty-Tichborne was born in Paris in 1829. His father, James Doughty-Tichborne, later the tenth baronet, seems to have been a good-natured but dull English squire, very much dominated by his half-French wife. The latter was a natural daughter of a Princess de Bourbon-Conti by an Englishman of good family and a Member of Parliament named Henry Seymour, of Knoyle, Wiltshire; on the other hand, she was a spoiled beauty, capricious, possessive, jealous, hating her English relatives and determined to bring up Roger and his younger brother Alfred as Frenchmen. However, Roger's father succeeded in getting him to England where he spent three years at Stonyhurst, the well-known public school for Catholic boys, before going into the army, which he did against his mother's wishes. He eventually sent in his papers because he had failed to obtain the transfer to an Indian regiment he wanted.

By this time Roger had fallen in love with his cousin Katharine Doughty, who was an heiress in her own right. But when he told her mother Lady Doughty, who was his aunt by marriage, he met with determined opposition. For one thing, Roger and Katharine were first cousins, which is a prohibited degree for marriage in the Church of Rome, although dispensations are sometimes granted. Then Roger was an excessive smoker, and also had a taste for alcohol and naughty French novels which alarmed the prudish Lady Doughty, who was a daughter of Lord Arundell of Wardour, head of another old Catholic family. On the other hand, Roger was the heir to a considerable estate, and his wife would be the female head of the Doughty-Tichborne family. Accordingly Lady Doughty and her husband Sir Edward proposed that until she came of age Katharine, who was their only surviving child and heiress to the Doughty estates, should not be bound in any way to Roger and should be free to choose any other eligible husband, notwithstanding which Roger should consider himself engaged to her. Although he was deeply in love with Katharine, Roger in effect rejected this one-sided proposal and in the manner of disappointed lovers of those times planned a long voyage to foreign parts, in this instance South America and Mexico. The last time he saw Katharine before leaving England he gave her a copy of a paper in which he vowed to build a church to the Holy Virgin at Tichborne if they were married 'before three years are over at the latest'. He told her that he had given the original to Vincent Gosford, the land agent at Tichborne and his closest friend, but that Gosford did not know that he was giving her a copy.

In January 1853, Roger Tichborne sailed for Valparaiso, which he reached on 19 June. Shortly after his arrival in that port he received news from England that his uncle Sir James Doughty, Katharine's father, who had been born Tichborne and had assumed the surname Doughty on succeeding to the Doughty estates in Lincolnshire and Surrey, had died. This meant that Roger's father James, who was Sir Edward's younger brother, inherited Tichborne Park, as well as the baronetcy, thus becoming the tenth baronet and being known as Sir James Doughty-Tichborne.

For the next twelve months or so, Roger travelled in Chile, crossed the Andes from Santiago to Buenos Aires, and eventually made his way to Rio de Janeiro. After writing home for money to be sent to him in Jamaica, where he intended to call on his way to Mexico, he embarked at Rio on 20 April 1854 in the good ship *Bella* bound for New York. Four days later, another vessel picked up some pieces of wreckage including a long boat bearing the name *Bella*, from which it was assumed that the *Bella* had foundered with all hands. No further authentic news of her was ever heard, and the underwriters paid the insurance. Meanwhile Roger's will, which he had executed before leaving England, was admitted to probate. With one exception his death was acknowledged by the members of his family, including his cousin

Katharine who got married, in 1854, to Sir James Radcliffe, a baronet with an estate in Yorkshire. The exception who cherished the notion that Roger was still alive was his mother, now Lady Tichborne; and any old salt who turned up at Tichborne with a tale, no matter how improbable, that the *Bella*'s passengers and crew had been saved, was certain of getting money from her.

In 1862, Sir James Doughty-Tichborne died, and was succeeded by his younger son Alfred, who assumed the title and estates. Alfred had recently married his cousin Teresa Arundell and hoped she would produce an heir to carry on the Doughty-Tichborne line. However, the Dowager Lady Tichborne refused to recognise Alfred as the heir and caused advertisements in English, French and Spanish to be inserted in *The Times* and various overseas newspapers, asking for 'any clue' of Roger and any other survivors of the *Bella* and promising 'a handsome reward for any well-authenticated particulars'. She then took up her residence again in Paris.

The prosecutor summarised the case against the accused in the following words:

In the year 1854, Roger Charles Tichborne, the heir to a baronetcy and to great estates, was believed to have perished at sea; no tidings of him were received, nor of any of those who were supposed to have shared his fate, for eleven long years, at the expiration of which time the Defendant, who was then living at Wagga-Wagga in New South Wales, came forth from the shambles and announced himself as the long-lost heir and entitled to a baronetcy and a rent roll of somewhere about £25,000 a year.

His claim was resisted, and in order to establish it, proceedings were taken in the Court of Chancery, and also by an action of ejectment, for the purpose of recovering the family mansion [Tichborne House]; and in the course of those proceedings the Defendant swore, first of all, that he was Roger Charles Tichborne who was supposed to have been drowned; secondly, in order to give apparent colour and confirmation to that statement, he swore that he had in July or August 1852, whilst upon a visit to his uncle Sir Edward Doughty at Tichborne House, basely seduced his uncle's daughter, his own cousin; and, thirdly, it being suggested that the defendant was Arthur

Orton, the son of a butcher at Wapping, the Defendant swore that he was not that person. . . .

Each of these assertions is alleged to be false, and is charged in the indictment as perjury wickedly and corruptly committed by the Defendant.

It was established that Arthur Orton was born in Wapping in 1834, being the youngest of the butcher George Orton's twelve children, so that he was five years younger than Roger Tichborne. At the age of fifteen he went to sea but deserted his ship on reaching Valparaiso. He then made his way up country to Melipilla, where he remained for the next eighteen months, receiving much kindness from a family named Castro. He returned to England in 1851 and entered his father's business, becoming an expert slaughterman. However, he was restless, and in the following year he emigrated to Australia, landing in Hobart, Tasmania, where for a time he worked as a butcher's assistant. After a while he moved to the Australian mainland, where he was occupied in a variety of ways, as stockman, mail-rider, and also, it was believed, as bushranger and horse-thief. He eventually turned up at Wagga-Wagga, under the name of Thomas Castro, which he took from the family who had befriended him in Chile. Here he worked again as a butcher's assistant and for a time as a butcher on his own account until he failed. While in Wagga-Wagga, in 1864, he married an illiterate domestic servant named Ann Bryant, who already had a child, declaring himself at the wedding ceremony to be Thomas Castro, a Chilean and a native of Chile, and giving his age as thirty, which was the correct age of Arthur Orton but not that of Roger Tichborne, assuming him to be alive.

At this time a man in Melbourne named Cubitt was in the habit of advertising in the London *Times* the virtues of his 'Missing Friends' Office in Australia'. In May 1865, the Dowager Lady Tichborne saw the advertisement and at once wrote to Cubitt, asking for his assistance in discovering the whereabouts of her missing son. The description she gave of him was this:

Roger Charles Tichborne is at present thirty-two years of age. . . . He is of delicate constitution, rather tall and thin, with very light brown hair and blue eyes.

Cubitt promptly advertised to this effect in the Australian newspapers, except that the words 'and thin' were omitted from the description, doubtless by accident. It may also be noted that Lady Tichborne erroneously stated Roger's age to be thirty-two, whereas it would have been thirty-six. Otherwise the Tichborne claimant, who was thirty-one and stout in build, might never have come forward, and a huge amount of time, trouble and expense would have been avoided.

Meanwhile the man in Wagga-Wagga who passed under the name of Thomas Castro was in financial difficulties, and an attorney named Gibbes to whom he went for assistance advised him to file his petition in the Insolvent Court. The debtor asked Gibbes whether he would be obliged to disclose any property to which he was entitled or in which he had an interest in the south of England. He told the attorney that the property was in Hampshire. He had a friend in Wagga-Wagga who came from this county and never tired of extolling its scenic beauties, and the merits of its gentry, and this may be why he picked on Hampshire.

Shortly after this conversation, the attorney saw Cubitt's advertisement, and recollecting his client's question about the property in Hampshire, the next time he saw him he asked, 'Shall I call you out loud by your real name?'

The man whom Gibbes knew as Tom Castro was smoking a wooden pipe at the time, which he thrust under the lawyer's nose. 'Are those the initials?' he asked. Carved on the underneath part of the bowl were the initials 'RCT'. Asked whether he had had the pipe 'ever since' Orton replied that he had only cut the initials about twelve months previously. Orton pretended to be upset that his real identity had been recognised, but this was apparently only a ploy since he now proceeded to borrow money from the lawyer.

Gibbes immediately wrote off to Cubitt, and the latter lost no time in letting Lady Tichborne know that he was on the eve of an important discovery. The unfortunate woman urged Cubitt to send Roger home to her at once, and told him that there was a Negro in Sydney named Bogle, who had been Sir Edward Doughty's valet for many years, and that he could help to establish the missing heir's identity; she also wrote to Bogle herself. A meeting between the two men duly took place in the Metropole Hotel, Sydney, at first without any recognition on either side. But eventually the allegedly missing heir appeared to recognise the old family servant. At the beginning Bogle was not quite convinced, but he was finally persuaded when he was engaged to accompany the claimant to England.

A lengthy correspondence ensued, the tone and substance of which should have put the old lady on her guard; but with an almost insane eagerness she made up her mind before seeing a single line of his handwriting that Tom Castro was her son. Nor was she put off by his illiterate letters, which contained some extraordinary statements such as that he had a brown mark on his side, which the real Roger never had, and that he had been involved in a case of cheating at cards in Brighton, an affair with which Roger had no connection. Eventually, in response to one letter, Lady Tichborne sent him £400 to cover his expenses for the voyage home, which he was able to supplement by raising a further sum from a local bank on the strength of his expectations. Before sailing from Sydney with his wife and the faithful Bogle as he did in September 1866, he made a will in which he left 'to my mother Lady Hannah Frances Tichborne the whole of my property in the isle of Wight'. Lady Tichborne always signed herself 'H. F. Tichborne'; however, the initials did not stand for Hannah Frances, as the claimant had wrongly guessed, but for Henriette Felicité. Also neither the testator nor any of the Tichbornes owned any property in the Isle of Wight. There was a similar non-existent bequest of 'the Hermitage estate', although it may be noted in passing that there was a Hermitage Wharf and a Hermitage Street in Wapping.

The claimant arrived by slow boat in London on Christmas Day 1866, his uncouth behaviour and misplaced aspirates having aroused much amusement on board as coming from an English baronet. Asked where they should put up, Bogle volunteered the information, which the real Sir Roger would unquestionably have known, that they should go to Ford's Hotel, Manchester Square. 'That's where the family always went,' said Bogle. Although it was Christmas Day and bitterly cold, the claimant left his wife and comfortable hotel immediately after dinner and took a cab to Wapping. After finding the Orton house in the High Street shut up, he made a number of inquiries in the neighbourhood about the family, sending in to one woman on whom he called a visiting card inscribed 'William H. Stephens, Australia'. The woman's reaction was immediate. 'Are you an Orton,' she asked her visitor. 'You look so like old George Orton!' This the visitor denied, but said he was a great friend of Arthur Orton, whom he described as one of the wealthiest men in Australia, adding that he was an Australian reported on his way to Ireland to investigate the Fenian conspiracy.

A few days later, the real Arthur Orton, who had never been in Hampshire in his life, went down to Alresford, where he put up at the Angel Inn as 'Mr Taylor of London'. By a stroke of luck the landlord of the Angel, a man named Rous, used to be employed as a clerk with the solicitors for the Tichborne and Doughty estates, Dunn & Hopkins. How Rous was won over is unclear, but he was soon driving the claimant to Tichborne Park where he saw the paternal mansion for the first time. Next day the claimant telegraphed Bogle in London to come down, and he spread the news around so cleverly that about three hundred people turned out to welcome the old Negro who was remembered affectionately in the neighbourhood. From the moment Bogle arrived, 'Mr Taylor' became 'Sir Roger', since Bogle proclaimed his belief that this indeed was the long-lost Tichborne heir.

Roger's younger brother Alfred, the eleventh baronet, had died eleven months previously. His wife was pregnant at the time and three months later she gave birth to a son and heir called Henry and referred to in the subsequent legal proceedings as 'the rightful heir', which indeed he was, although he had been born posthumously as the twelfth baronet. Shortly afterwards Teresa, Lady Doughty-Tichborne and her infant son moved out of the big house, which was let for a term of years to a Colonel Lushington.

Although Roger's mother had asked the claimant to come direct to Paris from Australia without going to England and seeing any of the family there, it was not until the end of January that he crossed the Channel. Instead of going to see her, he feigned illness, so that she came to his hotel where the meeting took place in a darkened room, the claimant lying muffled up and fully dressed on his bed with his face towards the wall. After leaning over and kissing him, she said, 'This is my son.' Mr Hopkins, the family solicitor, who was present, thereupon called in a servant and told him, 'You are a witness that she recognises him', and the old lady assented. Unsatisfactory as this identification was, she never departed from this belief until the day of her death eighteen months later. At the same time she accepted the claimant's wife and children and made him an allowance of £1,000 a year.

The conversion of Hopkins to the claimant's cause carried a lot of weight, since he was greatly trusted in the district, as did that of a local historian named Baigent, who had made a particular study of the Tichborne family pedigree. They were joined by the local MP, Mr Guilford Onslow, as well as by Colonel Lushington and others among the Hampshire gentry, while the villagers almost to a man hailed the claimant as the missing heir. Helped by Bogle and others, the claimant succeeded in eliciting a large number of facts which he used to remarkable effect. He was further aided by old Lady Tichborne, who let him peruse all the real Roger's letters and diaries, which the claimant used to supplement and embroider the account he gave of his own wanderings and adventures. He also took into his employment a couple of old carabineers, who had been servants of Roger Tichborne, and in a short time what he gleaned from them, added to his own tenacious memory, made him so completely master of the small details of regimental life that more than a dozen of Roger's brother officers not to mention many more private soldiers were convinced of the claimant's identity.

On the other hand, apart from Lady Tichborne in Paris, the rest of the family were convinced that the claimant was an impostor. This view was confirmed among others by Vincent Gosford, who to test the claimant asked him about the contents of the 'sealed package' which Roger Tichborne had left with him. The claimant said he had no recollection of it, whereupon Gosford tried to refresh his memory by saying that it contained directions or something of the kind to Miss Katharine Doughty. Again the claimant could not remember. Gosford added that although he had destroyed the paper he could recall its contents perfectly, and he politely intimated to the local banker, whose guests they were at dinner, that in his opinion the claimant could not be Sir Roger Tichborne.

In due course the claimant began a friendly action for ejectment against Colonel Lushington, and bills in chancery were also filed against the trustees of the Tichborne estate for possession. After some delay, the court directed that the issue should be tried in the Court of Common Pleas as to whether the claimant was the heir of the late Sir James Doughty-Tichborne. The trial of this action, which took place before Chief Justice Bovill, lasted for 102 days, between 11 May 1871 and 5 March 1872.

Asked in cross-examination by Sir John Coleridge, the Solicitor-General, who led for the trustees, about the contents of the 'sealed package' which he had previously stated had referred to an event which he hoped had not happened, the claimant declared that the event in question was the possible 'confinement of my cousin'. This produced a great sensation in court, particularly since Katharine, now Lady Radcliffe, and her husband were both present.

'Do you mean to swear before the judge and jury,' Coleridge went on, 'that you seduced this lady?'

'I most solemnly to my God swear that I did,' answered the claimant.

Counsel immediately produced the copy of the paper which had been given to Katharine Doughty and which was solely concerned with the late Roger Tichborne's vow to build a church and contained no reference whatever to any seduction.

It might be thought that this exposure would have finished the claimant, at any rate as far as the civil action was concerned. But the case went on until after Coleridge had opened the defence in scathing terms. 'The first sixteen years of his life,' the Solicitor-General said of the claimant, 'he had absolutely forgotten, while the few facts he had told the jury were either already proved or would be shown to be absolutely false and fabricated. Of his college life he could recollect nothing. . . . About his amusements, his books, his music, his games, he could tell nothing. Not a word of his family, of the people with whom he lived, their habits, their persons, their very names. . . . When he reappears in 1865 he has undergone a physical and moral miracle: a slight, delicate, under-sized youth has developed into an enormous mass of flesh.'

The first witness called for the defendant trustees was Lord Bellew, a schoolmate of Roger's at Stonyhurst who swore to having tattooed the initials 'RCT' on one of his arms, whereas the claimant denied that he had ever been tattooed and his arms showed no marks. Finally, after several members of the Tichborne and Seymour families had testified, the foreman of the jury rose and informed the court that the jury required to hear no further evidence. The claimant's counsel thereupon declared that his client 'elected to be non-suited'; but the judge ordered his immediate arrest for perjury and he was kept in prison until bail which had been set at £10,000 was forthcoming.

The delay of more than a year between the two trials was due to the fact that in the criminal proceedings stricter proof was required than in the civil action, and consequently evidence which had been taken on commission in France and Australia for the earlier trial was not admissible in the later one where the witnesses were required to testify in person. Lord Bellew repeated his former testimony about the tattoo marks, and the best that the defendant's counsel could do was to attempt to discredit Bellew by obliging him to admit that he had seduced a friend's wife and then eloped with her, having abandoned his own wife. The evidence of the tattooing was corroborated by numerous other witnesses including Lady Doughty and her daughter Katharine who also denied that she had ever been seduced. On his visit to Wapping in 1866 the claimant was shown to have asked in the most minute manner after all the Ortons and to have been identified as an Orton, including among others by an old sweetheart named Mary Anne Loder. In addition, convincing evidence was given by witnesses from Australia that Thomas Castro and Arthur Orton were one and the same person.

For the defence Dr Kenealy called Bogle, Baigent and others who had previously testified for the defendant, although on this later occasion the claimant could not enter the witness box again since at this date defendants in criminal trials were debarred from giving evidence in their own defence. Bogle repeated his earlier sworn statement that Roger Tichborne had no tattoo marks when he left England. Asked by Hawkins how he knew, the old Negro servant said he had seen his arms on three occasions. On each occasion Roger had rolled up his shirt sleeves looking for a flea.

'Same flea?'

'I suppose so.'

'Same time—ten minutes past eleven?'

'Yes,' the witness agreed.

'Then all I can say is,' remarked Hawkins, 'he must have been a very punctual old flea.'

When Baigent was giving detailed testimony about the Tichborne family pedigree, Hawkins's junior whispered, 'We might as well have the first chapter of Genesis and read that!'

'Genesis,' said the leader. 'I want to get to the last chapter of Revelations!'

Part of the defendant's story was that he had been rescued from the *Bella* by another vessel, the *Osprey*, which had gone on to Melbourne, although there were no maritime records showing the arrival of a vessel of that name there at the time stated by the claimant. However, Kenealy produced a certain Jean Luie, who swore that he had been a steward on the *Osprey* and had picked up the claimant in one of the *Bella*'s lifeboats. The claimant then gave his name as Rogers, said Luie, and the witness went on to relate with a wealth of seemingly veracious detail how he had treated him for sunstroke by keeping him continuously drunk on rum.

Unfortunately for this witness his portrait was published in the newspapers and someone who thought he recognised him came into court and after a quick look said, 'Why, this is Sorensen.' Sorensen turned out to be a swindler who had been in prison several times and had served one sentence for bigamy. He soon departed for prison again, this time for perjury.

In his concluding speech to the jury for the defence, Kenealy was so reckless in his remarks that he was reprimanded by the Lord Chief Justice. 'Is there a man in this country who believes this man to be Arthur Orton?' asked Kenealy pointing to his client. 'I believe the universal conviction of the people of England to be the other way.'

'Really you ought not to say that,' the judge broke in. 'We have nothing to do with people out of doors.'

'I hope we have,' retorted Kenealy, adding that if the jury acquitted the claimant they would receive the ovations of their countrymen.

In his summing up, Lord Chief Justice Cockburn severely castigated the defence counsel for using language 'outraging all decency' and really addressed not to the court but to the reporters in order that it might get into the newspapers. 'I am sure that the verdict you will pronounce,' he concluded his charge to the jury, 'will be received on all hands, except by fanatics and fools, as the judgment of twelve men who have brought to the consideration of this great cause the utmost vigilant attention, the most marked intelligence and the most earnest desire to discharge their high and solemn duty, according to what they believe in their hearts and souls to be the truth and justice of the case.'

It only took the jury half an hour, at the end of the longest English criminal trial on record, to find the defendant guilty of perjury. They were all agreed, said the foreman, that the claimant was not Roger Tichborne, but that he was Arthur Orton. On the question of Katharine Doughty (Lady Radcliffe), the jury found that she had not been seduced, and further that there was not the slightest evidence that Roger Tichborne had been guilty of undue familiarity with Miss Doughty on any occasion whatsoever.

The Tichborne claimant was thereupon sentenced to fourteen years' penal servitude. 'The marvellous growth and development of your knowledge as to the circumstances connected with the history of Roger Tichborne, and with the circumstances connected with his military life,' said Mr Justice Mellor to him in passing this unusually heavy sentence, 'leave it uncertain whether your original design was not enlarged by reason of the ease with which you found people ready to become your dupes, and, I fear, your accomplices.'

'Goodbye, Sir Roger! I am sorry for you,' said Kenealy as he shook hands with his client before he was removed in custody, a gesture which was calculated to show that the defence counsel thought that the verdict was wrong and the sentence unjust.

The result of the trial caused great excitement in the country, particularly among the poorer and less-educated members of the community who had subscribed to the defence and believed that the prosecution was the outcome of a conspiracy fomented by the Jesuits. At the present period in time, it may well appear extra-ordinary that the claimant should have deceived so many people so successfully and for so long. But it must be remembered that there was no cable communication between England and Australia in those days and the claimant displayed remarkable skill in using information which he had acquired from one person who had known the real Roger Tichborne to impress another. Popular support for the claimant thrived on the anti-Catholic feeling prevalent at the time and also on an element of class hatred, since the mob instinctively backed his claim to be a gentleman pre-cisely because he was not one, thus in a measure getting their own back on the aristocracy and landed gentry.

The sequel may be briefly told. Dr Kenealy, who had been disbarred for his unprofessional conduct at the criminal trial, continued to agitate for the case to be reopened. In 1875, he was returned to Parliament as MP for Stoke-on-Trent, pledged to advocate the plaintiff's cause. But when a few weeks later he moved in the House of Commons to refer the question to a Royal Commission only a single honourable member voted for his motion, which was rejected by a majority of 432. He failed to secure re-election in 1880 and died shortly afterwards.

In 1884 the claimant was released from prison, having earned full remission. He addressed a few public meetings only to find that people had largely lost interest in his cause. He appeared from time to time as a music hall turn and he also worked in a pub and in a tobacconist's. In 1895, driven by poverty, he signed a confession which he sold to the *People*, a popular Sunday newspaper, in which he admitted that he really was Arthur Orton, and that he had entered into the fraud at first as a lark, but one thing had led to another and his recognition by the half-crazy Dowager Lady Tichborne made him resolve to go on. He was afterwards said to have recanted, and when he died his remains were placed in a coffin engraved 'Sir Roger Charles Doughty Tichborne', together with the date of Roger's birth and his own death, which took place in obscure lodgings in Marylebone, appropriately enough, on April Fool's Day 1898.

In spite of the inscription on his coffin, the once celebrated Tichborne claimant was buried in a nameless grave in Paddington cemetery identified only by the number 1,470 section 2A. The 'rightful heir', Sir Henry Alfred Joseph Doughty-Tichborne, twelfth baronet, whose trustees were obliged to disburse nearly £200,000 in the expenses of the two trials, lived until 1910. His grandson Anthony, born in 1914, succeeded as fourteenth baronet in 1930. Sir Anthony Joseph Henry Doughty-Tichborne was destined to be the last of the line. He died on 18 July 1968, leaving no male heir; and the Tichborne baronetcy, which was one of the first dignities of its kind to be created by King James I in 1621, became extinct.

# The Assassination
# of President Garfield

The tragic episode which led to the trial of the killer of James
Abram Garfield, twenty-first President of the United States, took
place in the ladies' waiting room of the Baltimore and Potomac
Railroad station in Washington DC on 2 July 1881. The President
had not, as it might perhaps appear, been prowling or peeping. He
was merely on his way from the White House to attend the com-
mencement exercises at Williams College, Mass., of which he was
a graduate, and he happened to be passing through the waiting
room which had been fenced off for the occasion of his official
journey. Suddenly a shot rang out followed by another, and the
fifty-nine-year-old President fell to the ground. The man who
fired the shots from the crowd of spectators, who had gathered at
the station expecting to see the President depart for New York,
was promptly seized and taken into custody. He turned out to be a
disappointed office-seeker and lawyer about forty years of age
named Charles Julius Guiteau, who admitted to being a supporter
of the Republican 'Stalwarts', that is the old guard of the Party,
which had unsuccessfully campaigned for the renomination of
General Ulysses Grant as the Republican Presidential candidate
for an unprecedented third term at the last Party Convention.

Guiteau gave as his motive for the shooting his desire to see a
Republican 'Stalwart' as President. 'I am a Stalwart,' he was
heard to exclaim after the second shot. 'Arthur is President now.'
Asked by the police officer who arrested him why he had fired at
the President, Guiteau replied: 'I did it to save the Republican
Party. I am a Stalwart among the Stalwarts. With Garfield out of

the way we can carry all the Northern states and with him in the way we cannot carry a single one.'

The arrested man was of slight build and below the average height. His complexion was described as 'sandy', and he had a moustache, beard and greying chin whiskers. It was ascertained that he had been born at Freeport, Illinois, on 8 September 1841, the son of L. W. Guiteau, a respected member of the local community who was for many years cashier of the Second National Bank of Freeport. Young Guiteau had been sent to Ann Arbor to study at the University of Michigan, but he seems to have been an unsatisfactory student, since he never took a degree, although he afterwards qualified as a lawyer and was admitted to the Chicago Bar. Here he specialised in defending prostitutes, even after contracting syphilis from one of them. He later moved his law practice to New York, where he misappropriated some client's money for which he went to jail. He then joined a strange socialist community at Oneida in New York State and after that became a lay preacher. By the time he was thirty, his father clearly thought him mad. 'I have been ready to believe him capable of almost any folly, stupidity and rascality,' the elder Guiteau wrote of his son at this time. 'Indeed if I was called as a witness upon the stand, I am inclined to think I should testify that he is absolutely insane and is hardly responsible for his acts.' Had he lived, the elder Guiteau would no doubt have testified in this sense at his son's trial, but he died a few weeks after the shooting and before the matter came before the Washington Grand Jury, which it did on 4 October, when a True Bill was returned against Charles Guiteau for the murder of President Garfield.

The luckless President, who to his surprise secured the Republican nomination in the Presidential election in 1880 as a compromise candidate, cancelling out the stronger claims of Grant and Senator James G. Blaine from Maine, had literally trodden the long, hard road from log-cabin to White House, being the son of a poor Ohio farmer who had died when Garfield was a baby, so that he had known real frontier hardship as he grew up. His inauguration as President, following his defeat of the obscure candidate whom the Democrats had chosen as their standard-bearer in the election, took place in March 1881, so that he had enjoyed barely four months of office before he succumbed to Guiteau's bullets. Of these the first had struck Garfield near the left shoulder and had passed out by the shoulder blade, while the second had struck him in the back just above the left kidney. It was this shot which was eventually to prove fatal, although at first it was not thought that the President was in any serious danger. As the summer wore on he began visibly to fail in spite of the exertions of his doctors, and he eventually died on 19 September. He was automatically succeeded as Chief Executive by the Vice-President, Chester A. Arthur, who belonged to the 'Stalwart' branch of the Party.

The trial of Charles Guiteau for the murder of President Garfield began before Judge Walter S. Cox, associate justice of the Supreme Court, in Washington on 14 November 1881. Owing to frequent adjournments mostly occasioned by the prisoner's outrageous behaviour, which turned the proceedings into something of a farce, the trial lasted intermittently for more than two months. The only lawyer whom the prisoner could find to undertake his defence was his former brother-in-law George Scoville, whose sister Guiteau had married. (She was working as librarian in the YMCA in Chicago when Guiteau first met her, but he had deserted her within a year or two of their marriage and she had divorced him.) At the outset of the trial the services of a more senior counsel, Mr Leigh Robinson, were obtained by the defence, but on the opening day after he had formally pleaded not guilty, Guiteau declared that Mr Robinson had been briefed without his knowledge and demanded his retirement from the case. This the judge refused. The prisoner then produced a roll of manuscript and attempted to deliver a speech until stopped by the judge who observed that 'this is not the proper time' for such a recitation. The jury was then empanelled, a long drawn-out process, since many of those on the panel admitted that they had already formed the opinion that Guiteau should be hanged and they consequently had to be stood down. Eventually a liquor dealer named Hamlin was accepted by the defence as the first juror and the remainder of the jury were empanelled at the next day's sitting.

The prisoner continued to object to having Mr Robinson as his leading counsel and succeeded in writing a letter to the newspapers amplifying his objections, an action strongly disapproved of by Scoville. Finally, on the third day of the trial, District Attorney Corkill opened the case for the prosecution and proceeded to call two witnesses who had been present at the time of the shooting. These were James Blaine, who had become Secretary of State in the Garfield administration, and Señor Camacho, the Venezuelan Chargé d'Affaires; each gave his version of what had happened at the railroad station on 2 July.

Guiteau's counsel clashed with another prosecution witness who had seen the shooting when the latter was cross-examined about Guiteau's appearance at the time. 'He had a bad face, according to my opinion,' said this witness.

'I do not want an opinion from you,' snapped Scoville. Nevertheless he got it as the same witness admitted to having frequently and 'most decidedly' expressed the opinion that Guiteau should be hanged. At this some of the jurors nodded approvingly.

Another angry scene occurred when Scoville asked the judge to take measures to prevent his client from giving out unauthorised communications to the Press. This made Guiteau uproarious, abusing the judge, counsel and the court officials. The judge thereupon told him that if he did not keep quiet he would have him removed from court. 'I do not care if you do,' answered the prisoner brazenly. 'The Court of Appeal will reverse your decision and I will get a new trial. You have no right to remove me.' The shouting match terminated with an assurance from the judge that he had indeed authority to remove him and he would certainly do so if Guiteau persisted with his disturbances. Eventually the prisoner quietened down.

On the fifth day, Mr Scoville announced that he wished to change the prisoner's plea to one of insanity, and this was accepted. In the course of his remarks to the bench, the defence counsel stated that his client acknowledged the killing. Immediately Guiteau was on his feet. 'No, your Honour,' he protested. 'We acknowledge the shooting but not the killing.' He went on to say that on 25 July the President's physicians had announced that their patient had not been fatally shot. 'My bullet was not fatal,' Guiteau went on. 'Garfield's death was caused by malpractice. I was only inspired to *shoot* the President. The doctors finished the work. . . . It is the Deity's act, not mine, and I except that He can take care of it. He has taken care of it very well so far.'

When the court adjourned at the end of that day, Guiteau was as usual placed in the prison van to be taken back to the jail where he was being held in the malarial swamps on the banks of the Potomac River. On the way a man on horseback rode alongside the van and quickly discharged two shots directly into the van, taking good aim at the prisoner. One ball passed through his arm, inflicting a painful but not dangerous flesh wound. The assailant then put spurs to his horse and galloped off. He was later caught and proved to be a religious enthusiast called William Jones, who had hitherto been considered a harmless lunatic. A few days later another crackpot patriot named Sergeant Mason took aim at Guiteau through the window of his cell, but the bullet missed its target and flattened itself against the wall.

When the court reconvened next morning, Guiteau attributed his escape to 'the intervention of Providence'. He went on to declare that he was not afraid to die, but he did not want to be 'shot like a dog' until he had vindicated his conduct.

At this stage in the proceedings, Mr Robinson intimated that he had had enough of his eccentric client and asked leave to retire from the case. 'I want Robinson to stay now,' exclaimed Guiteau. But the counsel insisted on withdrawing and the judge allowed him to do so.

When his leader had departed, Mr Scoville rose to open the defence. He said that the plain question for the jury to decide was whether the prisoner had killed President Garfield, and if so whether his mental condition at the time was such as to render him responsible for his action. In developing the argument in favour of his client's insanity, defence counsel claimed that the burden of proof that he was sane at the time rested with the prosecution. 'I never feign,' the prisoner shouted at this point. 'I act myself, sane or insane.'

His counsel went on to refer to Guiteau's career as a lawyer in Chicago, how he had given it up to join the Oneida community, how he had helped the evangelists Dwight L. Moody and Ira Sankey, how he had been an unsuccessful lecturer and writer, and how he had depended on the Lord to pay his debts. Again Guiteau interrupted his counsel to say: 'I left a $5,000 a year law business to serve the Lord. I was happier than ever when I was selling my lectures on the street, for I was working for the Lord.' Later, a defence witness from Boston deposed that when Guiteau came to that city to lecture he boasted that he 'belonged to the firm of Jesus Christ & Co.'

The prisoner's brother John Guiteau and a string of other witnesses, lay and medical, took the stand and stated that in their view the prisoner manifested varying degrees of insanity. A doctor, who had examined him some years previously, stated that he had found him insane, 'but emotionally rather than intellectually, the judgment being impaired and not the intellect,' as evidenced by his 'pseudo-religious feelings'. He had come to the conclusion that Guiteau ought to be placed under restraint.

Another doctor from Chicago named James Kennon testified that in his opinion Guiteau was suffering from a form of paresis. 'Give us English, Doctor,' the prisoner interrupted. 'We are all plain people and do not understand Greek.'

Dr Kennon went on to explain that in 'original insanity' the cranium was divided into two equal parts, of which one part was larger than the other.

Guiteau joined in the laughter which this paradoxical remark produced. 'That is my case exactly,' he observed to the accompaniment of more laughter. 'Only one side of my head is smaller than the other—the doctors who examined me the other day found it so!'

A more serious note was introduced by Senator Logan of Illinois, the prisoner's home state. The Senator described how he had been 'besieged' by the prisoner in Washington to get him a job. He thought, hardly surprisingly, that there was 'something wrong in the prisoner's mental arrangement'.

Guiteau's landlady then testified that he was nervous and abrupt in his actions and moreover that he had failed to pay his bill. From the dock the prisoner loudly protested this evidence, as he did generally with other witnesses who spoke of his 'peculiarities', interrupting them impatiently and declaring their statements to be nonsense.

When it became known that the prisoner would himself take the witness stand, the court was more crowded than ever, particularly with fashionably dressed women carrying opera glasses which they raised to their eyes from time to time without any objection from the judge.

Guiteau began by reading from the written statement which he had been stopped from doing at the outset of the trial. 'I propose that all the facts shall go to the jury and the court,' he declared. 'Any facts in my career showing whether I or the Deity fired that shot are of vital importance.

'I only did what the papers said ought to be done. Since the shooting they have deified the President. I want them and the doctors who killed him to share the odium with me. I never would have shot him of my own volition, notwithstanding the newspapers, had not the Deity commissioned me to do the deed. . . . I am not a murderer. The Lord inspired my act, as in the case of Abraham and others in the Bible.'

He went on to deliver a long, rambling speech, bringing in his allegedly lucrative practice as a barrister, his life in the Oneida community, his work as a lecturer, and his unsuccessful attempt to establish a paper in New York called *The Theocrat*, which eventually got him 'run down' and demoralised. 'When you are down,' he said, 'everyone gives you a kick.' Then, comparing his case to that of the Apostle Paul, he exclaimed, striking his fist on the table in front of him, 'I strove to frighten the world, just as Paul did. I had no money and no friends. I had just as rough a time as the Apostle Paul did.'

Describing his work as a lecturer, Guiteau referred to his fellow lawyer and lecturer from Illinois, former state Attorney-General Robert G. Ingersoll, who gave public lectures attacking the fundamentalist teaching of the Bible. 'Ingersoll lectured that there was no hell and people came in crowds,' said Guiteau. 'I lectured that there was a hell and nobody wanted to hear me.'

Asked by his counsel about his application for office, he said that he wanted to be appointed an American consul in France, either in Paris or Marseilles, on account of his French antecedents. He had written on the subject to President Garfield and had gone to the White House to see him, on which occasion he handed the President a copy of a speech he had made in the recent Presidential election campaign. It was the only time he saw the President, he said. He did not get the job. 'I wish it to be stated here,' Guiteau declared, 'that my getting or not getting office had nothing whatever to do with my removing the President. That was an act of inspiration, done as a political necessity. I was urged on by the Divine Presence, since the President's removal was necessary to save the nation from ruin.'

Under cross-examination by the District Attorney, the prisoner admitted that he was 'physically a coward, always keeping away from personal danger'. But morally, he said, he was 'as brave as a lion', particularly when he thought that 'the Deity was backing him'.

2

Asked whether he believed in the Ten Commandments, he said that he did.

'How about "Thou shalt not kill"?'

At this question Guiteau bridled and pounded the table again. 'I decline to discuss that with you,' he shouted, and went on to say that the jury's simple duty was to determine whether or not the Deity had inspired him to do what he did. He had no doubts himself. 'The President's removal was an act of the Deity,' he repeated.

'Are you insane at all?' the District Attorney put the question bluntly.

'I am not an expert,' the prisoner replied with some cunning. 'Let the experts and the jury decide that.'

'Do you feel any remorse?' was the District Attorney's final question.

'Why of course I feel remorse—human remorse,' Guiteau answered after a moment or two's hesitation. 'I feel sorrow.'

It may be noted that in a statement which he had somehow succeeded in smuggling out of prison to the *New York Herald* he declared that the idea had occurred to him that 'if the President were out of the way, everything would go better'. It kept bearing down on him, he said, that 'the only way to unite the two factions of the Republican party and save the Republic from going into the hands of the rebels and the Democrats, was to quietly remove the President'.

Asked by his counsel in re-examination what he meant by the word 'remove' in relation to the late President, the prisoner answered that 'it implied no feeling of guilt'. He then said he 'felt tired and cross' and the court obligingly adjourned for his convenience.

On the nineteenth day of the trial, it was announced that President Arthur, who had been served with a subpoena by the defence, declined to appear in court as a witness. At the same time Garfield's successor in the White House intimated that he would be prepared to testify by affidavit and to answer any questions that might be put to him in writing. The new President did so a few days later in a statement in which he said that he was slightly acquainted with Guiteau, having seen him on a dozen or so occasions, but that he had never conversed with him except to return ordinary salutations, or in reply to his requests for employment as a political speaker in New York. 'Guiteau has rendered no services to the Republican Party that I know of,' the President's statement went on, 'and there is no ground for supposing that he would receive political preferment.' Nor, he added, did he (President Arthur) ever give Guiteau any reasons to think that he would have any influence with him.

When the prisoner's Congressman, Charles Farwell of Chicago, took the stand, he stated that Guiteau had proposed to him that if he (Farwell) would let him have $200,000 to purchase a Chicago newspaper called the *Inter-Ocean*, Guiteau 'would make him president'.

'That is false,' the prisoner interrupted with another characteristic shout from the dock, 'I never made such a proposition. I asked him to invest money in it.'

Another witness called by the defence was the editor of the *Washington Gazette*, who swore that Guiteau had 'made a perfect nuisance of himself about the Republican Headquarters'. This produced another outburst from the dock. 'You were a nuisance yourself. I would rather be hanged as a man than acquitted as a fool. I will not have any more of this kind of evidence.' Then, turning towards his counsel, Guiteau said to him, 'If you put any more of these cranky fellows on the stand, I will score you again. I am no fool and will not allow you to make me out one.'

A clergyman from New York, the Rev. Dr McArthur, whom the prosecution called in rebuttal, gave what the newspapers covering the trial described as a shocking story of the prisoner's immorality and depravity. 'We present this testimony,' the District Attorney informed the court, 'to show that what the defence calls insanity is nothing more than devilish depravity.'

District Attorney Corkill's remark was greeted with loud applause in court. This provoked another outburst from the prisoner, who shook his fist at the DA and shouted, 'It is the unanimous opinion of the American people that you are a consummate jackass, Corkill!' This was followed a little later by a further explosion when one of the medical witnesses advanced the theory that the prisoner's depravity was responsible for his having killed President Garfield. 'I think it a burning shame for the prosecution to harp on that word depravity,' Guiteau protested. 'I have been a consistent Christian all my life. Because I committed a sin to get rid of a woman I did not love, and owe a few hundred dollars, it is a burning shame for the prosecution to blacken my character.'

Another witness called by the prosecution in rebuttal was the lady herself, Guiteau's divorced wife, who had subsequently remarried. She declared that she 'never saw any signs of his insanity when living with him'.

Thereafter the court proceedings became more and more farcical. The prisoner suddenly showed unwanted solicitation for the jury's health. 'It would be a great misfortune if anything happens to the jury,' he said, and he went on to suggest that they should go for a four- or five-hour walk each day before breakfast. He would also frequently interrupt his counsel to say, 'You talk and talk and you don't amount to a snap!' Then turning to the spectators in the gallery he would exclaim, 'Scoville is making an ass of himself.' On being told to keep quiet by a court official, he roared at him, 'Mind your own business! I know my rights!' Once he called the judge an out-and-out liar, shouting and pointing his finger at him. 'It's an outrage! God will curse you if you hurt a hair of my head.'

On another occasion he brought the trial to a halt by screaming, 'I have seven or eight hundred letters from sympathisers, many from ladies expressing their sympathies and prayers for my acquittal.' This was probably true, since women did mob him with morbid sympathy, and he was pestered by female autograph hunters in court to sign their autograph books as well as photographs of himself which they had thoughtfully provided for the purpose. On New Year's Day, 1882, over two hundred persons, mostly women, responded to his public invitation to call on him in prison.

One of his admirers sent him a poem which he solemnly declaimed in court:

> We hope that your hour of freedom is near,
> For your stainless acquittal we heartily pray.
> God has confirmed the act . . .
> Beware, ye Americans!

As the trial drew to a close, the prospects of an acquittal rapidly faded. Anticipating the verdict, an enterprising manufacturer of refrigerator cars in Philadelphia named Ridgway proposed to

Guiteau that in the event of his being hanged he would be prepared to exhibit his body all over the country, 'beautifully frozen', while Guiteau's heirs would receive half the fees charged to view this example of the embalmer's art.

When newspaper reporters expressed doubts as to the feasibility of this idea, Mr Ridgway said 'Nonsense', and remarked that he had 'done better than that with some fish for the Government'. Guiteau himself was quite intrigued with the proposition when it was put to him, but finally said that it must be taken up through his lawyer.

Towards the end of the trial a plaster cast was allowed to be taken of his head. This necessitated shaving off his beard and moustache which gave him a madder and more haggard appearance than ever, but it caused no diminution in the numbers of women seeking his autograph.

The closing speech for the prosecution was made by a counsel from the District Attorney's office named Porter. This impelled the prisoner to intone from time to time, 'A saint from Heaven could not stand Porter's abuse.' On 25 January Judge Cox summed up the evidence quite fairly, taking only an hour and a half to do so, a considerable feat of compression in view of the unusual length of time the trial had taken. The jury were out for just under an hour, and when they filed back into the crowded court-room it was clear from their faces what their verdict was before the foreman actually pronounced it—'Guilty'.

Asked by the judge if he had anything to say why sentence should not be passed upon him, Guiteau replied, 'It was God's act, not mine. God will take care of it and won't let the American people forget it.'

Judge Cox thereupon sentenced the prisoner to death by hanging, the sentence to be carried out in Washington Jail on 30 June between the hours of 12 noon and 2 p.m. The date of the execution was dictated by procedural reasons, since the trial had run over into the next law term and no death sentence could be carried out in the same term in order to allow time for an appeal or a motion for a new trial. Such a motion was in fact made by Guiteau's counsel on 5 February but was overruled.

'May the Lord have mercy on your soul,' the prisoner shouted at the judge when he had heard the sentence. 'I'm not afraid to die. . . . I shall have a glorious flight to glory, but that miserable scoundrel Corkill will have a permanent job down below where the Devil is preparing for him.'

Guiteau was taken back to prison in a snowstorm. But when the day of the execution arrived the weather had changed to sweltering heat and the hooting, jeering crowd which surrounded the prison were refreshing themselves with lemonade and ice cream sold by itinerant Negro vendors. Meanwhile the condemned man had eaten a good breakfast, had a bath, read aloud to his spiritual adviser the Rev. William Hicks a poem he had written entitled 'Simplicity and Religious Baby Talk'.

'That's all right, that settles it,' he told the clergyman when he was given the news that President Arthur had refused to respite him. 'I want you to examine the scaffold and make sure it's all right too, so that there may not be any bungling. I want to be hung at 12 o'clock sharp.'

In the event there was no bungling, but there was a slight delay in the timing of the execution. This was occasioned by the prayers and other incantations which the condemned man insisted on delivering from the scaffold, where the final gruesome scene took place in the presence of 150 specially invited spectators. One particularly bitter prayer predicted that the nation would 'by this act incur eternal enmity as did the Jews by killing my Saviour. . . . The nation will go down in blood. My murderers will go down to hell. . . . President Arthur is a coward and an ingrate. . . . Farewell, ye men of earth!'

Finally Guiteau recited another poem he had written with the refrain:

> I'm going to the Lord,
> I am so glad,
> Glory Hallelujah!

As the executioner placed the black cap over his head and fixed the rope round his neck, the muffled words 'Glory! Glory!' continued to be heard until the lever was pulled and the trap door fell open.

In a letter written to the Rev. Hicks on the eve of his execution, Guiteau left his body to the clergyman 'provided it was not to be used for any mercenary purpose'. This ruled out the ingenious refrigeration already mentioned, but the minister did not feel debarred from letting the Government pathologist use the body for anatomical research. The skull was eventually placed among the permanent exhibits in the Washington Medical Museum, whence a few months later it was stolen. Its present whereabouts are unknown.

Guiteau's crime may be compared with the assassinations of two other American Presidents, Abraham Lincoln and John F. Kennedy, whose murderers were found guilty in law and rightly so. But there was this vital difference between the respective cases. If not actually insane, Guiteau acted with what is known today as 'diminished responsibility'. If this defence had been valid in his time, he would at least have escaped the hangman's noose, although he would probably never have regained his liberty.

# 3

# The Pimlico Mystery

When it became known in the spring of 1886 that Adelaide Bartlett was to be tried at the Old Bailey for poisoning her husband with fatal results, and that her clergyman friend the Rev. George Dyson would take his place beside her in the dock as an accessory to the crime, public interest was intense. So many spectators were expected to attend the trial, and in fact did so, that accommodation had to be specially provided for them in the shape of a stand which was constructed near the dock and blocked up one of the entrances to the court. In addition to the public gallery, the stand was packed to capacity, mostly by women, who had come to see the pretty French widow on trial for her life, together with the Wesleyan minister whom many people believed to be her lover. There was a general expectation too, which was not to be disappointed, that the trial would have strong, even sinister sexual undertones.

The trial opened on 12 April 1886 before Mr Justice Wills, a leading authority on the law of evidence and also a well-known mountaineer, who was later to try Oscar Wilde on homosexual charges and to sentence him to two years' imprisonment with hard labour. It has always been a rule in English poison trials that a Law Officer should appear for the Crown, and in this case the prosecution was led by the Attorney-General Sir Charles Russell, a hard-hitting Irishman, later Lord Russell of Killowen, and incidentally the first Roman Catholic since the Reformation to hold the office of Attorney-General and afterwards that of Lord Chief Justice of England. As her leading defence counsel, Mrs Bartlett had secured the services of Sir Edward Clarke, the most brilliant and sought after advocate of his day, who was known to take immense trouble with the preparation of his cases. In this instance he had put aside all other work and had spent ten days in the British Museum reading up everything he could discover about the properties and uses of chloroform, the substance which his client was alleged to have administered to the late Mr Edwin Bartlett.

The Rev. George Dyson was defended by another leading barrister, Sir Frank Lockwood, who as Solicitor-General was to prosecute in the second Oscar Wilde trial. But Lockwood had little to do for the Rev. Dyson apart from making an application to the court that his client should be tried separately. However, this turned out to be unnecessary, since at the outset the Attorney-General intimated that the prosecution intended to offer no evidence against Dyson and he was formally acquitted by the jury. In these circumstances it was obvious that the prosecution intended to call him as a witness. While this was expected to strengthen the prosecution's case against Adelaide Bartlett, it was also expected to help the defence, since it meant that the minister could be cross-examined on any statements he had made which would not have been possible had he remained in the dock.

At that date prisoners were not permitted to give evidence in their own defence, and this meant that Mrs Bartlett was unable to testify. Many people thought that this put defendants in criminal trials at a great disadvantage, but when they were eventually able to do so a dozen years later the privilege was to prove a two-edged sword, since if they chose to go into the witness box they were liable to be cross-examined, sometimes with disastrous results for themselves. Thus it can be said that the old procedure gave defence counsel opportunities for shining advocacy which they were later denied by the change in the law of evidence. It was certainly so with Sir Edward Clarke in the trial of Adelaide Bartlett.

The events leading up to the death of Edwin Bartlett, which Sir Charles Russell outlined in his opening speech to the jury, were full of dramatic interest which was to be sustained throughout the trial. The prisoner, who was dressed in black as if she was still in mourning for her husband, had been born Adelaide Blanche de la Tremoille in Orleans and was thirty years old. She was said to be the natural daughter of an Englishman of good social position. Nothing was known of her mother, whose name she presumably took, and very little of her early life apart from the fact that she was brought to England as a child. In 1875 she was living in Kingston-on-Thames and in the same house there lodged a man named Frederick Bartlett. The latter introduced her to his brother Edwin, who was a grocer and provision dealer. A few weeks later Edwin and Adelaide were married, being encouraged to do so by Adelaide's father, who put up a substantial sum of money in the way of dowry. This enabled Edwin Bartlett to extend his business, so that eventually he owned six shops in the neighbourhood of Brixton and Dulwich. Although she was nineteen at the time of her marriage, her husband, who was some ten years older, considered that her education was incomplete. Hence he sent her to school in Stoke Newington and later to a convent in Belgium, and she would spend the holidays with him in London. In 1877, her schooling being finished, the couple went to live in Herne Hill, where they were joined by the husband's father who had recently become a widower; he was a carpenter and builder also called Edwin. Shortly afterwards there was some domestic unpleasantness caused by the elder Bartlett accusing Adelaide of having had intimate relations with his other son Fred. The upshot was that he was forced to withdraw his statement and make a written apology. Adelaide never forgot nor forgave the incident.

Her marital relations appear to have been somewhat unusual. According to her, she was induced to enter into a compact with her husband, in consequence of 'certain peculiar views' held by him, that their relations 'should be of an entirely platonic nature'. Apparently the husband held that a man should have two wives, one for intellectual companionship and the other, as he put it, 'for service'. Adelaide fulfilled the former role, and the arrangement was adhered to, she afterwards told her doctor, except on one occasion which was due to her desire for motherhood. In 1881 she gave birth to a stillborn child, and so severe was her suffering that she resolved to have no more children. Generally she lived on affectionate terms with her husband, apart from the terms of the marriage compact which she said distressed her at first. On the other hand, her husband purported to admire her physically and liked to show her off to his male acquaintances, whose attentions to her he apparently enjoyed.

Two years later, they went to live at Merton, near Wimbledon, and it was as the result of attending the local Wesleyan chapel that they met the minister George Dyson, a handsome and attractive pastor who had recently graduated from Trinity College, Dublin. They became friends and it was not long before the three of them were on Christian name terms. 'Would that I could find words to express my thankfulness to you for the very loving letter you sent Adelaide today,' wrote Edwin to George in a letter which was subsequently quoted in court. 'It would have done anybody good to see her overflowing with joy as she read it whilst walking along the street, and afterwards as she read it to me. I felt my heart going out to you. I long to tell you how proud I felt at the thought I should soon be able to clasp the hand of the man who from his heart could pen such noble thoughts.'

Edwin Bartlett suggested that his wife's education should be continued under the minister's tuition, and this the Rev. Dyson was only too glad to do, spending hours with Adelaide when her husband was at business. When the Bartletts moved to Pimlico, so assured was the reverend visitor's position that an old coat and slippers were kept for him. Indeed the maid became accustomed to seeing them side by side on the sofa, and once she found Adelaide sitting on the floor with her head reposing on George's knee. George visited her when she and her husband spent a long summer holiday in Dover, and since the minister's stipend did not amount to more than £100 a year Edwin Bartlett would send him a first-class rail ticket. Eventually he told the minister that he was making a new will leaving everything unconditionally to his wife and asked him to be the executor, to which Dyson agreed with apparent reluctance. He told Bartlett that there was no denying the fact that he was 'growing very attached' to Adelaide, and asked him whether it would not be better to discontinue his friendship with them. 'Why should you discontinue it?' asked Edwin, adding that he 'hoped they should have some pleasant intercourse', and to facilitate this end presenting him with a season ticket so that he could come into London regularly. The Rev. Dyson would now kiss Adelaide openly in her husband's presence, walk out with her, and even entertain her in his bachelor quarters. 'My husband threw us together,' she said afterwards. 'He requested us, in his presence, to kiss, and he seemed to enjoy it. He had given me to Mr Dyson.'

On their return to London in October 1885, the Bartletts went to live in furnished apartments at 38 Clapperton Street,

Pimlico, where they occupied a sitting room and bedroom, which communicated with folding doors. Edwin Bartlett was a strong healthy man, and three years previously he had been accepted by an insurance company as a first-class life, although Adelaide told George Dyson that for some years he had suffered from a painful internal complaint for which she had nursed and doctored him with chloroform to soothe his pain. His teeth also gave him trouble owing to their decayed condition and he had a number of extractions at this time.

On 10 December, a local doctor, Alfred Leach, who had not previously attended him, was called in and found him suffering from indigestion and also mercury poisoning which the patient attributed to his having taken a pill of unknown strength and constituents. Dr Leach also found his teeth in a bad state and diagnosed that he had necrosis of the jaw. Meanwhile Adelaide continued to nurse her husband with conspicuous devotion, sitting up with him night after night. On being advised by the doctor to get some rest, she replied, 'What is the use? He will not sleep unless I hold his toe.' Adelaide then suggested calling in another opinion, giving as the reason that her husband's friends would accuse her of poisoning him if he did not get better soon. So a Dr Dudley was summoned, but apart from the patient's depression, sleeplessness and the condition of his gums, he did not consider that anything was radically wrong with him. Dr Dudley consequently told him he should get up and go out every day. Dr Leach gave him some purgatives, and finding his health better took him out for a drive. During his illness he was visited by his father and also by George Dyson, who at Mrs Bartlett's request got her some chloroform. Edwin rapidly improved and on New Year's Eve was well enough to go to the dentist who removed another tooth.

Whatever may have been wrong with Edwin Bartlett, he had an excellent appetite. On New Year's Eve he had oysters for lunch, and he dined off jugged hare, which he said he enjoyed so much that he could eat three a day. For supper he had more oysters, bread and butter, and cake and ordered a large haddock for breakfast next morning. After supper the maid made up the fire, and Mrs Bartlett told her not to go into the room again but to bring some beef tea and leave it outside the door, which she did.

At four o'clock in the morning, the landlord Frederick Doggett was awakened by Mrs Bartlett. 'Come down,' she said. 'I think Mr Bartlett is dead.' Mr Doggett, who by a strange chance was Registrar of Deaths for the district, found his lodger lying on his back in bed. He was perfectly cold and must have been dead for two or three hours. 'I had fallen asleep with my hand round his foot,' explained Mrs Bartlett. 'I awoke with a pain in my arm, and found him lying on his face. I put him in the position in which you see him, and tried to pour brandy down his throat—nearly half a pint.' When Mr Doggett entered the room, he detected a strong smell of anaesthetic and saw on the mantelpiece a wine-glass three-quarters full of what smelt like brandy with ether in it. But according to him and also Dr Leach who arrived shortly afterwards there was no bottle of chloroform on the mantelpiece. Dr Leach asked her if her husband could have taken poison. 'Oh no,' was the reply, 'he could have got no poison without my knowledge.'

She was told there would have to be a post-mortem on the body and an inquest. She was also told that the rooms must be sealed pending investigation by the authorities and that she must leave the house. Accordingly she went to stay with friends in Dulwich, Mr and Mrs Mathews, being accompanied there by George Dyson who had called at the house on the following morning. On the way he asked her whether she had used the chloroform he had procured for her. 'I have not used it,' she replied. 'I have not had occasion to use it. The bottle is there just as you gave it to me.' According to her, the bottle remained on the mantelpiece from the time of her husband's death until next morning when she re-moved it and put it in a drawer in the bedroom. She added that it was still there when she returned to the house on 6 January. She then took it away and threw it out of the window of a train in which she was travelling between London and Peckham Rye.

Meanwhile the post-mortem examination revealed that Edwin Bartlett's stomach contained over eleven grains of chloroform; 'almost as strong as a freshly opened bottle,' said the pathologist. At the adjourned inquest which followed, the coroner's jury returned a verdict to the effect that Edwin Bartlett had died from chloroform administered by his wife for the purpose of taking his life, and that the Rev. George Dyson was an accessory before the fact.

There could be no doubt that Bartlett's death was due to the

chloroform found in his stomach. The question posed by the
Attorney-General was, how did it get there? He dismissed any
suggestion of suicide or accident. It was clear, said Sir Charles,
that the deceased was first partially chloroformed and then, when
he was semi-conscious, liquid chloroform was poured down his
throat.

The first prosecution witness to enter the box was Edwin
Bartlett Senior. He related how he called on his son during his
illness and how he said he was better and hoped soon to be at
business again. He also repeated what his daughter-in-law had
told him about Edwin's death. 'He died with my arm round his
foot; he always liked to have my hand on his foot.'

Asked by Clarke in cross-examination whether he disapproved
of his son's marriage, the witness admitted that he 'certainly did
not much approve of it', though he did not disapprove of it.
Questioned about the letter of apology he had signed, he stated
that he knew it to be false but that he had signed it at his son's
request 'because it would make peace with him and his wife if I
did'. Asked in re-examination to elaborate on the charge he had
made against Adelaide, the elder Bartlett said that she had run
away and been absent for a week or more, during which time he
and Edwin were sure that she had gone off with the other son
Fred, who had since departed for America.

After the landlord and his wife and several other minor witnesses had briefly testified, the Rev. George Dyson was called.
He was in clerical dress and had closely trimmed whiskers and a
heavy black moustache. He described how the prisoner had asked
him to get her some chloroform for external use on her husband,
which she said she sprinkled on a handkerchief to soothe him. He
purchased several small amounts in four separate bottles, telling
the chemist in each case that it was required to remove grease
stains. On returning home, he poured the contents of the four
bottles into one large bottle to which he transferred the poison
label, and next day he gave it to Mrs Bartlett 'whilst out for a
stroll on the Embankment'. He accompanied her back to her
lodgings in Clapperton Street, where he saw her husband who was
up and dressed and 'seemed brightened' by the fact that he had
been out for a drive. Nothing was said about the unusual purchases
the witness had made. The Rev. Dyson stated that he subsequently threw away the four smaller bottles.

Sir Edward Clarke cross-examined with masterly skill, his questions being purposely friendly and sympathetic, since he realised that the more he could associate the minister's actions with those of his client in the dock, the more he would be able to strengthen the instinctive reluctance of the jury to send her to the gallows while the Rev. Dyson passed unrebuked to freedom.

The witness first confirmed that he had met Mrs Bartlett on 9 January at the house of Mr and Mrs Mathews, the friends with whom she had gone to stay in Dulwich.

'On that day you spoke to her about the chloroform?'

'Yes.'

'And she was indignant?'

'Very indignant.'

'And she said, why didn't you charge her outright with having given chloroform to her husband?'

The witness agreed that she had used words to that effect, and that it was from her lips that he first heard the suggestion. The minister added that he had not spoken to her since that day.

'Was there any secret between you, or any secret understanding between you, apart from her husband?'

'None,' answered the witness emphatically.

'Was there any impropriety between you and Mrs Bartlett?'

'There was not,' said the Rev. Dyson. However, he added that he had kissed her.

'That would be an impropriety—you do not defend that?'

'No.'

'You mean to say,' the judge interrupted, 'it was only in her husband's presence.'

'And out of his presence,' the minister admitted after a slightly embarrassed pause.

'You became aware,' Clarke continued, 'that at a very early period in your acquaintance Mr Bartlett had peculiar ideas on the subject of marriage?'

The witness agreed that this was so and that Mr Bartlett had suggested there might be one wife for companionship and another wife for service.

'Were both of them to be bedfellows?' the judge again broke in.

'He never mentioned that to me, my lord.'

'I want to know,' said Mr Justice Wills, 'why you went to three different shops to buy the chloroform?'

'Because I did not get as much as I wanted at one shop.'

This answer did not satisfy the judge. 'Why did you not say to the first man, "You have given me a little bottle—I want four or five times this quantity"?'

'Because I thought he would want to know what I wanted it for, and I did not wish to enter into a long explanation.'

'Why not?' snapped the judge.

'Because I thought he would not understand that Mrs Bartlett was skilled in the use of medicines.'

'Why did you say it was for taking grease spots out of clothes?'

'He asked me what I wanted it for,' replied the minister. 'I do not defend that, my lord. It was simply that I wanted to avoid an explanation. That was the only idea in my mind.'

Mrs Alice Mathews confirmed what passed at the meeting between Adelaide Bartlett and George Dyson at her house, when she had shown indignation at the latter's suggestion that it might be proved that she had given Edwin chloroform. George Mathews, her husband, who followed her, was asked in cross-examination about a certain book which he said Mrs Bartlett had lent him. It was by Dr T. L. Nichols and was entitled *Esoteric Anthropology: The Mysteries of Man*. It dealt with the physical relations between the sexes and particularly their regulation by birth control Abstinence was recommended; but, as this was a counsel of perfection other methods of contraception were described for the reader's information. The witness said that he had not read the book, which had been returned to Mrs Bartlett by his wife.

However, another witness said she had done so. This was a trained nurse and midwife, Annie Walker, who had attended Mrs Bartlett during her confinement. She had been recommended to Adelaide by the author's wife Mrs Nichols, who helped her husband in his work and who had been consulted by Mrs Bartlett. 'When I visited her after her confinement,' said Nurse Walker, 'I saw Mr Bartlett. As far as I could judge, they were living together as man and wife, and they were on affectionate terms together.'

Cross-examined by Sir Edward Clarke, Nurse Walker said that she had not used chloroform at the confinement and so far as she knew Mrs Bartlett had no knowledge of it and its uses.

'You have looked through this book?' Clarke went on, holding up a copy of *Esoteric Anthropology*.

'I have.'

'There is nothing immoral or indecent in this book, is there?'

'Not anything.' The witness said that the Bartletts had made no attempt to conceal the book and it lay about their place quite openly.

Dr Alfred Leach confirmed his professional visits to the late Edwin Bartlett, the treatment he prescribed, and the patient's symptoms after death. He also related the details of his conversation with Mrs Bartlett when she had told him of the marriage compact with her husband and their allegedly platonic relations except on the one occasion of the birth of the stillborn child. The doctor was not a very satisfactory witness, as he was inclined to qualify his answers by self-conscious personal explanations. But if there was one thing that Dr Leach was clear about, as the judge afterwards reminded the jury, it was that when he first saw his patient lying dead there was no bottle of chloroform upon the mantelpiece.

An officer in the Metropolitan Police, who was employed by the coroner, described how he had searched the rooms in Clapperton Street when they had been unsealed. His most interesting discovery turned out to be one of Edwin Bartlett's suits of clothes, in the right-hand trousers pocket of which he found 'four or five of what are popularly called French letters'.

The prosecution called two expert medical witnesses, and one of them agreed in cross-examination that there was no recorded case of murder by liquid chloroform. One doctor tried the experiment on six patients and all resisted. The other succeeded only with children and not with sleeping adults, who all woke up at once. Both agreed that the liquid would enter the windpipe and cause choking, burning the windpipe and leaving traces. Such traces were not revealed by the post-mortem.

Finally the prosecution called servants and others who testified that the Bartletts habitually occupied the same room. With that the case for the Crown was closed. Sir Edward Clarke rose, and intimated that he did not intend to call any evidence for the defence. He then went straight on to address the jury.

The defence counsel's first task was to discredit the prosecution's theory that Mrs Bartlett had caused her husband's death by forcing chloroform down his throat. If he was conscious, the first attempt must have failed through the patient's resistance. Then, if he became insensible, some of the chloroform must on the medical

evidence have got into the air passages, but there was no trace of
any there. As against this Sir Edward put forward his theory that
Edwin Bartlett had deliberately taken his own life in a fit of
depression, accentuated by the following circumstances.

'Mr Bartlett had so behaved as in fact to have given or
dedicated his wife for the future to Mr Dyson. Then he desires
to resume his rights, but is resisted, and on this night when he
has suffered during the day . . . he is told by her that the consent which he has given with regard to Dyson's relations is
treated by her as an irrevocable decision, that he has ceased to
enjoy the rights that a husband may exercise, that she has taken
him at his word, and that from this time onwards co-partnership must remain co-partnership and shall never be allowed
again to pass into the associations of marriage. He was grieved,
he appeared very grieved. . . .'

Counsel went on to invite the jury to sketch in their imagination
what then took place.

'Suppose she left the room as usual to wash, and he had
placed on the mantelpiece this bottle of chloroform. There was
a wine-glass there—that wine-glass was found afterwards—and
while she was away it was perfectly easy for him without leaving
his bed, lifting himself only on his elbow, to pour into this wine-
glass the less than half a wine-glass of chloroform which may
have constituted that fatal dose. . . . Having drunk it, he
resumes his recumbent position, the chloroform passes down
his throat and reaches his stomach . . . within two or three
minutes he might be passing into a state of coma. She returns
and goes to sleep, and her husband's coma deepens into
insensibility, and insensibility passes into death.'

In his closing speech to the jury, which as Attorney-General he
had the right to make last even in cases where the defence called
no witnesses, Sir Charles Russell attempted to discount the
suicide theory by putting forward an alternative—that the fatal
draught might have been handed to the deceased in a glass of
brandy and gulped down by him supposing it to be some medicine.
Immediately Clarke was on his feet protesting strongly that this

theory had not been advanced before. In the event the defence counsel was supported by the judge, who ruled that it was now too late to bring it up and directed the jury to pay no attention to it.

As soon as Russell sat down and before the judge began his summing up, Clarke was again on his feet, this time to ask if he could recall Nurse Walker to answer a single question. Apparently the nurse had come to him and volunteered the information. The judge agreed and Annie Walker again stepped into the witness box.

'At the time you nursed Mrs Bartlett in her confinement,' Clarke asked her, 'did you become aware from anything she said to you with regard to its having been the result of a single act?'

'Yes, sir.'

The judge leaned forward to ask, 'What was it?'

'That it happened only once—on a Sunday afternoon.'

'She said so?' the judge persisted.

'Both of them did,' replied Nurse Walker. And what was more, the witness added, they both said that on other occasions 'there was always some preventive used'.

'You say you had that from both of them?'

'From both of them,' the witness repeated.

Mr Justice Wills summed up the evidence quite fairly, but he could not disguise his prejudice against the prisoner, and he had some scathing things to say about her and her husband in the context of their sexual relations. First, there were the French letters which were found in the dead man's pocket. 'It is an unpleasant subject,' said the judge, who plainly disapproved of these articles. 'The case is full of unpleasant subjects.' Another such subject was the book *Esoteric Anthropology*, which explained how contraception could be practised and which the judge stigmatised as 'garbage', scattering its poison and doing its mischief under the garb of ostentatious purity. 'And then what becomes of this morbid romance about the non-sexual connection?' asked the judge, clearly showing that he did not believe it on the basis of what Nurse Walker had said. 'The whole foundation for that baseless illusion is swept away by the one sentence which you heard in the witness box today.'

The jury were out for just over two hours. 'Do you find the prisoner Adelaide Bartlett, guilty or not guilty?' the clerk of the court asked the foreman.

'We have well considered the evidence,' the foreman replied, 'and although we think grave suspicion is attached to the prisoner, we do not think there is sufficient evidence to show how or by whom the chloroform was administered.'

'Then you say that the prisoner is not guilty, gentlemen?'

'Not guilty.'

The spectators in court cheered loudly and were soundly rebuked by the judge who told them their conduct was an outrage and a court of justice was not to be turned into a theatre by such 'indecent exhibitions'. Sir Edward Clarke, for the only time in his career, broke down and sobbed in relief. He too was cheered when he appeared that night at the Lyceum Theatre to see Sir Henry Irving and Ellen Terry playing in *Faust*.

The subsequent history of Adelaide Bartlett and George Dyson is not known for certain. According to one account they eventually married, according to another they never set eyes on each other again.

However, one thing is certain, and that is what a distinguished surgeon told the Lord Chief Justice, who passed it on to Clarke with a note of congratulation on his triumph. 'Mrs Bartlett was no doubt quite properly acquitted,' said the surgeon, 'but now it is to be hoped that in the interests of science she will tell us how she did it!'

# 4

# Poison in the Mails

The trial of Roland Burnham Molineux has been described as one of the historic criminal trials of the century in the United States—the century being the last century, since it took place in New York City's Central Criminal Court between 14 November 1899 and 11 February 1900. The accused was indicted for the murder by poison of Mrs Katherine J. Adams; it was alleged that the poison had been administered in error and was really intended for her nephew Harry Cornish, the sports director of the Knickerbocker Athletic Club. The trial aroused immense public interest owing partly to the peculiar features of the crime and partly to the prominent position held in New York society by its principal characters in the case. An agile, debonair man of thirty-two, constantly smiling, Molineux was the reigning champion horizontal bar performer; like his alleged intended victim Cornish he was a committee member of the Knickerbocker Athletic Club. He professed to be a chemist and in fact was manager of a colour factory in Newark, New Jersey, although apart from a little technical training his education did not go beyond the high school equivalent. His father, General Edward Leslie Molineux, was a hero of the Civil War in which he had displayed conspicuous gallantry, and since the war had been a prominent figure in Brooklyn politics and was well known throughout New York. He was a director of a firm of colour makers in Brooklyn and a wealthy man.

The trial judge was the Hon. John W. Goff, Recorder of New York. Roland Molineux was defended by two leading city lawyers, Bartow Weeks and George Battle. The prosecution was led by the Assistant District Attorney James W. Osborne. Old General

Molineux, with his white beard and skull cap, sat throughout the trial at the defence counsel's table and from time to time would lean forward and in full view of the jury give his son a literal pat on the back.

The selection of the jury took a fortnight and was made from a panel of over five hundred names.

After the jury had been empanelled and the prisoner had formally pleaded not guilty, the prosecutor addressed the jury. The curious story he recounted began on the previous Christmas Eve, when Harry Cornish found in his mail box in the Knicker-bocker Athletic Club a cardboard box of the kind used by Tiffany's the jewellers, wrapped in manila paper and addressed to him. He opened the package in his office. At one end he found a silver toothpick holder and at the other, separated by tissue paper of the sort jewellers use for packing, what appeared to be a small bottle of bromo-seltzer. By taking off the outside wrapper, Cornish was able to fit the bottle into the holder, which he placed on his desk. There was an envelope in the box, but it contained no card or message. He threw the manila paper wrapper into the wastepaper basket in his office, but on second thoughts retrieved it and cut out the inscribed portion, thinking he might sometime be able to recognise the handwriting. He laughed at what seemed to him a joke on the part of some acquaintance in sending him a bottle of bromo-seltzer for Christmas, and several club members who came into his office that morning shared the joke with him and thought it a funny thing.

Cornish, who was divorced, lived in an apartment on West 84th Street, near Central Park, with his aunt Mrs Adams and her daughter Mrs Rodgers. When he told them about the mysterious present he had received, they also joked with him, saying it must have come from a female admirer and that he was afraid to bring it home as it probably had her name on it. A couple of days later, Cornish did take the bottle and the silver holder home with him and presented them to Mrs Rodgers, saying they were no use to him and she might have them. Mrs Rodgers accepted the gift and remarked that the design on the holder matched the design of the silverware on her dressing-table.

Next morning Mrs Adams had a headache and her daughter suggested that she take a dose of the bromo-seltzer. Cornish, who was present, mixed a teaspoonful of the preparation in the bottle with a glass of water and gave it to his aunt. 'My, how bitter it is!' she exclaimed after drinking from it.

'Why, that's all right!' said Cornish, as he took the glass and drank down what was left.

A few moments afterwards, Mrs Adams collapsed on the floor, 'like six foot of chain' as Cornish put it. When the doctor arrived, he found her face ashen pale, her breathing stertorous, and from her breath came an odour of bitter almonds. Shortly afterwards she died. Meanwhile Cornish was seized with a violent attack of vomiting. The fact that he was thus able to throw up the contents of his stomach doubtless saved his life. At all events he recovered. An autopsy followed on the body of Mrs Adams and this revealed that she had died from cyanide poisoning. The contents of the bromo-seltzer bottle were analysed and these were found to contain a lethal amount of cyanide of mercury. Further examination revealed that the bottle was not a genuine bromo-seltzer bottle and that the label had been removed from a genuine one and carefully pasted on the bottle which had been sent to Harry Cornish.

Police inquiries produced the first clues. The silver bottleholder was traced to Hartdegen's jewellery store in Newark, New Jersey, where it had been sold by Miss Emma Miller on 21 December to a man with a sandy beard, whom she said had come into the store and asked for something to hold a bottle of bromoseltzer for a lady's dressing-table. What she had sold him was really designed for toothpicks or matches. The Press then stepped in. A wigmaker near the store stated he had sold a red wig about 21 December to a man like the subject of a photograph a reporter showed him: the photograph was of Molineux. Then a clerk in a drug store told a newspaper reporter that he had sold two bottles of bromo-seltzer and two small bottles of bromo-caffeine to a man with a sandy moustache who resembled Molineux.

The newspapers, one of which, the New York *Journal* offered $5,000 for information leading to the arrest of the murderer, tracked down two men in New York, Joseph Koch and Nicholas Heckmann, who operated accommodation addresses for the convenience of customers to whom they rented private letter boxes to which mail could be sent. 'You can have a business address on Broadway for only 50 cents a month', was how Koch advertised. Heckmann operated from West 42nd Street. The former stated that he had rented a letter box to a man who gave his name as

'H. Cornish', while Heckmann said he had done the same to a man by the name of 'H. C. Barnett'. Both addresses, 1620 Broadway and 257 West 42nd Street, were often used by customers for the receipt of letters containing remedies for sexual debility, which the recipients naturally did not wish to be sent to their home addresses. ('Remedies can be sent by Mail or Express to suit the convenience of Patients.') The newspapers combed the files of patent medicine firms with the result that a firm in Cincinnati came forward and stated that as far back as 31 May 1898 they had received a written application signed 'H. C. Barnett' for a sample box of pills and another similar application on 21 December 1898 signed 'H. Cornish'. Both these applications were found to be in the same handwriting, and when they were compared by the secretary of the Knickerbocker Club with the handwriting on the fatal package addressed to Harry Cornish the resemblance was seen to be very marked.

It was now recalled that the real Henry C. Barnett, a produce broker, who also belonged to the Club, had received a box of Kutnow's powder through the mails addressed to him at the Club in the previous October. He was in the habit of taking this as a cure for simple ailments, and soon afterwards he took a dose of its contents. He immediately became ill, attributing his illness to 'those damned Kutnow powders', and saying that he was 'a damned fool' to take anything sent by strangers. The doctor called in diagnosed diphtheria from a membrane in his throat. However, subsequent analysis of the powders showed the presence of cyanide of mercury. Barnett died in November, but his physician was of the opinion that, if he had been poisoned, he had shaken off the effects and that his death was due to the after-effects of diphtheria.

Although Barnett and Molineux were on friendly terms, they were rivals for the hand of a lady named Blanche Chesebrough. She was said to have rejected Molineux as a suitor in favour of Barnett. However that may be, she became Mrs Molineux eleven days after Barnett's death.

Molineux was known to dislike Cornish and in the circumstances it was inevitable that Molineux should have been served with a subpoena to testify at the inquest of Katherine Adams.

'You claim to be entirely and absolutely innocent of this crime?' the District Attorney asked him at this hearing.

'Entirely and absolutely innocent,' was the confident reply.

On the other hand, Heckmann identified Molineux as the man to whom he had hired his letter box, although Molineux denied this. ('I want to say I never saw him in Forty-Second Street and I never rented a letter box from him.') Also seven well-known handwriting experts testified that in their opinion the 'Barnett' and 'Cornish' letters and the name and address on the fatal package when compared with Molineux's admitted handwriting were undoubtedly the work of the same writer. In the result the coroner's jury found that Mrs Katherine Adams had met her death by mercuric cyanide poisoning administered by Harry S. Cornish to whom the poison had been sent in the mails by Roland B. Molineux. Some suspicion had fallen on Cornish, but the coroner ordered his immediate discharge and the arrest of Molineux. The latter was taken to the Tombs prison and was subsequently charged with the murder of both Mrs Adams and Barnett. But owing to various technical flaws in the original indictment he was released on bail, rearrested, released again, and finally arrested for a third time on the sole charge of murdering Mrs Adams.

Summarising the prosecution's case at the trial, the Assistant District Attorney alleged that Molineux had killed Barnett out of jealousy and had gone on to kill Cornish out of hatred. Cyanide of mercury, the substance used in each instance, was never medically prescribed and could only have been prepared by someone like Molineux with a knowledge of chemistry.

The first witness was the doctor who had been summoned to the Adams apartment immediately after she had swallowed the fatal dose. Dr Edwin Hitchcock described her peculiar pallor and laboured breathing, how he had felt her flickering pulse and concluded that she was near death. Putting his finger in what he at first took to be a bottle of bromo-seltzer, he continued, he brushed off all traces of the mixture except one small particle. 'I placed that on my tongue and the instant I did I got a metallic taste,' he said, 'and I could detect the odour of almonds which is the characteristic odour of the cyanogen group, of which prussic acid is the base, and then I knew I was in contact with the most deadly poison I had ever heard of.'

The handwriting experts were then called to testify that the writing on the poison package addressed to Cornish, though disguised, displayed identical characteristics to admitted specimens

of Molineux's writing, particularly in the breaks between the 'e'
and the 'i' and between the 'i' and the 'a'—also that the initial 'f'
had an angle and a loop in the down stroke occurring in both, as
well as in the handwriting of the letters ostensibly signed by
Cornish and sent from the accommodation address. They gave
their opinion that the writing on the package was undoubtedly
Molineux's.

The experts were followed on the witness stand by a young
woman who answered to the name of Mary Melando. The
daughter of a New Jersey policeman, she admitted to having been
seduced by Molineux at the age of thirteen and afterwards to have
lived with him nominally as his housekeeper in his private
quarters at the Newark factory. She had recently been caught in a
disorderly house in Newark as the result of a police raid and been
released at the intercession of Molineux. She had no wish to
testify and her presence in court had been obtained as the result
of a ruse. Since she lived in New Jersey, she could not be served
with an effective subpoena by a New York court. Consequently
two dashing young New York detectives struck up an acquaintance
with her and a girl friend, took them both on a spree to what they
thought was another town in New Jersey but which turned out to
be in New York State. Melando was then forcibly held by the
New York police in custody, and in these circumstances it is
hardly surprising that she gave her evidence with considerable
reluctance and in the event had to be treated as a hostile witness.
Nevertheless she was able to state that she had seen several sheets
of peculiar blue paper with crescent markings in Molineux's
drawer in his room in the factory and that she herself had used
some sheets of the paper and the envelope to match, similar to the
letters written for the patent medicine remedies, of which one was
addressed to one such firm by Molineux and signed with his real
name and New Jersey address.

John Adams, the secretary of the Knickerbocker Athletic Club
—he was not related to the dead woman—gave evidence of the
quarrels between Cornish and Molineux as to how the club's
athletic activities should be run, of how Molineux threatened to
resign unless Cornish was removed from his office as athletic
director, and of how in the event Molineux did resign, in March
1898. Cornish himself was next called and he strongly denied that
he had written the letters signed either 'H. S. Cornish' or 'H. C.

Barnett' to the drug companies nor had he ever used any blue paper with crescent markings—indeed he had never seen such paper until it was handed to him in court. He went on to describe what happened after he received the poison package and took it home to the Adams apartment.

Mr Weeks began his cross-examination by asking Cornish whether he was a married man when he first came to the Knicker-bocker Athletic Club in 1896. Cornish replied that he was, though he was not living with Mrs Cornish at the time.

'Where was your wife?'

'In Chicago.'

'What has that got to do with it?' the judge interrupted.

'Does that not go at all to affect the witness's story?' Weeks queried back.

'Oh, no,' said Judge Goff. 'Many a man is not living with his wife whose word is as good as that of any other man. That is not an act of moral turpitude or moral deformity that would attach any penalty to it whatever. That is a matter of private life.'

Cornish stood up well to the cross-examination and his credibility was unimpaired. However, Weeks got him to admit that he went down town the day before he received the poison package and was within a few feet of the General Post Office where it appeared from the postmark that the package had been mailed.

Emma Miller, the salesgirl in Hartdegen's store, confirmed the sale of the silver holder from her sales book as being on 21 December. Asked by defence counsel whether Molineux was the purchaser, she said no. 'I am positive of that,' she added. However, in re-examination by Mr Osborne, she admitted that she had certainly seen the defendant in the store on that day.

Koch and Heckmann repeated the evidence they had given at the inquest, Heckmann saying that he had known the defendant by sight for five years.

'Did you know his name?' the judge asked Heckmann.

'No, sir.'

'Well, then, how did you come to write down the name Barnett?'

'He mentioned it to me.'

'When you wrote it down, did you know whether or not it was his true name?'

'No, sir,' replied the witness.

Under cross-examination, Heckmann agreed that he had accepted $350 from a newspaper in return for identifying the defendant, which he had done by a ruse in the presence of a private detective in the Newark factory. 'That is Mr Barnett all right,' he said he had told the detective at the time. 'He is my customer.'

Gustave Kutnow, a member of the firm of Kutnow Brothers, stated that his business was selling Kutnow's powder.

'And what is Kutnow's powder?'

'Kutnow's powder is an evaporation of the Carlsbad mineral springs, made in a pleasant tasting form. It is a pleasant tasting effervescent salts.'

Replying to further questions from the prosecutor, the witness said that his firm was in the habit of despatching sample tins of powder to any member of the public who wrote in for a sample tin with his name and address. He was shown one of the firm's sample tins which he identified. It was addressed to 'H. Cornish, Esq., 1620 Broadway'. He also identified the letter in response to which the same was sent out, and which (so the handwriting experts had testified) was written by Molineux.

The only other prosecution witness of any importance was Dr Henry B. Douglass, who attended Barnett in his last illness and reported his death to the New York Health Board. In reply to the prosecutor, he said he believed that his patient died from the after-effects of streptococcus diphtheria.

'Did you tell anybody connected with the Health Board that Barnett had received through the mails a package of Kutnow powder containing cyanide of mercury?'

'I did not.'

'Now,' Mr Osborne went on, 'Barnett had told you that he received this package anonymously through the mails, didn't he?' This was a leading question and strictly speaking inadmissible, but neither the judge nor defence counsel protested it.

'Mr Barnett had told me that he had received a box of Kutnow powder through the mail, purporting to be,' replied the witness. 'I had to account for a certain amount of mercurial stomatitis and for that reason I sent the box to be analysed.'

'Because he showed symptoms of having taken mercury?'

'Yes, that is why I took the box, trying to find the cause of that.'

'Well, now,' said Osborne, 'you know that Van Horne and

Ellison [the analysts] made a report that this Kutnow powder contained cyanide of mercury?'

'Yes, sir,' the doctor admitted.

'And you knew that he was suffering from diarrhoea that you attributed to mercury?'

'Moderately.'

'And yet you never reported to the Health Board one solitary thing about this mercury?'

'No.'

After the prosecution had called its last witness, Mr Weeks who led the defence, rose. Most of those in court thought that he was about to call his witnesses or at least to submit a reasoned argument that there was no case against his client to go to the jury. In fact, what he said was very brief and to the point.

'May it please the Court, after a very careful consideration of the evidence presented in this case, and with a full sense of the responsibility resting upon the defence, we believe that the prosecution has failed to establish the charge made against this defendant, and that no conviction can or should be had upon the evidence presented, and we rest the case.'

The jury thereupon retired and after an absence of eight hours, during which at their request they were provided with a set of the handwriting exhibits, they returned to announce they had found the defendant guilty of murder in the first degree.

For this crime the death sentence was mandatory. When he was brought up for sentence three weeks later, Molineux was asked by the clerk of the court whether he had anything to say why sentence should not be pronounced upon him.

'Of the crime of which I stand convicted,' he declared, 'and for still another crime with which I am charged, I am absolutely and entirely innocent. All of the evidence——'

'You are not charged with another crime,' the judge broke in.

The prisoner then raised his hands dramatically and went on: 'The handwriting experts who have testified against me, Your Honour, may give their opinion, they may give their reasons, what they believe, what they think, but I know that these hands never put pen to paper to address that poison package or to write the disputed letters.'

Molineux paused for a few seconds, lowered his hands, and placed them on the bar of the dock. Then he said quietly: 'And now, Your Honour, I am prepared to hear you sentence me. I am not afraid, because I am not guilty.'

Sentence was duly passed, and the prisoner was removed to the Death House in Sing Sing Jail, there to await the arrival of the hangman. Meanwhile Molineux's lawyers lodged an appeal, and as it was expected that it would be some time before this would be heard General Molineux and his wife took a house nearby in Ossining so as to be near their son whom they were allowed to visit at regular intervals. At the same time a petition for his pardon was got up urging that in view of what had recently happened in the Dreyfus case in France no conviction based on handwriting should be allowed to stand. Nothing came of this movement and the mills of justice continued to grind at their usual leisurely pace. Eventually the appeal was heard by seven judges in June 1901 and the court reserved judgment. Four more months elapsed before the judgment was delivered, on 15 October 1901. This set aside the verdict of the lower court and ordered a new trial.

The delay between hearing and judgment in the appellate court was due to a difference of opinion among the judges. A majority of four of the seven judges held that evidence tending to show that Molineux had poisoned Barnett, as well as sending the package to Cornish, was inadmissible, while the minority took the view that it was rightly admitted on the ground that it showed a common scheme. (The point was to come up fifteen years later in the celebrated Brides in the Bath trial in England, where the minority view in the Molineux appeal was adopted.) All the judges agreed, however, that the hearsay statement of Dr Douglass as to Barnett's receipt of the Kutnow powders through the mail should not have been admitted and this alone was sufficient reason for ordering a new trial.

The new trial took place a year later with a fresh jury and another judge. This time Molineux was defended by Frank S. Black, a former Governor of New York State. He testified in his own defence, denying that he had mailed the package and pleading an alibi. This was supported by a professor at Columbia University who swore that Molineux was with him at the time the prosecution alleged that the package was mailed. The defence also called handwriting experts who differed completely from those who gave their opinion for the prosecution.

A surprise witness for the defence was a grey-haired policeman's wife from Brooklyn, who testified that she had actually seen the fatal package being mailed. She was at Broadway and Vesey Street, Manhattan, at 3.50 p.m. on 23 December 1898, she said, when a man bumped into her. She noticed that he took the package out of his pocket nervously and held it for a few moments in his hand. She looked at the package and read what was written on it. It was like the superscription on the relevant exhibit. Then the man crossed Broadway to the General Post Office and she saw him drop the package into the box. She was asked was the defendant the man she had seen. No, he positively was not, she replied.

'Do you identify Cornish as the man who had the package and mailed it?' This question was put to her in cross-examination.

'Well,' she said, 'he looks very much like him.' Then, after she had appealed for advice to the judge who told her to go on, she added: 'Well, I am pretty sure he is the man.'

Mr Black in his concluding speech for the defence charged Cornish with having committed the murder, alleging that Cornish wanted to get rid of Mrs Adams so that he could have her daughter Mrs Rodgers to himself. On the face of it this was a most improbable accusation, but it served as a useful red herring with the jury. In the event the jury took less than half an hour to find the prisoner not guilty. Thus, after two-and-a-half years in shadow of the gallows, Roland Molineux was finally set free.

He now turned to writing. He had already recorded his impressions of life in the Death House, based partly on his letters to his family. This work was published under the title *The Room with the Little Door* and had a considerable success. Thereafter he became a writer of romantic fiction for the Sunday supplements of the New York *Herald* and *Tribune*. Finally, in 1913, he wrote a melodrama of prison life for the theatrical producer David Belasco which he called *The Man Inside*. After Belasco had put the play on, the author's conduct became markedly peculiar. One night he was ejected from the theatre for causing a disturbance and shortly afterwards he went into a sanatorium in Long Island for treatment following a nervous breakdown. At two o'clock one morning he succeeded in getting out of this establishment and going for a run dressed only in a sports shirt and bath robe. He knocked down several people who stopped to watch him, before being seized and locked up pending medical examination. In the result he was committed to a lunatic asylum. He was already suffering from syphilis in an advanced stage, one of the results of his loose mode of living which had led his wife Blanche to leave him and get a divorce. It also appeared that he used to consort with notorious Chinatown characters and he admitted to smoking opium.

On 2 November 1917, the once celebrated Roland Molineux died in the Kings Park State Hospital for the Insane, according to the hospital records, from 'General Paralysis, Cerebral Type, due to syphilitic infection and characterised by progressive mental deterioration, leading to complete dementia and terminating fatally.'

The Molineux case will long be remembered not only for the tragic story it tells but also as a leading authority on the law of evidence in American criminal trials.

# [5]

# The Good Shoemaker
# and the Poor Fishpedlar

No trial between the two world wars aroused greater con-
troversy both inside and outside the United States than that of
two lowly Italian immigrants named Sacco and Vanzetti, who
were twenty-nine and thirty-one years old respectively at the
time of their arrest. It was a trial which had strong political over-
tones, since both its central figures were on their own admission
pacifists and anarchists—that is to say, they were opposed to war
and to all kinds of organised government which they felt to be evil
and against the higher nature of mankind. On 5 May 1920 they
were arrested and afterwards charged with murder. They were
not brought to trial until just over a year later, at Dedham, a small
town in Massachusetts about ten miles from Boston. More than
six years were to elapse before they ended their lives in the electric
chair at the Massachusetts State Prison.

Public attention was focused on the trial for several reasons, the
origins and unorthodox political beliefs of the prisoners, the
probative value of the circumstantial evidence adduced, the professional behaviour of the trial judge, and above all the unprecedented delay in carrying out the death sentence. By left-wing
elements all the world over, Sacco and Vanzetti were regarded as
sacrifices to capitalist tyranny, and even today, nearly half a
century after they died, their memory is still honoured in Communist and Socialist demonstrations, particularly in the land of
their birth.

Actually there were two trials, and it is the second with which
we are mainly concerned here. Since the first was said to have
affected the second, it is necessary to give a brief account of the

3

earlier one which solely concerned Vanzetti. But first a few words
about the two men themselves.

Nicola Sacco was born on 22 April 1891, the third of seventeen
children of a fairly prosperous peasant family in Torremaggiore,
an Adriatic village in the foothills of the Appenines. Although the
elder Sacco owned olive groves and vineyards and had married
the daughter of a well-to-do local wine merchant, he was a Socialist
and his son Nicola inherited his political sympathies. At the age of
fourteen Nicola left school to work in the fields, where he proved
himself a hard worker and a reliable son. Three years later,
attracted by the accounts of life in America given by a friend of
his father's who had settled in Milford, Mass., Nicola and his
elder brother Sabino emigrated. Sabino found life in the New
World uncongenial, but Nicola stayed on, working in a road gang
and a foundry as an unskilled labourer. He was later employed in a
factory where he acquired a certain skill as a shoemaker in the
Milford Shoe Company. Here he met and married Rosina
Zambelli, the daughter of another Italian immigrant. He joined
the local anarchist club and also an Italian dramatic society with
which he and Rosina would put on performances to raise small
sums of money for the printing of anarchist pamphlets which he
would help to distribute. He was a fond husband and a devoted
father to his two children, Dante, his son, born two years after his
marriage, and Ines, his daughter, who arrived shortly after his
arrest. He had a noticeable charm of manner and was popular in
his social circle in Milford where no one ever believed that he was
guilty of such a crime as murder. The only offence of which he
had been previously convicted was participating as a speaker in a
socialist demonstration without a police permit during the First
World War, for which he was fined.

Bartolomeo Vanzetti was born on 11 June 1888 in the Pied-
montese village of Villafalleto in north-west Italy, where his
father, like Sacco's, was a relatively prosperous peasant who
owned a small holding where he grew fruit, mostly peaches and
grapes. He was a model pupil at school winning among other
awards the second prize for religious catechism. But there was no
living to be made in the village when he left school, and so his
father sent him to work in a city pastry shop where he laboured
from seven in the morning until ten at night. He worked in
similar jobs in other cities including Turin, then as now a strong

socialist centre where he absorbed the teachings of Marx. His mentality was more rigid than Sacco's and he was much more the agitator type. He once told the Massachusetts State Prison psychiatrist that 'where he came from in Italy there was a castle above the town and one family living in it had been oppressing the ordinary people in the valley for eight hundred years'. The psychiatrist replied that 'it wasn't so in America, that a family scarcely lasted three generations here'.

Vanzetti arrived in America in June 1908, two months after Sacco. Like him he turned his hand to a variety of jobs, including being a pastry cook, a bricklayer's assistant, a fishpedlar and a loader in the Plymouth Cordage Company, a rope factory where he led a strike and was consequently blacklisted in the other local factories. He first met Sacco in 1916, and in the following year, as the result of the United States coming into the war, he and Sacco fled to Mexico to escape being called up for military service. They returned to Massachusetts after the Armistice, when Sacco went back to shoemaking and Vanzetti to fishpeddling. Vanzetti was unable to obtain any factory employment owing to his reputation as a strike leader, but Sacco's reputation was clean from the point of view of management-labour relations.

The immediate post-war months were a difficult time for left-wing immigrants who were suspected of being 'Reds' and were marked down as sympathisers of the Bolshevik Revolution in Russia. A series of outrages in the spring of 1919, culminating in a number of bombs being sent through the mails, resulted in the arrests and deportation of many Communists, anarchists and other 'radicals'. Several of Sacco's and Vanzetti's friends were caught in the net, and in April 1920 Vanzetti went to New York to make inquiries about them; he was advised to hide his anarchist literature since more police raids were possible.

The following specimen of compromising literature was found in Sacco's possession at the time of his arrest and was later produced at his trial:

Fellow workers, you have fought all the wars. You have worked for all the capitalists. You have wandered over all the countries. Have you harvested the fruits of your labours, the price of your victories? Does the past comfort you? Does the present smile on you? Does the future promise you anything?

Have you found a piece of land where you can live like a human being?

On these questions, on this argument, and on this theme the struggle for existence Bartolomeo Vanzetti will speak. Admission free. Freedom of discussion to all. Take the ladies with you.

On the morning of Christmas Eve 1919, there was an attempted hold-up in the streets of Bridgewater, a manufacturing town some thirty miles south of Boston. A truck carrying the wages of the employees of the White Shoe Company was held up by a car in which sat a party of foreign-looking men, whom several witnesses swore to be Italian. Two of these men fired, one with a shotgun, at the driver of the truck, who being armed returned their fire. The bandits thereupon concluded that their attempt must fail and they accordingly drove off. In the course of their inquiries the Bridgewater police found an Overland car in a local garage which had been brought in for repairs. The police believed that it was owned or was being driven by an Italian named Boda for the purposes of the attempted hold-up and they told Mr and Mrs Johnson, who ran the garage, to let them know immediately if anyone came in for the Overland.

On 15 April 1920, nearly four months after the Bridgewater incident, another hold-up took place in the neighbouring town of South Braintree, this time successfully and with fatal results. Two employees of the Slater and Morrill Shoe Company, a cashier named Parmenter, and a guard named Berardelli, were transferring the weekly pay roll amounting to nearly $16,000 from one factory to another along the main street of South Braintree about three o'clock in the afternoon. They had nearly reached their destination when they were fired upon and killed by two men who had been leaning against a fence. At the same time a car drove up, the two men threw the boxes containing the cash into the car, jumped in themselves and were rapidly driven off, firing at on-lookers as they did so and throwing pieces of rubber hose studded with nails into the road so as to puncture the tyres of any car which might pursue them. They succeeded in passing a nearby level-crossing just as it was about to be closed.

Two days later a Buick car was found abandoned in a wood not far away. Leading from it were the tracks of a smaller vehicle, which the police felt might be those of the Overland which had been left in the Johnsons' garage. As for the Buick, this was known to have been stolen in the previous November, while its number plates were also stolen. The police were convinced that it had been used both at Bridgewater and South Braintree.

On the evening of 5 May, Boda called at the garage to collect his car. He was accompanied by Sacco and Vanzetti and a third Italian named Orciani. While Boda was talking to Mr Johnson, Mrs Johnson under the pretext of fetching some milk went into the house of a neighbour and telephoned the police. Her husband pointed out to Boda that the car did not have proper licence plates, and either because of this or because (as was alleged by the prosecution) the men realised that Mrs Johnson was telephoning the police, the Italians left without the Overland, Boda and Orciani on a motor cycle and the other two on foot. Later that evening Sacco and Vanzetti were arrested on a street car and both were found to be armed with revolvers. They were taken to the local police station where they were charged with being in possession of firearms without a permit, to which they pleaded guilty. They were also asked their reason for visiting Bridge-water that evening and about their whereabouts on various other dates. Nothing was said of the two outrages for the time being, though the newspapers began to speculate about their possible participation in them. Boda and Orciano were also picked up, but were allowed to go after questioning, Boda departing hurriedly for Italy and Orciani satisfying the police that he had been at work on the days of both crimes.

While Sacco and Vanzetti were being held in custody, witnesses who had been at Bridgewater and South Braintree were brought in to identify them. Sacco was able to prove that he had been working in his factory on the previous Christmas Eve, so that he could not be charged with the Bridgewater crime. However, unfortunately for him, he had had the day off on 15 April and so he was charged with the South Braintree murders. Vanzetti, being a self-employed fishpedlar at Plymouth, was unable to produce an alibi for either day and so he was charged with both crimes. Since the two crimes had been committed in different counties of Massachusetts—Plymouth and Norfolk—the respective indict-ments were presented by different grand juries. It was afterwards suggested by the defence that the prosecution deliberately

arranged for the Bridgewater case against Vanzetti to be tried first
in the hope that he might be convicted and when he came up for
the second trial with his co-defendant Sacco the latter might be
regarded as under a cloud. However, the prosecution pointed out
that the Plymouth grand jury happened to be in session and could
indict Vanzetti at once, whereas the Norfolk grand jury was not
due to meet before September. Anyhow Vanzetti was indicted
without delay and stood trial for the attempted hold-up in
Bridgewater before Judge Webster Thayer at Plymouth on
22 June 1920.

Five witnesses called by the prosecution claimed to identify
Vanzetti in the unsuccessful hold-up, though the descriptions they
first gave the police did not always tally with Vanzetti's actual
appearance. One testimony came from a newsboy who had taken
refuge behind a telegraph pole during the shooting and from this
vantage point had caught a glimpse of the criminal. 'I could tell he
was a foreigner,' said the boy, 'I could tell by the way he ran.'
Under cross-examination this witness admitted that he might have
been anything except a Chinaman, a Japanese, an African or an
American. Two things told against Vanzetti. One was that when
he was arrested he was found to be in possession of gun cartridges
similar to those found in the abandoned Buick car. Secondly, he
did not give evidence in his own defence, having been advised by
his defence counsel that if he took the stand his political views
would be elicited with disastrous results. On the other hand, more
than twenty people, customers and acquaintances, but all Italian,
swore to having seen him in Plymouth on Christmas Eve, and some
of them had bought eels from him for the Christmas Eve feasts.
Several of these witnesses were discredited in cross-examination,
but there was general agreement that Vanzetti always wore a long
flowing moustache, whereas some of the prosecution witnesses
had deposed that the chief bandit at Bridgewater had a neatly
trimmed moustache.

Vanzetti was found guilty and sentenced to imprisonment for
ten to fifteen years. A few weeks later he was indicted along with
Sacco by the Norfolk grand jury for the South Braintree murders.
Their trial opened on 31 May 1921 in the court house at Dedham,
Norfolk County, also before Judge Thayer. No mention was made
at this trial of Vanzetti's conviction in the other case, but the
newspapers drew attention to it in terms which, had it happened

in England, would certainly have resulted in their editors being immediately committed to prison for contempt of court.

There was considerable sympathy for the prisoners in liberal circles throughout the United States, concerned over the Government's repressive policy towards radicals, and this resulted in a substantial defence fund being raised which amounted to some $50,000 by the time the trial had ended and which afterwards reached as much as five times that amount. The prisoners could therefore afford the best counsel. In the event Sacco's defence was led by Fred Moore, a prominent 'labour lawyer' from California, whom it was hoped would be able to counteract or at least expose the anticipated prejudice of a New England judge and jury from such a conservative community as Dedham. Vanzetti was represented by two outstanding local advocates, the brothers Jeremiah and Thomas MacAnarney, while the prosecution was conducted by the District Attorney, Frederick G. Katzmann, assisted by Harold P. Williams. The latter opened the case for the State on 7 June after some delay caused by the defence challenging all but seven of the five hundred citizens who had been summoned to serve as possible jurors. The remaining five actual jurors were selected from a further panel of two hundred produced by the sheriffs.

The killing of Parmenter and Berardelli was not disputed by the defence. The sole issue to be decided at the trial was the identity of the killers. The prosecution claimed that Sacco did the actual shooting, while Vanzetti was riding in the car and was thus as guilty in law of the murders as Sacco. Mr Williams was afterwards criticised for not referring in his opening speech to what in the American phrase is called 'consciousness of guilt'—that is behaviour by the prisoners tending to show that they were guilty of the crime. It is true that such a reference was made by Judge Thayer in his summing up, but the earlier omission to do so explicitly was unfortunate since 'consciousness of guilt' was an important link in the chain of circumstantial evidence on which the case rested. According to the prosecution it was evinced by the conduct of the prisoners when they went to the garage for Boda's car, by the revolvers found on their persons and by the lies admittedly told by them to the police when they were arrested.

The trial exhibited a mass of conflicting testimony on the identity question, fifty-nine witnesses going on the witness stand for the prosecution and ninety-nine for the defence. Mrs Johnson, for example, was positive that Sacco was one of the men who called at the garage on the evening of his arrest. Another important prosecution witness was the policeman who arrested the prisoners on the street car. He described how he boarded the car and asked them where they came from.

'I said, "What was you doing in Bridgewater?" They said, "We went down to see a friend of mine." I said, "Who is your friend?" He said, "A man by the —— they call him Poppy." "Well," I said, "I want you, you are under arrest".' Then, according to the police witness, Vanzetti put his hand in his hip pocket, and the policeman said, 'Keep your hands out on your lap or you will be sorry.' At this point, Vanzetti in the dock shouted at the witness, 'You are a liar!' As to Sacco, according to this witness, he denied having a gun on him when he and his companion were arrested as 'suspicious characters', although in fact they were both armed.

The local police chief testified that Sacco and Vanzetti denied knowing Boda, the owner of the Overland car, or visiting the Johnson garage. He went on to recall his conversation with Sacco at the time about his revolver.

'You had a revolver in your pocket when arrested?'

'Yes,' answered Sacco.

'Why did you carry it?'

'To protect myself. Lots of bad men.'

'Why did you carry so many cartridges?'

'Well, I go to see my friend. We go into the woods and fire them.'

A cap picked up at the scene of the murder was produced by the prosecution and stated to belong to Sacco, who denied owning it. Two firearms experts were also called. One of them stated that in his opinion the fatal bullet had been fired by Sacco's revolver; the other stated that the bullet was 'consistent' with having been fired by his revolver. Sacco's employer testified to his good reputation as a steady worker, but he was obliged to admit that Sacco had not been at work on the day of the murders.

For the defence other firearms experts testified that in their view the bullets had not been fired by Sacco's revolver. Otherwise the evidence called by the defence was designed to prove an alibi for both prisoners. In Sacco's case, he swore he had gone to the Italian consulate in Boston on the day of the murders to arrange for a passport to return to Italy, and a deposition in support of this was taken in Italy from a clerk who had formerly worked in the consul's office. Other witnesses, mostly Italian, were called to state that though they had seen the murderers they were not Sacco and Vanzetti. A number of Italians swore abilis, but not always convincingly since their sense of loyalty to their fellow countrymen led them into contradiction and confusion over dates.

Both prisoners testified in their own defence. Vanzetti, who took the stand first, admitted that he had been to the Johnsons' garage on the night of his arrest, although he had previously denied this. Asked why he wanted to use Boda's car, he replied that it was to move a supply of anarchist literature to a safer place than his home and the homes of friends. This was the first mention in the case of his and his co-defendant's political opinions, and was deliberately introduced by the defence in order to provide the most convincing answer to the prosecution's case.

Vanzetti went on to explain why he had lied to the police when he was arrested. 'Because in that time there was a deportation,' he said, 'and the reaction was more vivid than now and more mad than now.' Both he and Sacco had lied, he stated, because they would be liable to be deported if it were known that they had fled to Mexico in 1917 in order to evade military service. As for lying about the revolver Vanzetti said that it was not to incriminate his friends, from one of whom he had bought it four years previously in Boston. 'It was a very bad time,' he said, and he armed himself in self-defence especially because he had to take money, a hundred dollars or more at a time, to Boston to buy fish. 'There were many crimes, many hold-ups, many robberies at that time.'

Sacco's reason for lying to the police was similar to Vanzetti's. 'I know some—most of the friends—Socialists, why they are slackers.' Sacco used the term 'slacker' to connote the English term 'conscientious objector' in wartime. 'They got literature in the house. They got papers and everything—Socialist movement. That is why I thought they would do the same way as in New York and Chicago.'

On the thirty-seventh day of the trial, Judge Thayer summed up the evidence quite fairly and dispassionately, and it is difficult to fault his directions to the jury, although he was subsequently the target for much abuse from Sacco–Vanzetti partisans. Every prisoner, he said, no matter what his nationality, class, position, education, politics, or religion, was entitled to the same rights, privileges and consideration. 'I therefore beseech you,' the judge continued, 'not to allow the fact that the defendants are Italians to influence or prejudice you in the least degree. They are entitled, under the law, to the same rights and considerations as though their ancestors came over in the *Mayflower.*'

On 14 July 1921, the jury found both Sacco and Vanzetti guilty of murder in the first degree. '*Siamo innocenti,*' cried Sacco from the dock, raising his hand. 'They kill an innocent man. They kill two innocent men.' They were not brought up to hear Judge Thayer pronounce the mandatory death sentence until 1 November, a lengthy adjournment necessitated by the appeal procedure. It was the first of a series of delays, which culminated in the death house of Charlestown Prison seven years later. Such a long intervening period between conviction and execution may well seem gruesome and barbaric to English readers who will recall that when the death penalty used to be inflicted for murder in England the maximum time between dismissal of the appeal against conviction and the carrying out of the sentence was three weeks. The inordinately long delay in the Sacco–Vanzetti trial was due to the efforts of their supporters, including their legal advisers, in exhausting every device to save their lives by way of motions for new trials and stays of execution. In deference to public agitation Governor Fuller of Massachusetts appointed an independent committee presided over by President Lowell of Harvard University, but the Lowell Committee found after prolonged investigation that Sacco and Vanzetti were guilty of the South Braintree murders 'beyond all reasonable doubt'. Meanwhile a young Portuguese gunman Celestino Madeiros confessed to being implicated in the crime and declared that Sacco and Vanzetti were not. However, the Supreme Court of Massachusetts confirmed Judge Thayer's finding that Madeiros's confession fell short of establishing his guilt or in creating reasonable doubt about the guilt of Sacco and Vanzetti. This judgment was handed down on 5 April 1927 and two days later the prisoners were brought up again to hear the death sentence confirmed by Judge Thayer.

'You know I am innocent,' declared Sacco from the dock. 'That is the same words I pronounced seven years ago. You condemn two innocent men.' When it came to Vanzetti's turn to speak, he said: 'Never in our full life could we hope to do such work for tolerance, for justice, for man's understanding of man as we now do by accident. Our words—our lives—our pains—nothing! The taking of our lives—lives of a good shoemaker and a poor fish-pedlar—all! That last moment belongs to us—that agony is our triumph.'

Still the defence persisted in its efforts. After two Federal judges had refused to issue a writ of Habeas Corpus, Sacco and Vanzetti were made ready for electrocution on the evening of 10 August 1927. Their trousers had already been slit and their hair cut to facilitate the passage of the electric current through their bodies, when news came that Governor Fuller had post-poned the execution for twelve days so that the Supreme Court could decide whether or not to issue a writ of error. With that court's refusal to do so, the last hopes of the condemned men vanished.

Also in the death house at this time was Madeiros who had been sentenced for another murder. Shortly after midnight on 22 August, Madeiros, Sacco and Vanzetti were executed in that order, while the jail was surrounded by machine-guns and besieged by a crowd of excited sightseers and partisans. Sacco's last words were, 'Long live anarchy!' in Italian and in English: 'Farewell my wife and child and all my friends. Farewell, Mother.' Vanzetti protested his innocence to the last: 'I have never committed any crime but sometimes some sin. . . . I am innocent of all crime, not only of this, but all. I am an innocent man. I wish to forgive some people for what they are now doing to me.'

Opinions remain sharply divided on the Sacco–Vanzetti trial. My own feeling is that Vanzetti was innocent but that Sacco may well have been guilty. However, on one aspect of the matter there is general agreement. Justice was too long delayed and it would have been better served if the sentence on both prisoners had been commuted to imprisonment. Six years waiting for execution is an ordeal which no prisoner, even if guilty, should have to undergo in any civilised country.[1]

[1] This is by no means a record. In May 1948, Caryl Chessman was sentenced to death for kidnapping with intent to commit robbery, then a capital offence under Californian state law. He was not executed until twelve years later.

# 6

# Landru, the French Bluebeard

Throughout the morning of 7 December 1921 a curious crowd of spectators gathered outside the Court of Assize in the Palais de Justice at Versailles. The entrance was guarded by police and troops, who turned away almost everyone who tried to gain admission to the small and shabby court room, since there was only accommodation for a handful of people inside apart from the court officials and lawyers concerned with the trial. It was a case which had already attracted world-wide interest, since the accused man was said to have had relations of one sort or another with no less than 283 women and to have murdered ten of them, having previously seduced them and persuaded them to hand over their money and property to him for safekeeping or investment.

Punctually at one o'clock in the afternoon President Gilbert in red robes and gold-braided hat took his place on the bench accompanied by two assessors. The uniformed soldiers on duty in their steel helmets presented arms smartly and the usher rang his bell calling everyone in court to order. Immediately below the judicial bench was a table containing the grim exhibits in the case, pieces of charred clothing and human bones. At a sign from the President, a little door at the side of the court room opened and the prisoner appeared, escorted by three gendarmes; two of whom stood on either side of him and one behind as he stepped into the appointed place in court which served as a dock. A tall red-bearded figure, he looked a rather weary old man, although in truth he was only fifty-two. His complexion wore the familiar prison pallor, since he had been in custody for more than two years.

The President's first duty was to establish the prisoner's

identity. 'Your name is Landru?' he asked the man on whom every eye in court was firmly fixed. 'Henri Désiré, son of Alexandre Julien and Henriette Flore Landru? You were born in Paris on 12 April 1869, and your last residence was 76 Rue de Rochechouart?'

'Yes,' Landru quietly replied.

The Clerk of the Court thereupon rose to his feet and proceeded to read the Indictment, a document of enormous length, which it took the Clerk three hours to do and which occupied the greater part of the first day of the trial. It was an extraordinary story of forgery, swindling, seduction and multiple murder. For the most part Landru listened to this appalling account with an air of apparent unconcern, his bearded face bent forward between his shoulders. Only once did he look up and scowl in the course of the lengthy recitation of his misdeeds. That was when the Clerk uttered the phrase, 'exploitation of women'. An audible titter ran round the court room at the mention of the 283 women with whom Landru was stated to have had 'relations'.

Landru's usual technique was the familiar one of the matrimonial advertisement. Here is a typical example which appeared in *Le Journal*, a Paris morning newspaper, on 1 May 1915:

> Widower with two children, aged forty-three, with comfortable income, affectionate, serious, and moving in good society, desires to meet widow with a view to matrimony.

Among the women who replied to this advertisement was a forty-four-year-old widow named Madame Anna Collomb, who gave full particulars of her family and fortune, and incidentally stating her age as twenty-nine. In due course she received a letter from a Monsieur Cuchet, who described himself as a director of a factory in Montmartre. At the meeting which followed Cuchet told Anna Collomb that he was a war refugee, an engineer from Rocroi, and had left everything before the advancing Germans and had come to Paris to build up his business afresh. He added that he had a car, a little apartment in town and a modest place, the Villa Ermitage, at Gambais, near the forest of Rambouillet, not far from Paris. He now wished to marry and settle down, he said. The result was that Madame Collomb found Monsieur Cuchet most attractive and, as they say, fell for him in a big way.

However, after a while his ardour for the lady began to cool. The truth was that he had several other affairs on hand at this time since there had been many replies to his advertisement and he could not spare all the time that the infatuated Anna Collomb demanded. However, they eventually came together again, she gave up her own apartment and went to live with her lover in his flat in the Rue Chateaudun, while she gave him her furniture to put into store. She also visited the villa at Gambais where Landru was known as Monsieur Fremyet. Elsewhere and with other women he had different aliases, Petit, Dupont, Diard and Guillet. He had another villa at Vernouillet on the River Seine near Paris. He also had a second apartment in Paris, 76 Rue de Rochechouart, not to mention a wife and four children who lived at Clichy, where he ran a garage.

On Christmas Eve 1916, Mme Collomb invited her sister Mme Pelat to Gambais to meet her lover. M. Fremyet ingratiated himself by saying that he would soon regularise their position by marrying his mistress, after which they would be moving to Nice. That was the last Mme Pelat saw of her sister and M. Fremyet. After writing to both of them at Gambais and receiving no reply, she addressed a letter to the local Mayor, asking him if he could tell her where M. Fremyet was and how to get into touch with him.

It so happened that not long before this the Mayor had received a similar request from a certain Mlle Lacoste about her sister Mme Celestine Buisson who had also visited the villa in Gambais and had disappeared. On making inquiries the Mayor learned that the Villa Ermitage was occupied by a M. Dupont, of whom there was likewise no trace. The Mayor suggested that Mlle Lacoste and Mme Pelat should get into touch with one another. In due course they met and compared notes. Both women had seen the occupier of the villa and they agreed that Cuchet-Fremyet and Dupont were singularly alike. Meanwhile the police were investigating another disappearance, that of a genuine Mme Cuchet. It appeared that Jeanne Cuchet and her son André had gone to live with a certain M. Diard in his house at Vernouillet in December 1914 and had not been seen or heard of since. After making further inquiries, the police were satisfied that Cuchet, Fremyet, Dupont and Diard were one and the same person. On 10 April 1919, a warrant was issued for the arrest of the individual whose identity corresponded with any of these aliases.

Next day Mlle Lacoste happened to be walking along the Rue de Rivoli when she suddenly saw the unmistakable figure of the man she recognised as M. Dupont. He had a smartly dressed young woman on his arm and Mlle Lacoste saw them enter a shop. She followed them inside where she heard the man order a white china dinner service to be sent to his apartment. After the two had left the shop Mlle Lacoste continued to follow them but eventually lost them in the crowd. She thereupon went to the nearest police station and reported her suspicions. On following up this clue, the police learned that the dinner service had been ordered by M. Lucien Guillet, an engineer, of 76 Rue de Rochechouart.

The following morning Landru was arrested in his apartment and told he would be charged with murder. He protested that he was Lucien Guillet, born at Rocroi in 1874, and seemed shocked that he should be accused of a capital crime. He was then searched and the police discovered a black loose-leaved note-book in his pocket which he made an unsuccessful attempt to dispose of by throwing it out of the window.

The note-book revealed that Landru kept a meticulous account of his daily expenses. For instance, on the day he invited Anna Collomb to Gambais, he had recorded one return ticket and one single ticket to the local station, similarly with Celestine Buisson. The note-book also showed that the replies to his matrimonial advertisements had been carefully classified and information had been filed about their fortunes, children, relations and so on. The names were briefly marked under the following heads:

1. To be answered *poste restante.*
2. Without money.
3. Without furniture.
4. No reply.
5. To be answered to initials *poste restante.*
6. Possible fortune.
7. To be further investigated.

The first police searches of the Villa Ermitage and the house at Vernouillet revealed nothing of importance, but later a stove was discovered in which Landru was alleged to have burnt the bodies of his victims after he had cut up the bodies. Afterwards 295 bone fragments of human bodies were discovered. These were believed to belong to three corpses; there was also a miscellaneous collection of women's clothing, buttons, and trinkets of various kinds.

Besides the Mesdames Buisson, Collomb and Cuchet and the latter's eighteen-year-old son, seven more women whom Landru knew were stated to have disappeared without trace. They were Mme Thérèse Laborde-Line, widow, aged forty-seven, and a native of Buenos Aires whom Landru called 'bresil'; Mme Desirée Guillin, a widow, aged fifty-nine, formerly a governess, who had inherited 22,000 francs which Landru drew out of her bank account with a forged signature, having also sold her furniture; Andrée Babelay, a servant girl, aged nineteen, whom Landru met in the Metro; Mme Louise Jaume, a married woman, aged thirty-eight, who was separated from her husband, and whose money and furniture Landru appropriated after he had taken her to Gambais; Mme Anne-Marie Pascal, a divorceé, aged thirty-three, and a struggling dressmaker of easy morals, whose furniture and personal belongings were found in Landru's garage; and Mme Marie-Thérèse Marchadier, a prostitute turned brothel-keeper, who gave up her establishment and went with Landru to Gambais, after parting with her furniture. All eleven names with accompanying particulars appeared in the sinister black note-book which Landru had tried to hide from the police when he was arrested.

On the second day of the trial, President Gilbert examined the prisoner on his past record. 'You have received seven sentences for fraud, Landru,' he remarked. 'Your parents were honest and decent folk. Your father was for a long time a fireman in the Vulcain Ironworks. Your mother worked at home as a dressmaker. After her death, your father, who had retired to the Dordogne, came to Paris to see you but found you were in prison. He was so upset by your conduct that in 1912 he committed suicide in the Bois de Boulogne.'

As the prisoner did not dispute these facts, the judge went on: 'You were a clever boy at school and earned high praise from your teachers. On leaving school you were admitted as a subdeacon to a religious establishment?'

'Only for a short time,' Landru added.

'Perhaps it was there,' said the judge, 'that you learned that unctuous manner which has been one of your chief methods of seduction, and which has helped you to capture the trust and affections of so many women.'

President Gilbert paused, but the prisoner remained silent. 'Then,' continued the judge, 'you took up more profane occupations. Not far from you there lived your cousin Mme Remy, who had a young daughter.'

'She had two,' Landru interrupted.

'Very well. One of them became your mistress, and you had a daughter born in 1891. Two years later you regularised the position, married her and acknowledged the child. In all you had four children?' Landru nodded his agreement.

'You had a lot of different jobs,' said the judge. 'Clerk in an architect's office, agent, toy salesman and so on. In fact you had no definite, stable occupation.'

'Which proves how inadequate were the inquiries which were made about me,' Landru again broke in. 'The police are often inefficient.'

'Yet,' said the judge, 'when the magistrate confronted you with this information you had nothing to say?'

The prisoner threw up his hands as if amazed at such official stupidity. 'It was not my business to guide the police,' he exclaimed. 'Have they not been accusing me for the past three years of deeds which the women who disappeared never for one moment reproached me with?'

These words produced some laughter among the onlookers in court which the judge suppressed by calling for silence. 'It is you,' he emphasised his words by pointing a finger at the prisoner, 'it is you who have made it impossible for these women to complain. That is as clear as anything.'

Asked to explain to the jury why the names of so many women were in his note-book, at first he was evasive. Finally when pressed by the judge, he said: '*Eh bien! Voila!* It is the list of a businessman, who entered the names of his clients with whom he did business.' He had bought these women's furniture from them to help them during the war, he explained, intending to sell it back to them when the German armies had been driven out of France.

'Why then recruit your clients by means of matrimonial advertisements?' the judge asked.

'Just a little business ruse, very innocent,' Landru replied. 'It flattered their conceit.' The prisoner let his gaze wander in the direction of the jury, as if to say what a clever answer he had given. But they did not look at all convinced. Then he turned again to the judge and said: 'You say that some of these women have not been found. Perhaps they will turn up during the trial.' Needless to add, none of them did turn up.

During the succeeding days a string of relatives of the ten women who had vanished came forward to testify to the occasions when they had last seen the women in question, usually in Landru's company. Others testified having seen dense smoke coming out of the chimneys of the houses which Landru had occupied at Gambais and Vernouillet, accompanied by a most offensive stench. Indeed one of the neighbours complained about it to the police at Vernouillet. However, this was at a critical stage of the First World War, and though the police did call at the house they eventually dropped the matter as they had more serious matters to think about at that time than malodorous smoke from a domestic chimney, particularly when Landru assured them that he had only been burning some refuse. There were also stories of portions of putrified human flesh being recovered from a lake near Gambais by fishermen.

One witness who attracted particular attention was the pretty young woman who had been with Landru when he went shopping in the Rue de Rivoli, and as events fortunately turned out for her was 'the one that got away'. She gave her name as Fernande Segret, her age as twenty-nine, and her occupation as 'lyric artiste'. She described how she had become engaged to Landru whom she knew as Roger Guillet, how her mother had described him as a impostor and an adventurer, and how despite this warning she had insisted on going to live with him as his mistress. She was deeply in love with him, she said, and wished to marry him.

'I went to Gambais seven or eight times,' said the nubile Fernande Segret. 'The villa was not what you would call well furnished. In one room there were some guns and cartridges which he knew well how to use.'

'Do you know what means your fiancé had?' the judge asked her. 'How did you live?'

'Landru told me his garage brought in a good deal, enough for our needs. I went there one day, and was rather disappointed as there was only one apprentice working in the place, for he had told me he had a considerable business there.'

Asked if they ever had any quarrels, pretty Mademoiselle Segret replied that they had two she remembered in particular. One was when a letter came for him addressed in another name. The other was when she began to look through some of his papers in their flat in the Rue de Rochechouart and he flew into a great rage. 'I promised not to do it again,' she added, 'but I showed my astonishment since all my correspondence was read by him.'

There was 'a delicate point' he wished to clear up, said the judge to this witness. She had told the examining magistrate that in her sexual relations with the accused she had found him extremely passionate but at the same time quite normal.

'Is that right?'

'Oh, yes,' replied Mademoiselle Segret. 'Very normal.' What President Gilbert was trying to ascertain was whether Landru was a sadist and pervert. Apparently he was not, though the medical evidence pointed to his being a dangerous psychopath, though well aware of what he was doing.

In his speech to the court, the chief prosecutor declared: 'I demand the extreme punishment—death for Landru, the murderer of Vernouillet and Gambais. He is entirely responsible for his deeds. The doctors have certified this, and the ability which he has shown here is proof of his sanity. He had no pity on his victims. Why then should you have pity on him?'

It took the jury an hour and a half to find Landru guilty on all charges except two—only in respect of those of defrauding the domestic servant Andrée Babelay of her property (she had virtually none) was he acquitted.

Prompted by Landru's defence counsel, the jury surprisingly added a recommendation to mercy, calling upon the President of the Republic to reprieve the condemned man. However, the judge sentenced him to death by the guillotine, to be carried out publicly in front of the prison where he was confined.

'Be brave!' one of the officials said when they came to fetch him as was customary between five and six o'clock in the morning. 'I *am* brave,' replied Landru. Asked if he would make his confession to the priest and hear Mass, he exclaimed, 'Never on your life!' Anyhow, he added, 'I cannot think of keeping these gentlemen waiting.' He also refused the usual offer of a glass of rum and a cigarette.

As he was led out into the prison yard, he shivered a little in the cold morning air, since he was wearing thin trousers and an open-necked shirt. Then the prison gates were flung open and for a minute or two he faced a cordon of troops holding back the spectators who had collected at that early hour in front of the guillotine which had been erected in the square outside the prison.

In a matter of seconds the executioner and his assistant strapped him face downwards on the platform of the guillotine. Then the razor-sharp knife fell and Landru's head rolled into the waiting basket below as blood spurted out in great jets from the headless trunk.

Justice, French-style, had been done and, what is more, had been seen to be done in gruesome fashion.

The Landru story has a curious tail-piece. Sixty odd years later a film entitled *Landru* and scripted by Françoise Sagan was made and publicly shown. Fernande Segret, whom everyone thought was dead as she had not been heard of for years—in fact she had been working as a governess in the Lebanon—suddenly turned up and sued the film company for 200,000 francs damages. She got 10,000. She then retired to an old people's home in Normandy where she eventually killed herself, saying she was tired of people pointing to her as 'the woman in the Landru case'.

# 7

# The Victory Bond Swindle

One of the most colourful characters ever to appear in the dock of the Old Bailey was Horatio William Bottomley, Member of Parliament, financier, company promoter, journalist, public orator, newspaper and magazine proprietor, theatrical backer, racehorse owner, gambler and bankrupt. He was twice acquitted in spectacular trials in which he was charged with fraud and conspiracy, and in another trial the magistrate refused to convict him of promoting an illegal lottery, though the evidence against him was clear. It was the fourth and final trial, which opened at the Central Criminal Court before Mr Justice Salter on 18 May 1922, that proved his undoing. This time he was accused on twenty-four counts of fraudulently converting to his own use more than £150,000 entrusted to him by members of the public for investment in his so-called Victory Bond Club and three other enterprises. Mr Travers Humphreys, perhaps the greatest criminal lawyer of his time in England, led the prosecution. Bottomley, as was his wont, conducted his own defence.

By this date, the sixty-two-year-old defendant looked bloated and dissipated. 'In truth, it was not I who floored Bottomley,' said Humphreys after the trial. 'It was drink. The man I met in 1922 was a drink-sodden creature, whose brain could only be got to work by repeated doses of champagne.'

Both Bottomley's parents died when he was a child and in consequence he was placed in an orphanage school. He ran away from school to become, successively, an errand boy, a clerk in a solicitor's office and a shorthand reporter in the Law Courts, where he acquired considerable legal knowledge as well as forensic skill. For many years he pretended to be the illegitimate son of the

celebrated atheist Charles Bradlaugh, whom he strikingly resembled. Actually his father was a tailor's foreman who ended his
life in a lunatic asylum. But he did have a somewhat tenuous
connection with Bradlaugh through his mother who was a sister of
Bradlaugh's friend George Holyoake, the founder of the Co-operative Movement. His first business venture, a small suburban
weekly newspaper, ended in bankruptcy and prosecution for
fraud. He was acquitted and the judge who tried the case was so
impressed by his conduct of it that he advised him to become a
barrister. However, as an undischarged bankrupt he was unable to
obtain admission to any of the Inns of Court, so that he turned
instead to the shadier occupation of promoting Australian gold
mining companies.

By the time he was thirty-seven, it was estimated that Bottomley
had made £3 million in this way. However, his companies failed
regularly, as evidenced by the fact that in the first five years of the
present century he was served with sixty-seven bankruptcy
petitions and writs. At the same time Bottomley was recklessly
extravagant in his personal expenditure. He started a racing stable,
and although he won the Cesarewitch and other prizes on the
turf, he squandered large sums on various theatrical enterprises,
besides a luxurious flat in London, a large country house in
Sussex, where he kept his racing stables, and a villa in the south of
France. He posed as a philanthropist and this helped to secure his
election to Parliament as Liberal MP for South Hackney in 1906.
Three years later he was again charged with fraud and acquitted.
But shortly afterwards he was made bankrupt for a second time so
that he had to resign his seat in Parliament.

The outbreak of war in 1914 provided Horatio Bottomley with
a fresh opportunity for self-advancement and incidentally self-
enrichment. He told his friends he would break with his 'sordid
past', in which he had latterly been involved in the organisation of
gigantic lotteries and sweepstakes. He now became a recruiting
officer for the armed forces and stumped the country making
patriotic speeches (for not less than £50 a time), exhorting the
young men of Britain to join up with the colours. These speeches,
added to his propaganda articles in the *Sunday Pictorial*, for
which he was likewise well remunerated, made him a nationally
known figure. He was consequently able to pay off his old
creditors and to obtain his discharge from bankruptcy.

At the General Election in 1918 he got back his old parliamentary seat in South Hackney, this time as an Independent. Shortly afterwards the Government floated a Victory Loan, in which the smallest bonds were of a nominal value of £5 and were issued at £4 5s. Bottomley conceived the brilliant idea of forming a club, so that the 'little man' and the 'little woman' could share in the loan by subscribing smaller sums with the accumulation of which Bottomley would buy Victory Bonds or National War Bonds in the name of the club. Interest on the club's holding of stocks, and the bonuses, represented by the Government's annual redemptions, were to be combined in a fund which would be distributed by lot among the subscribers, who would also be entitled to withdraw their subscriptions at any time and get their money back in the same way as Government Premium Bond holders can do today. Bottomley invited the public to subscribe in units of 15s 6d, which represented the purchase price of a £1 share, the proceeds of which he undertook to incorporate in the Club's funds.

The public fell for the scheme in a big way. Between June 1919 and the end of the year Bottomley received subscriptions to the amount of nearly half a million pounds. Some of this he handed over to the Treasury Department, but much of it—so it was alleged—Bottomley applied to bolster up various companies in which he was interested or else barefacedly transferred to his own pocket. In October 1921 the Chancery Court appointed a receiver to examine Bottomley's enterprises. At the same time he quarrelled with an associate named Reuben Bigland, who proceeded to publish a defamatory pamphlet about him in which he described the Victory Bond Club as Bottomley's 'latest and greatest swindle' and how he 'gulled poor subscribers to invest one pound notes' in the Club. Bottomley then prosecuted Bigland for criminal libel. Bigland put in an elaborate written plea of justification, but in the event he was not called upon to prove his accusations, since Bottomley abandoned the prosecution and Bigland was formally acquitted. This made Bottomley's own prosecution inevitable.

Since Bottomley was still an MP, the normal practice would have been for the Crown to be represented by one of the Law Officers. But such was the legend of Bottomley's invincibility in the courts that Mr Lloyd George's Government, which was highly nervous about the proceedings, declined to instruct either the Attorney-General or the Solicitor-General. However, they offered Humphreys any King's Counsel he might choose to lead him, but Humphreys refused the offer. Though he had no specialised knowledge of accountancy, Humphreys put aside all other work to prepare the prosecution case, had an extra table brought into his chambers in the Temple, and worked for weeks with the Government accountants, so that he eventually became as familiar with the questioned figures as Bottomley himself.

The preliminary proceedings took place in March 1922 at Bow Street Magistrate's Court. On his way to the court, Bottomley waylaid the prosecutor's clerk and asked for a few minutes interview with his master. Humphreys consented provided his junior counsel was present.

Bottomley asked for two favours at the interview. First, he wanted a short adjournment each day at 11.30, so that he could have a pint of champagne, which he said he simply could not do without if he was to get through the morning. He added that he would call it his 'medicine' to the magistrate. Humphreys agreed provided that the magistrate had no objection, and this was conceded. Secondly, Bottomley wanted Humphreys to suppress the name of a certain lady into whose account, which he had opened for her in the same bank, he had paid various Victory Club subscriptions. Humphreys agreed provided Bottomley would state that the account was his own private one. If there was any attempt at prevarication, said the prosecutor, the lady would be put into the witness box. In the event the hearings before the magistrate went according to plan, and Bottomley was duly committed for trial.

In his opening speech to the jury at the Old Bailey, Humphreys showed how very large sums from the Victory Bond Club had passed to its founder. For example, there was a payment of £5,000 for the upkeep of racing stables in Belgium, and another to a wine merchant for over a hundred dozen bottles of champagne, while a company, which was merely an alias for Bottomley himself, benefited by £20,000. Many thousands more went to one of his numerous lady friends who acted as another go-between. Altogether over £150,000 in cheques drawn on the Club's account had been diverted in this way. Books dealing with the Club accounts were absent, there were never any Club trustees except Bottomley, and there was never any regular audit. Since the Club's affairs had been taken over by the receiver, 85,000 persons had written in claiming back their money, but of course it was impossible to call these people as witnesses. The fraction Humphreys did put into the witness box could, however, be taken as a fair cross-section of the whole.

A colonel who said he was a regular reader of Bottomley's weekly *John Bull*, in which the attractions of the Victory Bond Club were extensively puffed, stated he had lost £10,000 which he had invested in it. At the other end of the scale were domestic servants, unemployed, needy widows and the like who had been persuaded to part with a few pounds, amounting sometimes to all their savings. Many were deluded by the following advertisement:

A New Road to Fortune
£1 gives you an opportunity of winning £20,000.

One woman, named Mrs Alice Twichett, said she sent £10 to Bottomley after reading the advertisement. In April 1921 she wanted her money back. She wrote four letters and eventually forwarded the certificates. But she never got a penny back. Another woman witness who had invested £5 eventually received a letter giving the result of the draw, after she had asked to have her £5 returned.

'You did not get a prize?' asked Humphreys.

'No,' replied the witness.

Only one witness, a retired naval officer, who was also a regular reader of *John Bull*, admitted when cross-examined by Bottomley that he had no grievance against him, and that he did not charge him with the fraudulent conversion of the £4 he had invested in the bonds. However, this witness also admitted that he had been asked to subscribe for a French Premium Bond, but he did not part with any more money. This was a new scheme of Bottomley's by which Victory Bonds could be exchanged for French Government Bonds, Bottomley making a profit on each exchange.

A stockbroker gave evidence to the effect that Bottomley had owed him £10,000 since 1912, and eventually the debt was settled through an arrangement by which Bottomley gave the broker scrip of National War Bonds for that amount.

'In exchange for the £10,000,' Bottomley asked the witness in cross-examination, 'did I claim against you a considerable number of shares?'

'Yes, under the settlement,' the broker agreed.

'On very favourable terms, as it happened?' Bottomley continued.

'I should think so, undoubtedly.'

Humphreys asked the witness one extremely pertinent question on re-examination. 'Just tell me the name of the company in which those shares were?'

'John Bull Limited.' This was, of course, Bottomley's magazine company. By that time *John Bull*, though still edited by Bottomley, had been taken over by Odhams Press.

An official of the Midland Bank, who had been employed by Bigland to make investigations, gave particulars of the Victory Bond account and the account of another Bottomley concern, the Northern Territory Syndicate. A cheque for £25,000 drawn on the Victory Bond account was paid into the Northern Territory account, and shortly afterwards the sum of £5,000 was withdrawn from the latter to purchase Belgian francs in order to defray the expenses of Bottomley's racing stable at Ostend.

'Are you satisfied,' Bottomley asked this witness, 'that considerable sums of money, other than subscriptions, were paid into the Bond Club's account?'

'The bank would not know whether the credits were or were not subscriptions to the Club,' replied the bank official. 'Considerable sums were paid into the Victory Bond Club account which were cheques drawn in your name.' He added that the bank would know nothing of the ins and outs of the account. The cheques were simply paid in.

Bottomley went on to ask the witness whether he could say from his investigation of the Victory Bond Club account how many debits represented repayments to subscribers for their money. The reply was that he had not totalled them up, but there were a very large number of small items.

'I suggest that they came to nearly £50,000?'

The witness said he could not accept or deny that, but on being pressed by Bottomley he admitted he should have thought they were quite £50,000.

'Do you say,' Bottomley went on, 'it is or is not wrong to draw on a trust account, assuming that the moneys you draw out were due to you?'

'I think that is a lawyer's question and not a banker's question,' was the cautious reply. 'A great deal would depend as to whether the bank was suspicious.'

'Take the £25,000 transferred from the Victory Bond Club to the Northern Territory account. Would that appear a suspicious transaction?'

'It would all depend. I don't say it would be.'

At this point the judge, Mr Justice Salter, who was well nick-named 'Drysalter', broke in. 'Is it a question for the witness to say what he suspects? Is it not rather a question for the jury?'

Before opening his defence, Bottomley asked the judge to say if he was entitled to call 100,000 members of the Victory Bond Club, if necessary, to prove that they had their money back in full, by way of rebutting the few witnesses called by the prosecution. Mr Justice Salter refused to give any ruling but contented himself with saying that he would listen to any evidence placed before him and to any objections placed before him. He then directed Bottomley to proceed with his opening, which the defendant did with a strongly emotional appeal to the jury.

'You may have entertained a great opinion of me,' he said, 'and thought that, whatever my faults in days gone by, I have en-deavoured to do my duty to my King and country. Now you are asked to change your opinion, and to say that all the time I was an arrant humbug and scoundrel.' The only question for the jury, he went on, was whether he had dealt fraudulently with the funds and securities of the Victory Bond Club.

'You have got to find,' he declared, 'that I had the intention to steal the money of poor devils such as ex-soldiers who subscribed to the Club. You have got to find that Horatio Bottomley, editor of *John Bull*, Member of Parliament, the man who wrote and spoke throughout the war with the sole object of inspiring the troops and keeping up the morale of the country, who went out to the front to do his best to cheer the lads—you have got to find that that man intended to steal their money. God forbid!'

'I swear before God,' he concluded, 'that I have never fraudu-lently converted a penny of the Club's money.' But this in effect was just what Travers Humphreys's searching cross-examination revealed. Even his 'patriotism' was financially rewarding. 'Were you not paid for your patriotic speeches during the war?' the prosecutor asked him.

'Never a farthing for my recruiting meetings,' answered Bottomley. 'But later on, as lecturer on the war, I got certain remuneration.' He was a bankrupt at the time, he added, and had to get his living. Pressed for details, he agreed that his lecture receipts for a time averaged between £300 and £400 a week. In fact, he had made £27,000 out of his speaking campaign.

'So the war did you pretty well?' queried Humphreys.

'No, it did not,' replied Bottomley angrily. 'As a professional journalist and lecturer, I delivered a large number of lectures, as distinct from attending a large number of recruiting meetings. I was most desirous of clearing off my liabilities and getting back into Parliament. I am not at all ashamed of my work as a professional lecturer. . . . I think it is rather unfair to introduce this.'

However, there was nothing unfair about the way the prosecutor took Bottomley through the tangled web of his shady financial transactions, in which there was an occasional gleam of humour. For instance, his friend the eccentric Independent MP, Pemberton Billing, had bought the captured German submarine *Deutschland* for £5,500 and sold it to *John Bull* for £15,000 paid out of the Victory Bond Club account. But it did not become the property of the Club, since at that time the Club owed him (Bottomley) more money than the submarine cost. 'They could have the vessel now, if they liked,' Bottomley added amid laughter. The *Deutschland* was to be taken round the country on exhibition, but before she was ready an explosion took place on board injuring several people. The exhibition when it was mounted resulted in a considerable loss.

Questioned about a meeting of Club members he had called in the Cannon Street Hotel in January 1920 for the purpose of explaining the position to them, Bottomley said about 200 were present. 'Did they all speak?' asked Humphreys.

'Many of them at the same time,' said Bottomley, and his reply raised a laugh.

At the same time Bottomley had circulated a report in which it was stated that the stock of the Club consisted of £500,000 in bonds.

'Was that true?'

'Well', said Bottomley, 'it is not quite the phrase I should have used myself.' Nevertheless, he admitted responsibility for the report, in which it was also stated that the bonds were held by the Club's bank. In fact, what were left had been transferred to Bottomley's private accounts with the Credit Lyonnais in Paris.

It was practically the same thing, said Bottomley. Yet by February 1921 all the remaining stock had been sold. 'Is that practically the same thing as remaining with the Club's bankers?' For once Bottomley was at a loss for a reply.

In his defence Bottomley called two former members of his staff to prove that £3,500 had been repaid to Victory Bond subscribers. But not a single one of the 100,000 people who Bottomley had stated had been repaid the amount of their subscriptions in full appeared in the witness box.

In his final speech to the jury, Bottomley again reached the height of his characteristic rhetoric. 'You will not convict me,' he fulminated. 'The jury is not yet born who would convict me on these charges. It is unthinkable.' He then pointed to the large sword suspended above the Bench 'The sword of Justice will drop from its scabbard if you give a verdict of Guilty against me,' he went on. 'I say it with a clean conscience. I say it without one thought of fear or misgiving. I know my country and my country people, and knowing you, and knowing myself, and knowing the truth about this matter, without one atom of hesitation, one atom of fear. . . . I know by the mercy of God and the spirit of justice you will liberate me from this ordeal.' He thereupon burst into sobs, so affected was he by his own oratory.

But the jury were not impressed when they heard the judge's scrupulously fair summing up of the evidence. In less than half an hour they found Bottomley guilty on all counts, except one which was withdrawn on the judge's direction. Meanwhile the sword of Justice remained securely in its scabbard.

'Horatio Bottomley,' said the judge to the man in the dock, 'you have been rightly convicted by the jury of a long series of heartless frauds. These poor people trusted you, and you robbed them of £150,000 in ten months. The crime is aggravated by your high position, by the number and poverty of your victims, by the trust which they reposed in you. It is aggravated by the magnitude of your frauds and by the callous effrontery by which your frauds were committed. I can see no mitigation whatever. The sentence of the Court upon you is that you be kept in penal servitude for seven years.'

'I was under the impression, my Lord,' said the prisoner, 'that it was sometimes put to an accused person, "Have you anything to say before sentence is passed upon you?" '

'It is not customary in cases of misdemeanour,' replied Mr Justice Salter.

'Had it been so, my Lord,' observed Bottomley, 'I should have had something rather offensive to say about your summing up!'

With that remark Bottomley was taken to the cells below and thence to Wormwood Scrubs Prison. A few days later he was formally expelled from the House of Commons, after he had apologised, in a letter to the Speaker, for the slur he had brought upon it. His expulsion, he wrote, was 'a punishment far greater and more enduring than any sentence of any Court of Law. . . . But I have myself to blame, and all I can do is to ask Members of the House to judge me as they knew me.'

During his fourteen months at Wormwood Scrubs, Bottomley spent much of his time in the prison hospital before being transferred to Maidstone, where he recovered his health sufficiently to be put to work on stitching mailbags. This gave rise to one of the best stories about him, which showed that at least he had not lost his sense of humour. A visitor, who happened to be passing his cell and saw how he was employed, looked in and remarked, 'Ah, Bottomley, sewing, I see.'

'No,' replied Bottomley glumly, looking up. 'Reaping.'

After serving just over five years of his sentence, Bottomley was released on licence. A Sunday newspaper paid him £12,500 for a series of articles on his prison experiences, a considerable sum for those days. Some old friends, mostly money lenders who had done well out of him in the past, rallied round with more money, and he started a magazine which he called *John Blunt*, which he hoped would outstrip the old *John Bull*. It was a failure from the start as were his other journalistic ventures at this time. He was again made bankrupt and had to part with 'The Dicker', his large country house near the Sussex Downs. He was eventually driven to applying for the Old Age Pension, which was granted and then for some reason immediately withdrawn. His wife died, and in his last days he was cared for by an ex-musical comedy actress named Peggy Primrose, whose shows he had backed in more prosperous times. Finally he made a pathetic series of appearances at the Windmill Theatre, but after a few days he collapsed and was admitted to Middlesex Hospital.

He died on 26 May 1935. 'What a wasted life,' commented Travers Humphreys when he heard the news. 'What a pity!'

# 8

# The Gentleman in the Park

Late on the night of 29 September 1922, the telephone rang in the London home of the well-known King's Counsel, Sir Henry Curtis-Bennett. He took the call himself and heard the agitated voice of a solicitor who had briefed him in the past. Could he be at Marlborough Street Police Court at 10.30 next morning to defend a well-known Buckingham Palace official who had been arrested by the police on a charge of 'wilfully interfering with and annoying women in Hyde Park'? The official, who had been released on bail, was the seventy-one-year-old Sir Almeric Fitzroy, Clerk of the Privy Council and holder of two of the highest honours in the land, Knight Commander of the Bath and Knight Commander of the Royal Victorian Order, distinctions which are only conferred for exceptional service to the state and the person of the sovereign.

Sir Almeric's aristocratic family connections were what one might expect of a devoted courtier. Directly descended from King Charles II by his mistress Barbara Villiers Duchess of Cleveland, Sir Almeric was a grandson of the Duke of Grafton; his mother was the daughter of a peer, and he himself was married to the daughter of a baronet. As Clerk of the Privy Council, an office which he had held for the past twenty-four years, he was one of the most trusted courtiers, being responsible for keeping the records of the royal acts of state and having served three monarchs in this capacity, Queen Victoria, King Edward VII and King George V. No one connected with the court was more respected and few wielded greater influence than Sir Almeric Fitzroy. Consequently his arrest on such a charge was a society sensation of the first magnitude and every newspaper in the country carried banner headlines in reporting the affair.

Briefed with Curtis-Bennett as junior counsel was Sir Richard Muir, one of the most experienced criminal practitioners of the day. After meeting their client for a consultation at the police court, Curtis-Bennett immediately applied for a postponement of the trial so that he could prepare his defence. The magistrate accordingly remanded Sir Almeric for a week and granted him bail on his own surety.

At their consultation Sir Almeric told his counsel how he had come to be in the park when he was arrested. He had dined at his club and had previously arranged to meet his wife, who was dining with her mother, at 10 p.m. at Stanhope Gate, one of the entrances to Hyde Park, which is about half-way along Park Lane. It was a fine evening and he decided to walk.

The magistrate at Marlborough Street Police Court, who tried the case, was Mr Frederick Mead, an elderly and somewhat irascible judicial officer who seemed to have forgotten a good deal of his law, since an increasing number of cases where he had con-victed defendants had been reversed on appeal. When Sir Almeric duly surrendered to his bail and took his place in the dock, he knew so little of court procedure that he asked whether his wife could not sit with him in the dock. It was then explained to him that, since she was going to be a witness, this was not possible.

The Crown prosecutor immediately opened the case, which he described as a distressing one. 'The defendant is a man occupying a high position in the service of the state,' he said. 'He is a man advanced in years, and has occupied his position in association with the highest in the land. But the position of the defendant is of no account. The point is—is the charge proven or not?'

'Does he plead guilty or not guilty?' interposed the magistrate.

'Not guilty,' said Sir Henry Curtis-Bennett with marked emphasis.

Police Constable Herbert Gumbrill then took the stand. Replying to the Crown prosecutor, he said he was on duty inside Hyde Park near the Hyde Park Corner entrance on the night in question. Shortly after 9 p.m. he noticed a flashily dressed woman walking northwards. A gentleman, whom he identified as the defendant in the dock, passed her, turned round and followed her, eventually overtaking her and looking into her face. He appeared

4

to say something, while she gave the impression of being annoyed, moving her shoulders about and walking away from him. He was in evening dress and wearing a light overcoat and a trilby hat. A little further along he sat down beside two women on one of the park chairs.

'Was it a fairly well-lighted spot?' the magistrate asked.

'Yes, he was sitting underneath a lamp.'

The police witness went on to say that Sir Almeric looked into the women's faces and appeared to say something to them. But they turned their heads away from him and seemed to be annoyed. The constable went on to say that Sir Almeric had sat down beside another woman a little later on and that she got up almost immediately and went off. Finally, Sir Almeric returned to where the two women had previously been sitting together. There he sat down again and took his hat off. After he had looked into the remaining one's face and said something to her, the witness who had been following Sir Almeric for most of the past half hour, stated that he went up to him, accompanied by another constable, whose name was Brosman, and said he was going to take him into custody. Sir Almeric, according to the witness, then became very violent, threw his arms about and struck Constable Brosman in the face. He also struggled on the way to the police station and when they got there, kicking and shouting, 'I repudiate it,' as the charge was read over to him.

Curtis-Bennett began his cross-examination by asking the witness about the type of woman who frequented the park at that time of night. P.C. Gumbrill replied that some of the women were known to him but not this particular one who had come to the police station and made a statement incriminating Sir Almeric. Asked what he meant by describing the first woman whom Sir Almeric was alleged to have followed as 'flashily dressed', the witness explained that she appeared to be wearing a new costume and new shoes and hat. When he first noticed her she had gone about twenty yards.

'People were passing her both ways?'

'Yes.'

'And among all those you saw you noticed Sir Almeric?'

'Yes. The defendant was walking slowly and smoking a cigarette.'

'You are quite sure of that?'

'Yes.'

'Did he run after her?'

'Not exactly run. He hastened after her, and caught up with her in about twenty yards.'

'Did you hear him say anything?'

'No.'

'Did she stop at all?'

'No. She almost ran away.'

'You have not the remotest idea who she is?'

'No.'

Coming to the incident of the two women on the park chairs, Curtis-Bennett suggested that as he went up to these two ladies Sir Almeric took off his hat and then sat down. This the witness denied. But he agreed, in replying to further questioning, that the place was full of shadows and that it was difficult to distinguish faces until one was close up. (This was contrary to his statement when examined by the Crown prosecutor that it was a well-lighted spot and that the defendant was sitting under a lamp.) As for the third woman whom Sir Almeric was alleged to have sat beside and who got up immediately and went off, Curtis-Bennett suggested that this was not so.

'Do you know who she is?'

'No.'

'I suggest he sat down and lit a cigarette?'

'I did not see him light one. I saw him smoking afterwards.'

As for the fourth incident with the woman who subsequently accompanied them to the police station, giving her name as Mrs Dorothy Turner, the police witness insisted that she was annoyed by Sir Almeric's presence and looked at him as much as to say: 'Get out of this. I don't want anything to do with you.'

'You did not suspect the woman of doing anything?'

'No.'

'Did Sir Almeric, when you told him he was under arrest, tell you that he had an important appointment?'

'No.'

'He protested, did he not, over and over again, that he was being wrongly charged?'

'He was protesting the whole of the way to the police station.'

'That this was a misconceived charge?'

'Yes.'

'Denying that he had done anything wrong?'

'Yes.'

Mrs Dorothy Turner then went on the witness stand. She gave her age as twenty-four and said she was a widow and lived in Kennington, a working-class district south of the River Thames. Her husband, she went on, had been a warrant officer in the Navy and was killed in the war. On the evening of 29 September, she said, she went to keep an appointment in Hyde Park with a gentleman friend. A lady acquaintance went with her. After entering the park they sat on two chairs near the Achilles Statue. They had been there for about five minutes when they saw a gentleman pass several times and look into their faces. He came back once more and sat down beside her.

'Was it this gentleman?' asked the Crown prosecutor, indicating Sir Almeric in the dock.

'Yes.'

'Did he say anything?'

'He asked me what I was doing. I told him I was waiting for a friend, and I got up and walked away.'

'Did you notice him particularly?'

'Yes.'

'Did you give him any encouragement to sit beside you?'

'Not at all.'

'Were you there for any improper purpose?'

'No.'

Mrs Turner added that she went to see her woman companion on to a bus in Park Lane, after which she returned to where she had been sitting before. She had been there for about two minutes when the same gentleman came back and sat beside her.

'Did you ask him to?'

'No.'

'Did you give him any encouragement?'

'No.'

'Did he say anything?'

'Yes. He asked me to go for a walk across the park. I again told him I was waiting for my friend.' According to her, Sir Almeric then remarked, 'Your friend is a long time coming.'

'Do you ever go to the park for an improper purpose?' the Crown prosecutor repeated his earlier question.

'No, certainly not.'

'Are you a woman of loose life?'

'No.' When the police came up, she added, Sir Almeric struggled with one of the officers and hit him with a stick. As for herself, she went quite voluntarily to the police station.

'Were you or were you not annoyed by the defendant's action?' was the Crown prosecutor's final question to this witness.

'I was annoyed.'

Sir Henry Curtis-Bennett then informed the magistrate that he was not in a position to cross-examine the witness fully, but that he would ask her some preliminary questions. In reply to these, Mrs Turner stated that she had been employed at two hotels in Brighton, but had given up her job five months previously on account of ill-health. She went on to say that she had had an appointment on the evening in question for 9.30.

'Will you write down who the appointment was with?'

'No, I would rather not.'

'It was with a gentleman?'

'Yes.'

'In fact, did he turn up?'

'I do not know. We left for the police station before 9.30 and I then went home.'

'Do you know whether he came at 9.30?'

'No, I have not seen him since. He is a commercial traveller and has gone into the country, but I know he would have turned up, as he always does.'

'Have you heard from him since?'

'No.'

'Does he know your address?'

'Yes.'

'Have you communicated with him?'

'No.'

After seeking the witness to write down the name of her woman friend, which she again refused to do, Curtis-Bennett asked the magistrate to adjourn the case. The magistrate agreed, and Sir Almeric was accordingly remanded on bail for another week.

During this week Curtis-Bennett made a number of inquiries about Mrs Turner and discovered, as he suspected, that she was a prostitute. His resumed cross-examination was a model of its kind in dealing with a palpably untruthful witness.

'You told us you were the widow of a warrant officer in the Navy?'

'Yes.'

'What was his name?'

'Charles Turner.' The witness added that she was married in Brighton Register Office in 1916.

'Will you give me the exact date?' Sir Henry pressed her.

'I would rather not,' replied Mrs Turner. 'I do not see it has any bearing on the case at all.'

'We will see about that,' said Curtis-Bennett ominously. 'Won't you give me the date?'

On being pressed further Mrs Turner intimated that it was 24 March 1916. Her husband, she added, had died in 1918 and since then she had been drawing a pension from the Admiralty. This was paid every month and she drew it through her local post office.

Curtis-Bennett went on to question her about the last hotel where she worked in Brighton, which turned out to be the Queen's.

'You were well known there?'

'I do not know about being well known,' replied Mrs Turner, who was now looking distinctly uncomfortable. 'There were lots of other girls besides myself.'

Asked about the night she went to the park with the friend whose name she refused to give, Mrs Turner said that there were a great many people walking up and down. Sir Almeric passed her several times. 'We took notice of him because he kept passing us and looking into our faces.'

'You want to be careful about this,' Curtis-Bennett warned her again. 'Did he annoy you?'

'Yes.'

'We shall see. I suggest that, before Sir Almeric came up to you at all, as he passed you smiled at him?'

'No.'

'You would not do a thing like that?'

'No.' She repeated that she never went into the park for an improper purpose and did not lead a loose life.

'I suggest that when Sir Almeric came across he took off his hat?'

'I did not see him take off his hat.'

'Did you say to Sir Almeric that you were waiting for a friend?'

'Yes.'

'You suggest that this is all that happened?'

'Yes.'

'He got up and went away and that annoyed you?'

'Yes.'

'You saw Sir Almeric again?'

'Yes. He came up and sat down beside me.'

'Did you excuse the fact that you had been rather stiff when he spoke to you before?'

'No.'

'I suggest that you told him you were sorry you had been rather stiff and that you had seen a constable or two constables?'

'No.'

'And that you again remarked that it was cold and that Sir Almeric suggested to you that if you were cold you should go for a walk?'

'No. I only sat down the second time with him for two or three seconds and then I went to the police station.'

'You were thoroughly annoyed with what happened?'

'Yes.'

'Let there be no misunderstanding because we know all about you,' Curtis-Bennett remarked at this point. 'You have been living in Kennington for the past four months alone?'

'Yes.'

'I suggest that you were living there in two rooms—a bed-sitting room with a double bed in it, and a kitchen—with a man who goes by the name of Turner?'

'No.'

Curtis-Bennett looked at her severely. 'I think it fair to remind you that you are giving evidence on oath, and we have the address. Did you have these rooms for yourself and your husband?'

'No. I did not.'

'I have the landlady here.' Then, beckoning the court usher, he said, 'Let her be brought in.'

A woman then entered the court. Mrs Turner, who had turned deathly pale, agreed that she was her landlady.

'I suggest that you took these rooms for yourself and your husband?'

'No. I did not take them. And I decline to answer anything else.'

'You swore you were not living there with a man of the name of Turner,' Curtis-Bennett reminded her. 'While there is time, I will give you an opportunity of withdrawing that. Were you not living there right up to this morning?'

Mrs Turner did not answer, and a moment later fell back in a dead faint.

After she had been revived, Curtis-Bennett questioned her about the two Brighton hotels at which she had sworn she had been employed. The manageress of each was successively called and Mrs Turner failed to recognise either.

'I suggest you were never employed at the Queen's Hotel at all. Do you say you were or you were not?'

'I won't answer.'

'Do you still swear that you get a pension in the name of Dorothy Turner, the widow of a warrant officer named Charles Turner?'

Mrs Turner, by now looking completely wretched and conscious that she had been exposed as a blatant liar, looked down and did not answer.

At this point the magistrate intervened and spoke to the Crown prosecutor. 'To save time, have you any further corroboration of the police evidence?' The prosecutor intimated that he did not think so.

'I don't think you need trouble this witness further,' the magistrate remarked to Curtis-Bennett. Accordingly, after the prosecutor had admitted that he did not consider it to be his duty to rely on her evidence, Mrs Turner was allowed to leave the witness stand completely discredited and fortunate not to be arrested herself and charged with perjury.

After the other police officer, P.C. Brosman, had briefly confirmed what the other constable had said and described Sir Almeric's behaviour when he was asked to accompany them to the police station, Curtis-Bennett rose to open the case for his client. He began by pointing out to the court that this was 'a class of charge very easily made and very difficult to deal with'. No one knew better than the magistrate, he went on, that numbers of men had been convicted on the evidence of police officers that women appeared to be annoyed. What would have happened if the woman here had not gone on to the witness stand? Would the magistrate not have been left with the impression that the woman was a respectable lady sitting in the park, if such a thing could exist, at ten o'clock at night? 'Thank goodness that at least one of these women who are said by the officers to be annoyed has gone into the box and we have been able to cross-examine her!'

Here the magistrate interrupted to say that there was no evidence that this woman was annoyed. 'The police came up too soon, but there might have been others.'

'I must protest as strongly as I can at the attitude you are taking here,' Curtis-Bennett said to the magistrate with some heat. 'There is no evidence that Sir Almeric spoke to any other woman than Mrs Turner and the woman whose name she refused to write down. You kindly intimated that I need not continue my cross-examination of this witness. Nothing pleased me more, because it is very unpleasant for counsel to have to draw from an unfortunate being what her real life history is. But I think, when I was told to stop cross-examining, you had made up your mind that this charge was an ill-founded one and could not be substantiated. Otherwise I suggest I should have been allowed to go on cross-examining her. I am not entitled now to anticipate what I might have been able to get from her, but I had much more material to cross-examine her on.'

As for his client's behaviour in the park, he summarised it in these trenchant terms:

> 'It is a disaster that Sir Almeric should have had half an hour to wait for Lady Fitzroy, and that he walked in the park. What he did there was perfectly innocent. It has never been suggested that he made an improper suggestion to anyone, and the only reason this case has received such prominence is because of Sir Almeric's position.'

Curtis-Bennett also informed the court that he had been to Hyde Park the night before with his junior counsel Sir Richard Muir, and he suggested that it was impossible for the police officers to see what they professed to have seen.

Sir Almeric then went on to the witness stand, where he was examined by Sir Richard Muir, who asked him to describe his movements in the park. 'I went towards Stanhope Gate and then turned,' he said. 'As I did so I had the impression of a figure of a woman just stepping from the roadway on the path abreast of the Achilles statue. That woman I never followed and made no effort to overtake her. It is, therefore, morally and physically impossible that I looked into her face.'

'Are you conscious of having looked into the face of any other?'

'No, emphatically not.'

Sir Almeric went on:

'I continued my walk and as I neared Stanhope Gate I saw two women sitting on chairs. I paid no attention to them at first, but as I was passing I was struck by the likeness of one of them to someone I knew. As I got nearer I felt confirmed in my belief that I knew one of them. I therefore raised my hat and discovered I was mistaken, and wishing to repair the mistake by treating her with courtesy, I asked her what they were doing there so late. She answered that they were waiting to meet a friend, and went on to say that he might not come, as it might be too cold. It was then I suggested she should take a walk to warm herself. She seemed as if she would do so, but she decided to wait for her friend. I raised my hat and left her.'

Afterwards he sat down alone on another chair, he said, and smoked a cigarette for ten minutes or so, before returning towards Stanhope Gate.

'It was then between a quarter and ten minutes to ten. I there saw sitting alone, as I thought, the lady I had spoken to a quarter of an hour ago. I should have passed her but she gave me a cordial smile as if she had something to say to me. I stopped and she remarked, "I was sorry to have been so stiff when I last saw you, but there are one or two policemen about."

'These words were hardly out of her mouth when two of these gentlemen appeared, and not to put too fine a point upon it, with a use of brutal authority they told me and this woman to stand up. I did so, and protested with great vehemence against the arbitrary interference of the police with a perfectly harmless conversation. The policeman told me I must go to the station. I replied that was impossible as I had other business. They insisted, seized my wrist with violence, and caused me very acute pain. Naturally I struggled to free myself, and in my efforts it is very likely my stick touched one of the officers. If so, he was responsible for it.'

'Did you intentionally assault a police officer?'
'Emphatically no. It is ridiculous to suggest that a man of seventy should have tried to escape with swarms of young policemen on every side.'

Sir Almeric's cross-examination was brief. Asked by the prosecuting counsel why he had left his club so early, Sir Almeric replied that he had been travelling that day and had had no exercise. 'I went out in the evening, which was a beautiful one.'

'Then how were you going to spend the time in the park?'
'In rest and recreation.'

'What do you say about the incident described by the police—that it did not occur?'
'No, I don't think it did.'

'Did you know your presence in the park had become known to the two police officers?'
'No, not until the time I was arrested.'

Further questioned about what he had meant by asking the two women he sat beside what they were doing, he replied, 'Simply for the sake of saying something—I suppose I was curious.'

'Did they appear to be respectable?'
'Certainly.'

'Is it true that when the police officers came up you heard one of them ask the woman if she knew you?'
'I think I did.'

'Did you hear the woman say to the police officer in reply. "He asked me to go across the grass with him"?'
'No.'

'Did you say you spoke to the lady?'
'Of course.'

Lady Fitzroy, Sir Almeric's wife, was the only other witness for the defence. 'It was a common custom of my husband to meet me at some place on the way home,' she said. 'On this occasion it was to be Stanhope Gate, and I got there about ten o'clock. Finding he did not arrive, I went home.'

'When he did arrive home,' Curtis-Bennett asked her, 'did

he give you an explanation as to why he had not kept the appointment?'

'Yes.'

'You have seen the woman who has given her name as Turner? Did she call to your recollection anyone?'

'Yes. She is a younger woman, but has a striking resemblance to a mutual friend.'

Asked if she would write down that lady's name on a piece of paper for the magistrate's information, Lady Fitzroy said she would be glad to do so. But the magistrate intimated that he did not require it. When Curtis-Bennett sat down, the prosecutor said that he did not wish to cross-examine, and Lady Fitzroy left the stand.

Both Curtis-Bennett and his junior counsel confidently expected that the magistrate would now proceed to acquit Sir Almeric. But to their surprise, and indeed to the surprise of nearly everyone else in court, Mr Mead held that there were two incidents in which women were proved to have been annoyed by Sir Almeric, and he therefore imposed a fine of £5 and ordered him in addition to pay ten guineas costs. 'The charge is practically that he spoke to persons without knowing them and therefore without justification,' he said. 'If a man accosts women and sits by them, he does so at his own peril.'

'I deny it absolutely,' Sir Almeric interrupted.

'Of course there will be an appeal,' Curtis-Bennett told the magistrate. 'I very much regret, if this is your view of the case, that you should have intimated to me that I should discontinue cross-examination of the woman Turner. I would not have stopped it if I and my learned friend Sir Richard Muir had not formed the opinion you had made up your mind about the case and meant to acquit.'

'I regret the misunderstanding,' said the magistrate, 'but I am not responsible for it.'

There was a considerable public outcry in the Press about the verdict. 'It is an outrage,' thundered the *Sunday Express*. 'The villain in a melodrama always wears evening dress and has a name like Sir Almeric Fitzroy.' 'What are we to do to be safe in Hyde Park?' one correspondent wrote. 'Wear blinkers, a gag and a gas-mask. Is the Park to be open for the public pleasure or is it to be a happy hunting ground for the police?'

The appeal was heard a few weeks later at London Sessions before Sir Robert Wallace, the Chairman, and a bench of senior magistrates. After the two police officers had repeated their earlier evidence, incidentally disclaiming all knowledge that Mrs Turner had for months past plied her trade as a prostitute in that part of Hyde Park, the Chairman stopped the case, and allowed the appeal. The conviction must be quashed, he said, because the only person alleged by the police to have made a complaint that she was annoyed was the woman Mrs Turner whom the magistrate indicated that he could not believe. It was not enough for the conduct which the police saw to be such as in their opinion ought to annoy. There must be a definite complaint which was entitled to belief, and this was lacking in this case.

Curtis-Bennett immediately rose and applied for costs against the police on the ground that his client had been put to considerable expense to prove he was not guilty of the offence with which he had been charged. 'If the police had taken the trouble to go to Mrs Turner's house in Kennington,' he pointed out, 'if they had put one question to this woman, the answer would have been that she was living in one room with a man. If the authorities had gone one step further and telephoned to the Admiralty, they would have found out that she had never married a man—who, in fact, did not exist—and that she was not in receipt of a pension at all. Without any inquiry of any sort, although there were eight days elapsing between the time of the woman's statement and the time when she was before the magistrate, the police proceeded with the case on her evidence. What would have been the position had a humble man been charged under the same conditions as Sir Almeric, who has spent hundreds in order to find out the history of Mrs Turner? Her evidence would have been accepted.'

The Chairman was at first uncertain whether he had the power to accede to Curtis-Bennett's request, but after consulting his colleagues on the Bench he decided (rightly) that he had. In fact Sir Almeric's costs, which the police had to pay, amounted to £500, a record for a hearing which had taken only three days in all.

There is no doubt that the police slipped up badly in this case and that Curtis-Bennett was able to expose their over-zealous methods in patrolling Hyde Park. It also gave him considerable pleasure that largely as a result of his efforts he had been able to clear the character of such a distinguished public figure as Sir

Almeric Fitzroy of the charge of misbehaving in a public park. But the case had a moral, which Curtis-Bennett, in discussing it afterwards, recalled that he had heard from his father. He was later to pass it on to his son, who was to follow in his footsteps at the English Bar. 'Never walk across Hyde Park at night!'

# [9]

# The Killing of Percy Thompson

The trial which began in No. 1 Court at the Old Bailey on the morning of 6 December 1922 before a jury of eleven men and one woman was unquestionably the most sensational one of the year in England if not for the whole period between the two world wars. It aroused nationwide interest, so much so that when the court doors were opened there was a queue outside of more than fifty people which had formed during the previous afternoon and throughout the night for the few seats available in the public gallery. The accused were Frederick ('Freddy') Bywaters, a twenty-year-old laundry steward on an ocean liner, and his mistress Edith ('Edie') Thompson, a married woman, who worked as manageress-bookkeeper in a firm of wholesale milliners in the City of London and was eight years older than her lover. Just over two months previously, Edith's husband Percy Thompson, a thirty-two-year-old shipping clerk, had been killed near his home at Ilford, a small town in London's commuter belt, when returning late one night with his wife. Bywaters was charged with his murder, while Edith Thompson was charged with inciting her lover to carry out the killing after she had unsuccessfully tried to kill him herself giving him poison and mixing powdered glass with his food.

As soon as the judge, the venerable-looking Mr Justice Shearman, had taken his place on the Bench in the historic wood-panelled court-room, the accused were brought up by a policeman and a female wardress from the cells below where they had been anxiously waiting. As they took their places in the dock, Bywaters, a good-looking youth with curly dark hair, gave the impression of being a virile almost animal type, essentially a man of action,

determined and masterful. His companion, however, looked pale
and she trembled slightly as she followed Bywaters and gave her
plea to the Clerk of the Court as he had done: 'Not guilty.'

Edith Thompson's defence was in the hands of Sir Henry
Curtis-Bennett, King's Counsel, and a fashionable leading
advocate of the day in criminal cases. As his counsel Bywaters had
Mr Cecil Whiteley, another eminent KC and a prominent
criminal lawyer. The prosecuting team was led by the Solicitor-
General Sir Thomas Inskip, since it was customary for a Law
Officer of the Crown to prosecute in any case involving a poison
charge. Sir Thomas was a stern Sabbatarian and no criminal could
expect any mercy at his hands.

On the table in front of the Solicitor-General was a large bundle
of letters, sixty-two in all, which Edith Thompson had written to
Bywaters in the course of their love affair and which had been
recovered by the police, some in the house in London where
Bywaters had lived with his mother and others in his locker on his
ship. Some of them were to be described by the judge as 'gush'.
Certainly Edith analysed her feelings and emotions in remarkable
detail. Her favourite term of endearment for her lover was
'Darlingest', contracted to 'Darlint'. The letters breathed a
curious passion, in which the writer depicted herself as half
mother and half slave-mistress. She also described how she had
tried to do away with her husband on several occasions. 'You said
it was enough for an elephant,' she wrote in one letter. 'Perhaps it
was. But you don't allow for the taste making it possible for only
a small quantity to be taken.' And again: 'I'm going to try the
glass again occasionally—when it's safe. I've got an electric light
globe this time.' In fact, according to her, she used the light bulb
three times in his food, 'but the third time he found a piece—so
I've given it up—until you come home.'

They were foolish letters to write and even more foolish to keep.
Incidentally Edith Thompson never referred to her husband in
them by his Christian name, but always as 'he' or 'him'. In one
letter she wrote:

'Yes, darlint, you are jealous of *him*—but I want you to be—
he has the right by law to all that you have the right by nature
and love—yes, darlint, be jealous, so much that you will do
something desperate.'

In this letter she enclosed a cutting from a newspaper which described how a woman's death had been caused by taking a bowl of broth made from the carcass of a chicken which had been killed by rat poison. Other cuttings enclosed in Edith's letters contained headings like 'Patient Killed by an Overdose', 'The Poisoner Curate', 'Poisoned Chocolates', 'Masterful Men', and 'Woman the Consoler'.

Edith Thompson's counsel had been shown these highly compromising letters before the trial opened, since under the rules of criminal procedure the prosecution was bound to disclose them to the defence if it was intended to introduce them as evidence against her. Not only did they contain passages suggesting on the face of them that Edith had tried to kill her husband with poison and powdered glass, but they also plainly indicated that on at least one occasion she had aborted herself and had a miscarriage after becoming pregnant by her lover.

Thus Sir Henry Curtis-Bennett had to reckon with the prosecution showing that she was not merely an adulteress but also a self-abortionist as well as a potential murderess. The nature of her relations with her husband were also reflected in certain passages in the letters describing how, after Bywaters first went to sea, she rejected her husband's sexual approaches, but eventually yielded to him and became 'the dutiful wife' which she thought was the best course to allay his suspicions if she and Bywaters had to take what she called 'drastic measures'.

Realising that the letters were dynamite, Sir Henry Curtis-Bennett did his best to persuade the judge to rule that they were inadmissible as evidence against his client. Therefore, as soon as the jury had been sworn, Sir Henry jumped to his feet and with a glance in the direction of the bundle of letters informed the judge that he had an objection to make to certain evidence which he understood the Solicitor-General proposed to put before the jury. The jury were then sent out of the court-room while Curtis-Bennett and Inskip argued the point with the judge.

Briefly Curtis-Bennett's argument was that the letters could not and should not be admitted until the prosecution had shown that Mrs Thompson took some active part in the murder, if it was murder, of her husband. The Solicitor-General replied by submitting that they were admissible because she was being charged as a principal in the second degree, although she did not strike the fatal blow. 'The crime is one where one hand struck the blow,' said Inskip, 'and we want to show by these letters that her mind conceived it and incited it—the evidence of that is the letters that Mrs Thompson wrote to the man who struck the blow.'

Having listened patiently to the argument, the judge then gave his ruling. 'I think these letters are admissible as evidence of intention and motive,' he said, 'and I shall admit them.' Turning towards Edith Thompson's counsel, he added: 'I do not think you can contest that letters showing the affectionate relations between the parties are not evidence of motive in so far as they show affection.'

Sir Henry was overruled. He had done everything he could to exclude the damning letters; now he knew that the task before him was all the more difficult. He glanced at his client in the dock. Her face, almost hidden by the brim of her black velour hat, looked anxious and drawn.

The jury were then brought back to court, and the Solicitor-General proceeded to open the case for the Crown. 'May it please your lordship, members of the jury,' he began, 'on 4th October, a little after midnight, Percy Thompson was stabbed to death on his way home from Ilford station. He was in a dark part of the road, not over-well lit at the best of times, when he was struck, first of all, apparently from behind, and then in front, by some assailant. The only person present was his wife, Mrs Thompson, who is now in the dock. She is charged with Bywaters, who is said by the prosecution to have been the assailant, with the murder of Percy Thompson.'

It was a sombre tale which the Solicitor-General went on to relate. Husband and wife had been to the theatre, and as they were walking along the road from Ilford station to the terraced row of suburban houses in Kensington Gardens where they lived, a man suddenly jumped out of the shadows. Seizing Percy Thompson by the arm, he said, 'Why don't you get a divorce from your wife, you cad?'

Thompson, who appeared to recognise the man, replied, 'I've got her, I'll keep her and I'll shoot you.'

Thereupon the other pulled out a knife from his coat pocket. With this he stabbed Thompson several times, while Edith Thompson shouted, 'Oh, don't! Oh, don't!' The attacker then ran off and disappeared into the darkness. Meanwhile Percy Thompson fell to the ground, blood pouring out of his mouth. He was dead before a doctor, who had been summoned, arrived on the scene, followed by the police.

Edith Thompson was still in too hysterical a condition to tell the police very much except that her husband had been 'attacked by a strange man'. However, a woman named Mrs Fanny Lester, who lived in the same house with the Thompsons, was also questioned, and it was Mrs Lester who put the police on the track of the killer. She stated that about eighteen months previously Frederick Bywaters had lodged in the house for some weeks but had left after a row he had had with Percy Thompson, caused by the attentions Bywaters had apparently been paying Edith. The police also learned that Bywaters was a steward with the P. & O. line and this in turn led the police to find the letters Edith had written to him and which he would pick up at the various ports at which his ship called.

Bywaters was eventually traced to the home of Edith Thompson's parents who lived at Manor Park, near Ilford. There he was arrested and taken to Ilford police station where he was formally charged with the murder. Later that day Edith Thompson was picked up and taken to the same police station where she was likewise charged on the basis of the letters with being a principal in the murder or alternatively with being an accessory to it.

At this time neither she nor Freddy Bywaters knew that the other had been arrested. As she was being led past a window of the police station, she looked in and saw her lover sitting there obviously in police custody. The sight shook her extremely. 'Oh, God, why did he do it?' she cried, the words coming out involuntarily between stifled sobs. 'I didn't want him to do it.' Yes, she went on, it was Bywaters who had killed her husband.

Under police interrogation, Bywaters agreed with what his mistress had said. At the same time he did his best to shield her and insisted that she knew nothing of his intention to waylay Percy Thompson on their homeward journey from the theatre. Both prisoners signed statements confirming what they had told the police when they were arrested, and these statements were put in evidence by the prosecution in addition to Edith Thompson's letters.

The story of the fatal encounter which Bywaters told in his statement was as follows:

I waited for Mrs Thompson and her husband. I pushed her to one side, also pushing him up the street. . . . We struggled. I took my knife from my pocket and we fought and he got the worst of it. . . .

The reason I fought with Thompson was because he never acted like a man to his wife. He always seemed several degrees lower than a snake. I loved her and I could not go on seeing her leading that life. I did not intend to kill him. I only meant to injure him. I gave him an opportunity of standing up to me as a man but he wouldn't.

Bywaters stuck to this story when he went into the witness box on the third day of the trial, although he did qualify his admission, 'I only meant to injure him', by saying that what he really intended was 'to stop him from killing me'.

Nor could the Solicitor-General shake him in cross-examination about his mistress's compromising letters, for which the witness had a ready explanation.

'As far as you could tell, reading these letters,' Sir Thomas Inskip asked, looking sternly at the man on the witness stand, 'did you ever believe in your own mind that she herself had given any poison to her husband?'

'No,' replied Bywaters with an air of self-confidence, 'it never entered my mind at all. She had been reading books. She had a vivid way of declaring herself. She would read a book and imagine herself as the character in the book.'

He also stated in reply to the Solicitor-General that it was Percy Thompson who attacked him first.

The expression on Sir Thomas Inskip's face clearly showed that he did not believe the witness. 'Do you mean to suggest that he made the first assault upon you?' he asked incredulously.

'Yes, he did.'

'And that you then drew your knife?'

'I did.'

'Is it the fact that you never saw any revolver or any gun at that moment?'

'I never saw it, no,' Bywaters had to admit.

Mr Cecil Whiteley, KC, did something to repair the damage caused by this admission when he re-examined his client about the possibility of Percy Thompson having a gun. 'Although I never saw a revolver,' said Bywaters, 'I believed that he had one, other-wise I would not have drawn my knife. I was in fear of my life.'

'At any time have you had any intention to murder Mr Thompson?' defence counsel asked in conclusion.

'I have not,' replied Bywaters firmly and unhesitatingly. He added that he had met Mrs Thompson in a tea shop near her place of work on the afternoon of the killing, but he strongly repudiated the suggestion which had been made by the prosecution that the purpose of the meeting was to plot her husband's death.

The atmosphere of tension mounted when the usher called out 'Edith Jessie Thompson', and the prisoner left the dock to follow her lover on to the witness stand. There was no need for her to testify. Had she remained silent the prosecution could not have commented upon the fact. The only evidence against her consisted of the letters, and Sir Henry Curtis-Bennett would have preferred to have been left to deal with them himself in his speech to the jury rather than risk his client being cross-examined by the ruthless Solicitor-General and probably convicting herself out of her own mouth. However, Edith Thompson brushed aside all her counsel's objections, determined as she was on getting the lime-light. She realised the enormous public interest in the case, her counsel said afterwards, and decided to play up to it by entering the witness box.

The story of her relations with Freddy Bywaters which she told in her examination-in-chief was a curious one. She and her husband had known the Bywaters family for some years, she said, the acquaintance going back to the days when her brother and Bywaters were schoolmates. In June 1921, Bywaters was on extended leave from his ship, and he accompanied her husband and herself on a holiday they took in the Isle of Wight. At that time she and Freddy, she went on, were no more than friends. The friendship continued after Freddy went to live with the Thompsons as a paying guest until his ship was ready to sail.

'How did you become lovers?' her counsel asked her.

'Well,' said Edith, 'it started on the August Bank Holiday, I had some trouble with my husband on that day—over a pin!'

It was a fine sunny afternoon and all three were in the garden at the back of the house. Edith Thompson was sewing. Suddenly she looked up and said, 'I want a pin.'

'I will go and get you one,' said Bywaters.

When he returned with the pin, husband and wife were arguing, Percy Thompson saying she should have got the pin herself.
Edith Thompson then went into the house to prepare tea. Her
husband followed her and a further argument ensued as she was
laying the table in the sitting room. Her sister, Avis Graydon, was
expected, but she was a little late and, unlike his wife, Percy
Thompson did not want to wait for her. He went on to make some
uncomplimentary remarks about Edith's family and then began to
beat her. Finally he threw her across the room and she collided
with a chair which overturned. Hearing the noise from the garden,
Bywaters rushed in and told Thompson to stop.

'Why don't you come to an amicable agreement?' said Bywaters.
'Either you can have a separation or you can get a divorce.'

Thompson hesitated before replying. 'Yes—No—I don't see it
concerns you.'

'You are making Edie's life a hell,' said Bywaters. 'You know
she is not happy with you.'

'Well, I have got her and I will keep her.'

Edith went upstairs and Bywaters returned to his room. After a
short while she joined him there, when he comforted her and for
the first time kissed her on the lips. When he came back to the
sitting room, he extracted a promise from her husband that he
would not knock her about or beat her any more. But Thompson
flatly refused to take any steps towards obtaining a legal separation or a divorce from his wife. Shortly afterwards, Bywaters left
the house and went to stay with his mother.

During the next few weeks—he was due to embark early in
September—he and Edith met secretly from time to time. Most of
these meetings took place in tea shops or municipal parks such as
Wanstead or Epping Forest, near Ilford. There were not many
opportunities for more than hand-holding at dance teas and an
occasional embrace on a bench. It was the age of the *thé dansant*,
and at one of these occasions the orchestra played 'One Little
Hour', which became 'their tune'. However, just before Bywater's
ship sailed on 9 September the two became lovers, apparently
going to a small hotel for the purpose and registering under
assumed names.

Questioned by her counsel about the letters and the news-
cuttings, she explained that she had deliberately deceived her
lover into thinking that she wished to poison her husband, but

that she had no intention of acting upon what she had written. She had sent the letters with their suggestive enclosures, so she said, because she was anxious to keep Freddy's love. Occasionally he would go out with other girls, one of whom was Edith's un-married sister Avis, and Edith thought that he might be tiring of her.

When the Solicitor-General rose to cross-examine, it was not difficult for him to entrap her as Curtis-Bennett had feared he would. Inskip held up one letter in which she had written to her lover: 'Why aren't you sending me something? I wanted you to. . . . If I don't mind the risk, why should you?'

'What was it?' the Solicitor-General asked sternly.

'I've no idea,' Edith replied as nonchalantly as she could.

'Have you no idea?'

'Except what he told me.'

'What did he lead you to think it was?'

'That it was something for me to give my husband?'

'With a view to poisoning your husband?'

Edith paused before answering, not knowing exactly what to say and looking distinctly uncomfortable. 'That was not the idea,' she said at last, 'that was not what I expected.'

'Something to give your husband that would hurt him?' the Solicitor-General went on.

'To make him ill,' she blurted out.

Replying to further questions, Edith Thompson admitted that she had urged Bywaters to send the 'something to make him ill', instead of bringing it. 'I wrote that,' she added, 'in order to make him think I was willing to do anything he might suggest, to enable me to retain his affections.'

Again the Solicitor-General eyed her severely. 'Mrs Thompson,' he put it to her, 'is that quite a frank explanation of this urging him to send instead of to bring?'

'It is, absolutely,' was the unconvincing reply. 'I wanted him to think I was eager to help him.'

At this point, the judge leaned forward in the direction of the witness. 'That does not answer the question, you know,' he remarked.

There was little that Curtis-Bennett could do in re-examining his client to repair the damage caused by her replies to the Solicitor-General's questioning. But he did his best. For example, the phrase, 'He is still well', which she had used in one letter, he was able to show referred not to her husband but to a bronze monkey that Bywaters had bought in some foreign port and given her as a souvenir. Her defence counsel also made the most of her conduct on the night of the killing.

'As far as you could,' he asked her, 'from the moment you got to your husband, did you do everything you could for him?'

'Everything I possibly could,' echoed Edith Thompson.

Curtis-Bennett came back to this point in her favour when he made his closing speech to the jury. 'The letters provide the only evidence upon which the charge of murder is framed against Mrs Thompson,' he stressed his words deliberately. 'Everything that was done and said by her on that night shows as strongly as it can that not only did she not know the murder was going to be committed, but that she was horrified when she found her husband was killed.'

His client was no ordinary woman, counsel went on. 'She reads a book and then imagines herself one of the characters in the book. She is always living an extraordinary life of novels.' So far as her relations with Freddy Bywaters went, Sir Henry Curtis-Bennett made it clear that for his part he did not care whether they were described as 'an amazing passion' or 'an adulterous intercourse' or whatever. 'Thank God, this is not a court of morals,' he told the eleven men and one woman in the jury box, 'because if everybody immoral was brought here I should never be out of it, nor would you. Whatever name you give it, it was certainly a great love that existed between these two people.'

Mr Justice Shearman began his summing-up of the evidence to the jury with the ominous words: 'You should not forget you are trying a vulgar, common crime!' Edith Thompson's letters to her lover the judge proceeded to describe as 'full of the outpourings of a silly but at the same time a wicked affection'.

'Members of the jury, if that nonsense means anything,' he went on to say, 'it means that the love of a husband for his wife is something improper because marriage is acknowledged by the law, and that the love of a woman for her lover—illicit and clandestine—is something great and noble. I am certain that you, like any other right-minded persons, will be filled with disgust at such a notion. Let us get rid of all that atmosphere and try this case in an ordinary common sense way.'

The summing-up was strongly hostile to both prisoners. The red-robed and bewigged figure on the judicial bench left little doubt in the jury's minds that 'these two by arrangement between each other agreed to murder this man Thompson, and the murder was effected by the man Bywaters.' The impression was heightened by the sense of moral indignation expressed by the judge at the prisoners' sexual morals. In the event it took the jury just over two hours to find both prisoners guilty of murder.

'I say the verdict of the jury is wrong,' exclaimed Bywaters when he heard it. 'Edith Thompson is not guilty. I am no murderer. I am no assassin.' These words were echoed by the woman who stood beside him in the dock. 'I am not guilty,' she cried. And again, after both had been sentenced to death by hanging, she repeated, 'I am not guilty. Oh, God, I am not guilty.'

Both prisoners appealed on the grounds that the verdict was against the weight of the evidence and that the judge had mis-directed the jury. Each of the appeals was dismissed by the Court of Criminal Appeal, which saw no grounds for quashing the con-viction or ordering a new trial, the President of the Court describing it as a 'squalid and rather indecent case of lust and adultery' and one which 'exhibits from the beginning to the end no redeeming feature'.

At the time no woman had been hanged in England for fifteen years. Largely for this reason there was considerable public agitation that Edith Thompson should be reprieved and a petition for reprieve containing many thousands of signatures was sent to the Home Secretary with whom the final decision rested.

Three days before the date set for the execution, Bywaters had a meeting with his mother in the condemned cell in Pentonville Prison, where he was being held. He told his mother that he had no grievance against the law so far as he himself was concerned, and that execution had no terrors for him. 'I killed him and I must pay for it,' he said. 'The judge's summing-up was just, if you like, but it was cruel. It never gave me a chance. I did it, though, and I can't complain.'

His mistress's case was quite different, he stressed. 'I swear she is completely innocent. She never knew that I was going to meet them that night. . . . For her to be hanged as a criminal is too awful. She didn't commit the murder, I did. She never planned it.

She never knew about it. She is innocent, absolutely innocent. I can't believe that they will hang her.'

When this was reported to Edith Thompson's solicitor, the lawyer dashed through the night to make a last-minute appeal to the Home Secretary who had gone off to spend the weekend at his country house about two hundred miles from London. When he had read Bywaters's 'confession', the Home Secretary promised to give the solicitor his decision next day, the eve of the execution. He did so, but it was that there could be no reprieve for either prisoner and the law must take its course.

They were both hanged at the same hour, 9 a.m. on 9 January 1923—she at Holloway and he a quarter of a mile away at Pentonville. Freddy Bywaters met his end 'like a gentleman', as he told his mother he would, protesting his mistress's innocence to the last. Edith Thompson, however, had to be carried from the condemned cell to the scaffold by two wardresses as she was in a state of complete collapse during her last moments.

Edith Thompson's leading counsel was greatly upset by the verdict and its outcome, which he felt would have been different if she had taken his advice. 'She spoiled her chances by her evidence and demeanour,' he said afterwards. 'I had a perfect answer to everything, which I am sure would have won an acquittal if she had not been a witness. She was a vain woman and an obstinate one. Also her imagination was highly developed, but it failed to show her the mistake she was making. I could have saved her.'

Furthermore, Sir Henry Curtis-Bennett never ceased to deprecate the contemptuous manner in which both the Solicitor-General and the trial judge had described what he felt was really a great and sincere mutual love. Asked why the extreme penalty had in the circumstances been invoked in the case of his client, Sir Henry said simply: 'Mrs Thompson was hanged for immorality.'

# 10

# The Life and Death
# of a Playboy Prince

The trial of Marie-Marguerite Fahmy for the murder of her playboy husband Prince Ali Kamel Fahmy Bey, which began in London's Central Criminal Court on 10 September 1923, had all the elements of a drama of powerful passions. The accused was an attractive and sophisticated thirty-two-year-old Parisienne brunette of slender height and striking beauty. Her late husband, ten years her junior, was an abnormal and vicious young Egyptian of considerable wealth and worldly possessions, who was widely believed to have treated her with disgusting cruelty. He held the nominal post of attaché at the French Legation in Cairo and had obtained his princely title in return for making gifts to various Egyptian charities. Prince Fahmy's death, which his wife admitted she had caused by shooting him, had taken place during the night of the previous 9–10 July in the Savoy Hotel in London, where they occupied a luxurious suite of rooms. At the inquest which followed the killing, the coroner's jury returned a verdict of wilful murder against Madame Fahmy.

Mr Justice Rigby Swift presided at the trial. He was the youngest judge on the High Court bench, having been only forty-six at the time of his appointment three years previously, but he had already made his mark by his effective handling of jury cases. The prosecution was led by Mr Percival Clarke, son of the famous Victorian advocate Sir Edward Clarke. Marguerite Fahmy was represented by two leading King's Counsel, Sir Edward Marshall Hall and Sir Henry Curtis-Bennett, though in fact the defence was to be entirely handled by Marshall Hall, who had taken Sir

Edward Clarke's place as the most popular and sought after defence lawyer in the country.

Fahmy Bey, said Mr Percival Clarke in opening the case for the Crown, had inherited great wealth from his father, an engineer. He became infatuated with the accused, then Madame Laurent, a divorceé, whom he first met in Paris in May of the previous year. He followed her to Deauville where she became his mistress, and they lived there and in Egypt and Paris. In December Marguerite became a Moslem and there were civil and religious marriage ceremonies. Prince Fahmy returned to Cairo where he was later joined by his wife, who had remained in Paris, but at no time were they happy. Their natures seemed incompatible.

At the beginning of July 1923, the couple came to London and put up at the Savoy Hotel, accompanied by a secretary, valet and maid. On 9 July they had some disagreement because the wife wanted to go to Paris to have an operation which the husband wished to have performed in London. At supper in the hotel restaurant that night there was a violent quarrel during which Madame Fahmy, it was alleged, said to her husband: 'You shut up. I will smash this bottle over your head.' When the band leader came to her table and asked if there was any particular tune she would like to be played, she replied, 'I don't want any music—my husband has threatened to kill me tonight.' The polite maestro bowed gravely and said, 'I hope you will still be here tomorrow, madame.' After supper Prince Fahmy twice asked his wife to dance with him, but she refused, though she danced once with his secretary Seid Enani.

They went upstairs to their suite about 1.30 a.m. A violent thunder storm was raging at the time. Shortly afterwards a luggage porter was passing the door of the suite when Fahmy came out in his pyjamas and said to the porter: 'Look at my face! Look at what she has done!' The porter saw a slight red mark on his cheek. Then Madame Fahmy, who was in evening dress, came out and speaking hurriedly in French pointed to her eyes. The porter thereupon told them to go into their rooms and not create a disturbance in the corridor. The porter then continued on his way.

Hearing a whistle the porter looked back and saw Prince Fahmy stooping down, whistling and snapping his fingers at a little dog which had come out of their suite. A few moments later the porter heard three shots in quick succession and running back to the suite saw Madame Fahmy throw down a pistol. Her husband was lying on the floor bleeding from his head. 'Oh, sir,' said Madame Fahmy when the manager was summoned, 'I have been married six months which has been torture to me. I have suffered terribly.' The police and a doctor were sent for and the wounded man was removed to hospital where he died shortly afterwards. Marguerite Fahmy was then taken into custody.

Seid Enani was the first to give evidence for the prosecution, corroborating details of his late master's life and marriage. Cross-examined by Marshall Hall, he denied that he had any influence over Prince Fahmy which would have made his wife jealous.

'Was he in the habit of beating women?'

'He would dispute with them,' the secretary replied, 'but I have never seen him beat them.'

'You have known of his intimacies with many women?' Marshall Hall continued.

'Yes,' the witness agreed.

'You said that you tried to dissuade the prince from marrying her?'

'Yes.'

'Did you say he was an Oriental, and passionate?'

'Yes.'

'You were very much attached to Prince Fahmy?'

'Yes.'

'Was he infatuated with her at that time?'

'Yes, very much in love with her.'

Marshall Hall then quoted a letter written in French from Egypt by the Prince to Marguerite in terms of sickening flattery. The translation read in part:

> Your image pursues me incessantly. . . . Torch of my life . . . your head so haughty and majestic, brightly encircled by a crown which I reserve for it here. Yes, this crown I reserve for you on your arrival in this beautiful country of my ancestors.

'Everybody thought he was a prince, then?' Madame Fahmy's counsel asked the witness.

'We always refer to our ancestors,' was all the secretary could say.

'But they do not all wear crowns?'

'No.'

Answering further questions, Seid Enani said that it was in Cairo that the question of marriage first arose. Fahmy at first wanted her to live with him, but was the first to suggest marriage. Two of the stipulations in the contract were that Madame Fahmy would not be obliged to wear Egyptian clothes and that she would have the right to divorce her husband. She adopted the Moslem religion because Fahmy's mother had left him a large legacy on condition that he married a woman of that faith.

'When the religious ceremony took place, did Fahmy decline to allow the divorce condition to be inserted?'

'Yes.'

'After the religious ceremony, then, he could divorce her, as she was a Moslem, at a moment's notice and she could not divorce him, and he had the power to take three wives if he liked?'

The witness agreed that this was so. Marshall Hall then turned to the prince's treatment of his wife.

'Were people always set to watch her when she went out?'

'They were lately,' the witness again agreed.

'On February 21st was there a very serious scene? Do you know that he swore on the Koran to kill her?'

'No.'

'Do you know that she was in fear of her life?'

'No, I never knew that.'

'On the 23rd, did Fahmy take her on his yacht at Luxor?'

'Yes.'

'Were there six black servants on board?'

'Yes.'

'I suggest that from that moment Fahmy began to treat her with persistent cruelty?'

'I cannot say cruelty. He was a bit unkind.'

'The day he arrived at Luxor, did he smack her face, tell her she must not leave the yacht, and then kick her?'

'I have not seen him kick her. I knew he locked her in.' Further pressed by Marshall Hall, the secretary was obliged to admit that he remembered an incident when Fahmy struck his wife a violent blow on the chin and dislocated her jaw.

To drive home his point Marshall Hall went on to read from a letter which Fahmy had written to his wife's younger sister:

Just now I am engaged in training her. Yesterday, to begin with I did not come in to lunch nor to dinner and I also left her at the theatre. This will teach her, I hope, to respect my wishes.

With women one must act with energy and be severe—no bad habits. We still lead the same life of which you are aware—the opera, theatre, disputes, high words, and perverseness.

'When you came over from Egypt,' counsel continued, 'his treatment of his wife was the talk of the ship?'

'They were always quarrelling,' replied the secretary.

'Do you know that he locked her in her cabin for twenty-four hours and that the captain had to have her released?'

'I don't know that.'

'Was not the Madame Fahmy of 1923 totally different from the Madame Laurent of 1922?'

'Perhaps.'

'From a quite entertaining and fascinating woman she became miserable and wretched?'

'They were always quarrelling.'

'Did she say that you and Fahmy were always against her, and that it was a case of two to one?'

'Yes.'

Marshall Hall went on to suggest to the witness that Prince Fahmy was a man of vicious and eccentric sexual appetite, and that he had a homosexual relationship with Seid Enani which was notorious in Egypt. He showed the witness a coloured cartoon which had appeared in an Egyptian newspaper depicting Prince Fahmy, his secretary and a friend as 'The Light, the Shadow of the Light, and the Shadow of the Shadow of the Light'. While agreeing that he and his employer were represented in the cartoon, the witness loyally denied any unfavourable reflection on his or his master's morals. The judge then asked to see the cartoon, and when he had examined it he remarked that it did not reflect on anybody's moral character, except perhaps the artist's.

It was a masterly cross-examination. Marshall Hall did not attack the secretary's character, though he got very near to it at the end. Had he done so, this would have entitled the prosecution to attack that of Madame Fahmy, and it was of vital importance to her counsel's case that she should not be exhibited in the guise of an habitually loose woman. As it was, the secretary as the prince's paid employee did not admit a great deal, but he admitted enough to impress the jury by creating an atmosphere of intense sympathy for the accused woman who had been in the power of this decadent Oriental millionaire.

The porter, night manager and assistant manager of the Savoy Hotel followed the secretary into the witness box. In cross-examining the assistant manager, Marshall Hall again showed his characteristic skill and incidentally his knowledge of the French language. According to this witness, Madame Fahmy had said to him in French immediately after the shooting, 'Monsieur, what have I done? I have lost my head.'

The actual words used by Madame Fahmy were, '*J'ai perdu la tête*.' Marshall Hall put it to the witness that their real meaning was not 'I have lost my head', but 'I was frightened out of my wits'. The witness agreed and this interpretation was not challenged by the prosecution.

Robert Churchill, a gunsmith and expert on firearms, testified that the weapon used in the killing was a .32 Browning automatic of Belgian manufacture, capable of holding eight cartridges.

Prosecuting counsel asked him, 'Is it a weapon that continues to fire when the trigger is pressed, or does the trigger require pressure for each shot?'

'The trigger has to be pulled for each shot,' the witness replied. 'It is automatic loading, but not automatic firing.' The gunsmith added that the pull of the trigger was 8¼ pounds. It was not a light pull. The pistol had a safety grip and a safety catch and was not the sort to go off accidentally.

He was cross-examined at length about the mechanism of the weapon by Marshall Hall, who suggested that when the pistol was tightly gripped a very small pressure on the trigger would discharge each shot. The witness agreed that this was so and also that after one shot had been discharged through the barrel it would immediately be replaced by another. An inexperienced person might thus easily reload the weapon, believing that in fact he had emptied it.

Dr Gordon, who had been attending Madame Fahmy and had made arrangements for her to go into a London nursing home for an operation on the day after the killing, testified that he was called to the scene of the tragedy and asked Madame Fahmy what she had done. 'I have shot my husband,' she replied. She was in a

Arthur Orton, the Tichborne claimant

Roger Tichborne, heir to the
Tichborne baronetcy

LEADING CHARACTERS IN THE TRIAL
OF THE TICHBORNE CLAIMANT FOR
PERJURY

Lady Tichborne,
Roger's mother,
who recognised Arthur
Orton as her son

Arthur Orton in 1867
at Tichborne Park

The claimant's counsel Dr Kenealy shaking
hands with his client at the end of the trial
in Westminster Hall

The claimant's coffin showing the inscription:
'Sir Roger Charles Doughty Tichborne
Born 5th January 1829 Died 1st April 1898'

The President Henry A. Garfield

The Assassin Charles Guiteau

The shooting of President Garfield 2 July 1881

Adelaide Bartlett, accused of
murdering her husband

The Rev. George Dyson,
Mrs Bartlett's supposed lover

Mr Edwin Bartlett being cross-examined by Edward Clarke QC, MP,
during the trial of Mrs Adelaide Bartlett at the Old Bailey, 12 April
1886

Roland Molineux, accused of
fatally poisoning Mrs Katherine
J. Adams

General Edward
Molineux, the accused's
father

The envelope of the poison package

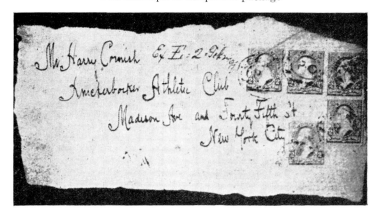

The address as written by Molineux at the request of the police

Nicola Sacco and Bartolomeo Vanzetti
shortly before they were sentenced
to death April 1927 at Dedham, Mass.

Judge Webster Thayer
the trial judge

District Attorney Frederick
Katzmann who prosecuted

Landru and Mlle Segret, 'the one who got away'

Landru in court

Horatio Bottomley addressing a recruiting meeting
in Trafalgar Square, London, in 1915

Bottomley arriving at Bow Street Police Court where he was
committed for trial October 1921. The notorious ex-solicitor Arthur
Newton is on Bottomley's right and his valet Rawson on his left

Sir Almeric Fitzroy, KCB, KCVO, Clerk to the Privy Council

Extract from
The *News of the World*
8 October 1922

# OYAL OFFICIAL IN DOCK. 9/10/22

## HARGE AGAINST CLERK TO PRIVY COUNCIL.

## YOUNG WIDOW'S STORY.

lborough-street was besieged yester-
y crowds of people curious to hear
ce against
Almeric Fitzroy, K.C.B., K.C.V.O.,
4 years Clerk to the Privy Council, and
r, therefore, of Royal Office.
meric, whose age is 71, was charged

ly interfering with and annoying

with both hands, in the left of which he
had a walking stick, and struck Constable
Brosman somewhat violently in the face
with the hand which held the stick.
Whether he meant it or not I do
not stop to inquire. The officer
has not thought fit to charge him."
Continuing, Mr. Muskett stated that defendant was taken to the station, and the

Sir Edward Marshall Hall, KC, who
defended Madame Fahmy

Madame Marguerite Fahmy, accused
of murdering her husband

Fahmy Bey in his Rolls-Royce outside the Savoy Hotel where he was fatally shot

Mr Justice Shearman
the trial judge

Sir Thomas Inskip, KC
Solicitor-General

JUDGE AND COUNSEL IN THE BYWATERS-THOMPSON MURDER TRIAL

Mr Cecil Whiteley, KC
counsel for Bywaters

Sir Henry Curtis-Bennett, KC, counsel
for Edith Thompson

(Left to right) Frederick Bywaters, Edith Thompson and Percy Thompson

Senator Albert Fall
Secretary of the Interior

President Warren Harding
President of the United States

Harry S. Sinclar (left) and Edward L. Doheny
(right) oilmen involved in the Teapot Dome scandal

The promissory note given by Fall to Doheny in return for a 'loan' of $100,000.
Fall's signature which Doheny tore off the note was later produced by Mrs Doheny

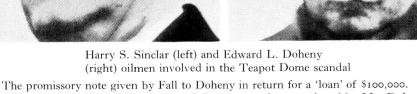
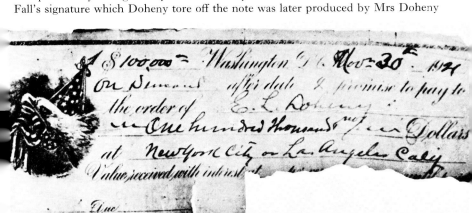

The Chicago home of Albert Leopold

The Chicago home of Richard Loeb

Leopold (left) and Loeb (right) conferring with their
counsel Clarence Darrow

The Minister, the
Rev. Edward Hall

The Choir Singer
Mrs Eleanor Mills

**QUIRIN** **BURGER** **THIEL**

**KERLING** **DASCH** **HAUPT**

Six of the eight German saboteurs who were landed in the
United States by submarine in 1942. All of them were captured
and tried by a military court *in camera* and condemned to death.
The sentences on Dasch and Burger were commuted by President
Roosevelt to imprisonment. The others were executed.

(*Left*) Compton Mackenzie and his wife
leaving the Old Bailey after his conviction
for contravening the Official Secrets Act

Coast Guard John Cullen who raised the alarm after four of the German saboteurs had landed at Amagansett beach, Long Island

Part of the court-room during the trial of the German saboteurs. The US Attorney General Francis Biddle is on the left and J. Edgar Hoover, Director of the FBI, in the middle. Colonel Carl Ristine, who defended Dasch is in the right foreground

Nancy Oakes and her husband, Count Alfred de Marigny, accused of the murder of her father, Sir Harry Oakes (*below left*) in the Bahamas

The windows of Sir Harry Oakes's bedroom at Westbourne, his house now part of the Nassau Country Club

The remains of Sir Harry Oakes as discovered by his friend Harold Christie

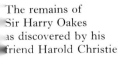

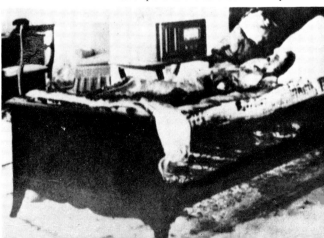

Karl Gustav Hulten alias
Lieutenant Richard Allen

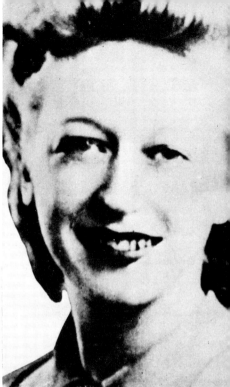

Elizabeth Jones alias
Georgina Grayson

Hulten's wife and mother trying
unsuccessfully to telephone
him from America on the eve of
his execution

Han van Meegeren
self-portrait

An art expert testifying at the trial of Van Meegeren for forgery. His picture *Christ at Emmaus*, painted in the style of Vermeer, is on the wall in the background

*The Last Supper* painted by Van Meegeren in the style of Vermeer

Eileen Gibson                    James Camb

Cabin 126 on the *Durban Castle*.
After having had sexual intercourse with her on the bed Camb was alleged to have
pushed the body of Eileen Gibson through the porthole into the shark infested sea

The Atom spies Morton Sobell, Julius Rosenberg and his wife Ethel being driven away from court

Sing Sing prison
The electric chair in which
the Rosenbergs were
executed

Judge Irving Kaufman who tried
and sentenced the Rosenbergs.
'Your crime is worse than murder
he told them

white evening dress trimmed with beads, and was very dazed and frightened.

'Did you see any marks of bruising on her arms?' asked the prosecutor.

'She showed me a scratch on the back of her neck about one and a half inches long, probably caused by a finger nail.' She told him her husband had done it.

Asked by Marshall Hall in cross-examination whether the marks on her neck were consistent with a hand clutching at her throat, the doctor said they were.

'When you visited Madame Fahmy for her illness, did you see her husband?'

'No. He was in the next room, and a black valet was outside Madame's door.'

Questioned about the nature of Madame Fahmy's illness, Dr Gordon agreed that she was suffering from a painful complaint which might have been caused by the conduct she alleged against her husband. The published accounts of the trial are silent on the nature of this conduct, but it may well be that Prince Fahmy forced his wife to have anal intercourse and may conceivably have communicated a venereal disease to her in the process.

After police evidence of the accused's arrest, the prosecution case was closed and Marshall Hall opened his defence with a speech to the jury, to whom he submitted that it would be impossible justly on the facts to find 'this poor, unfortunate woman guilty' of either murder or manslaughter. She was 'perhaps a woman of not very strict morality', he went on, because they had heard that she had been divorced and had lived with Fahmy before marriage. However, there was no doubt that, although they were infatuated with each other at the beginning, she made a terrible mistake in her estimate of his character. 'We know that women are sometimes very much attracted to men younger than themselves,' he told the jury, 'and he went out of his way, with all his Eastern cunning, to make himself agreeable and acceptable to her. But this was a man who enjoys the sufferings of women. He was abnormal and a brute. After marriage all restraint ceased and he developed from a plausible lover into a ferocious brute with the vilest of vile tempers and a filthy perverted taste. It makes one shudder to consider the conditions under which this wretched woman lived.'

5

Coming to the night of the tragedy, Marshall Hall recounted how Fahmy had called his wife into his bedroom and pointed to a heap of money on the table. She asked him to give her the French money, about 2,000 francs, for her travelling expenses to Paris for her operation. He told her she could not have it unless she agreed to a suggestion he made, apparently for abnormal sexual intercourse. She refused and he spat in her face, telling her to go to the devil. He then followed her outside in to the corridor, catching her by the neck and tightening his grip on her so that she feared she would be strangled.

Thanks to the judge's intervention, Marshall Hall went on, 'a new and wonderful piece of evidence' had come into his hands. This was the report of the prison medical officer, who was also the governor of Holloway Prison where the accused was taken after her arrest. He was called as the first witness for the defence and he described how Madame Fahmy, when she was admitted to Holloway, had three abrasions on the back of her neck which were consistent with having been caused by a man's hand.

Marshall Hall intended to call the accused next, but before he did so he informed the judge that it was necessary to discuss a point of law in the absence of the jury. When the jury had accordingly been sent out, the leading defence counsel said he had been told by the prosecutor that he (Mr Percival Clarke) proposed to cross-examine Madame Fahmy to show that, as she was a woman who lived an immoral life, she would therefore be a woman of the world well able to look after herself. 'The only effect of that,' observed Marshall Hall, 'would be to prejudice the jury unfavourably towards this woman. We know the effect of these suggestions.'

'Sir Edward has said she was an immoral woman,' the judge remarked, 'but he has said it in such a way as to give the impression to everyone who listened to his speech that she was an innocent and most respectable lady. It is a difficult thing to do, but Sir Edward, with all that skill we have admired for so long, has done it.' Mr Justice Swift then ruled that the evidence so far did not justify Mr Clarke in asking Madame Fahmy about her relations with any other men, but with regard to the dead man he might ask anything he liked.

When the jury returned to court, the judge said he did not propose to inform them of the legal discussion which had taken place, and added: 'I must now give instructions that you are not to be allowed access to any newspapers until the trial is over. I am sorry to deprive you of them. It must be very boring to be shut up all the evening without even a newspaper, but I am bound to do it.'

The prisoner was then called to testify in her own defence. Slowly and carefully through the medium of an interpreter, since she knew no English, Marshall Hall took her through the tragedy of her life with Prince Fahmy until the three fatal shots were fired. She said she had married her first husband M. Laurent in April 1919 and had divorced him a few months later for desertion. On the subject of her second husband's treatment of her, she said that his black valet was always following her about and used to enter her room when she was dressing. When she complained to her husband, he replied: 'He has the right. He does not count. He is nobody.'

She described how one day in Paris, when her young sister Yvonne Alibert was present, he had threatened her with a horse-whip, seizing her by the throat and throwing her backwards. He only stopped when her sister, who had a revolver in her hand, told him to desist. After the scene on the yacht, she described how Ali Fahmy had taken the Koran and sworn on it that he would kill her. Later she wrote to her French lawyer that she had been held literally prisoner on board the yacht for three days and that she bore on her arms 'the marks of my husband's gentleness'.

In further replies to her counsel, she said that she had never fired a pistol till the night of her husband's death. He had given it to her loaded, saying, 'It is all ready to fire'. She had often seen him unload his own pistol by opening the breach and taking out a cartridge. On that dreadful night, when he had tried to strangle her and she had been in an agony of fear, she had tried to do the same thing. But her hands had not been strong enough to pull back the breach cover fully, and she had struggled to extract the bullet by shaking the weapon in front of the window. While she was thus engaged, somehow the first cartridge went off and the bullet spent itself harmlessly out of the window. 'After the cartridge had been fired,' she said, 'I thought the revolver was not dangerous.' However, unknown to her the second cartridge had automatically come up into position.

'I know nothing about automatic pistols,' she said, as her

counsel handed the weapon to her. At first she shrank back from it, but eventually she took it in her hands. She tried, but was quite unable to pull back the breach cover.

'Why did you assent to come to London when you were so frightened?' Marshall Hall asked her.

'I had to come to London for family reasons,' she replied. 'I had always hoped he would change. Every time I threatened to leave him, he cried and promised to mend his ways. I also wished to see my daughter who was at school near London.'

With a sob punctuating every phrase, she told the story of the final scene.

'He advanced and had a very threatening expression. He said, "I will revenge myself." I had taken the revolver in my hand. . . . I went out into the corridor in front of the lift. He seized me suddenly and brutally by the throat with his left hand. His thumb was on my windpipe and his fingers were pressing on my neck.

'I pushed him away, but he crouched to spring on me, and said, "I will kill you." I lifted my arm in front of me and without looking pulled the trigger. The next moment I saw him on the ground before me without realising what had happened. I do not know how many times the revolver went off. I did not know what had happened.

'I saw Fahmy on the ground and I fell on my knees beside him. I caught hold of his hand and said to him, "Sweetheart, it is nothing. Speak, oh, please speak to me!" While I was on my knees the porter came up.'

Marshall Hall asked her two final questions in his examination-in-chief.

'When the pistol went off, killing your husband, had you any idea that it was in a condition to be fired?'

'None,' the witness answered emphatically. 'I thought there was no cartridge and that it could not be used.'

'When you threw your arm out when the pistol was fired, what were you afraid of?'

'That he was going to jump on to me. It was terrible. I had escaped once. He said, "I will kill you. I will kill you." It was so terrible.'

Mr Percival Clarke began his cross-examination by asking if her father was a cab-driver in Paris. Immediately the judge intervened. 'Does it matter whether he was a cab-driver or a millionaire?' he asked the prosecutor. 'I don't want a long inquiry into the lady's ancestry or into circumstances which may not be admissible.'

Counsel did not pursue this line. Instead he asked the witness, 'Can I correctly describe you as a woman of the world, a woman of experience?'

'I have had experience of life,' Madame Fahmy answered sagely.

Asked whether she had not gone to Egypt with the idea of marrying Prince Fahmy, she said that she had arrived at no decision but had merely 'accepted to be his *amie*'.

'Were you not very ambitious to become his wife?'

'Ambitious, no,' replied the witness. 'I loved him so very much and wished to be with him.'

Asked what she did when her husband was cruel, she said, 'Once only I boxed his ears when he had beaten me very much.'

'I was always alternating between hope and despair,' she went on. 'Some days he would be nice and I had new confidence in him, but the next day he would be bad again, and it was always the same.' Their physical relations she described as 'being never quite normal.' She added that when she went out to buy new dresses, her husband's secretary Seid Enani was always sent with her and she had to undress before him.

'Why did you not have him to protect you if you feared your husband?'

'He was not my friend. He obeyed my husband's orders, not mine.'

'Did you think that he was in league with your husband to ill-treat you?'

'Sometimes I have thought so, because I noticed each time I told him something he immediately went to my husband and told him what I said, and he always did whatever he could to make matters worse.'

On the whole Madame Fahmy stood up well to this cross-examination, particularly when she was asked about the pistol. 'I never intended to shoot it out of the window,' she said. 'I just wanted to get the ball out, and I tried to pull the thing back but I had not the strength to do it. As I was shaking it, it went off and I felt perfectly certain it was safe.'

'Did you not think that when you got rid of the cartridge you were depriving yourself of the only defence left to you if your husband assaulted you?'

'I never wanted to kill my husband,' the prisoner answered between sobs. 'I only wanted to prevent him killing me. I thought the sight of the pistol might frighten him. But I never wanted to do him any harm. I never did. . . . I never noticed that I had pressed upon the trigger. . . . I saw my husband lying on the ground before I could think or see what had happened.'

Marshall Hall had kept one important piece of evidence in reserve for re-examination. This was a letter Madame Fahmy had written to her lawyer, accusing her husband of being responsible should she disappear. It read in part:

> Yesterday, January 21, 1923, at three o'clock in the afternoon, he took his Bible or Koran—I do not know how it is called— kissed it, put his hand on it, and swore to avenge himself upon me tomorrow, in eight days, a month, three months, but I must disappear by his hand. This oath was taken without any reason, neither jealousy, bad conduct, nor a scene on my part.

'Is that letter true?' asked Marshall Hall holding it up.

'It is the exact truth,' Madame Fahmy answered with conviction.

After the prisoner's sister, maid and chauffeur had been called to corroborate the catalogue of Prince Fahmy's cruelties, Marshall Hall began his closing speech to the jury on the fourth day of the trial. 'She made one great mistake, possibly the greatest mistake any woman of the West can make,' he said of his client; 'she married an Oriental. I dare say the Egyptian civilisation is, and may be, one of the oldest and most wonderful civilisations in the world. But if you strip off the external civilisation of the Oriental, you get the real Oriental underneath. It is common knowledge that the Oriental's treatment of women does not fit in with the idea the Western woman has of the proper way she should be treated by her husband.'

Marguerite Fahmy's defender went on to make the jury's flesh creep with his description of the subtle means by which the prince had enticed her into his 'Oriental garden', after which she was constantly watched by his retinue of black servants. 'Why was this woman afraid?' he asked the jury and went on to supply the answer. 'Was she afraid that some of the hirelings of this man would do her to death? The curse of this case is the atmosphere which we cannot understand—the Eastern feeling of possession of the woman, the Turk in his harem, this man who was entitled to have four wives if he liked for chattels, which to us Western people with our ideas of women is almost unintelligible, something we cannot deal with.'

Marshall Hall had not finished when the court adjourned. He resumed his speech next morning with a reference to the storm on the night of the killing. 'You know the effect of such a storm when your nerves are normal,' he told the jury. 'Imagine its effect on a woman of nervous temperament who had been living such a life as she had lived for the past six months—terrified, abused, beaten, degraded.'

The advocate went on to stage what was perhaps the most remarkable theatrical performance of his professional career when with the pistol in his hand he described the shooting in detail, imitating Fahmy's stealthy crouch as he advanced on his wife. 'In sheer desperation—as he crouched for the last time, crouched like an animal, like an Oriental, retired for the last time to get a bound forward—she turned the pistol and put it to his face, and to her horror the thing went off.'

As he spoke the last words, the great advocate held up the pistol and pointed it for a moment at the jury. Then he paused and dropped the weapon so that it fell with a clatter on the court-room floor, just as it had fallen from the prisoner's hands in the corridor of the Savoy Hotel. It is impossible to describe the effect of this daring demonstration. Yet Marshall Hall always said afterwards that the final dramatic touch with the pistol was an accident and that he had not meant to drop it at all.

He concluded with two references. The first was to what the prosecutor's father Sir Edward Clarke had said in another sensational Old Bailey trial. 'To use the words of my learned friend's great father many years ago in the Bartlett case, "I do not ask you for a verdict—I demand a verdict at your hands".'

His second reference was to a modern best-selling novel by Robert Hichens called *Bella Donna*, in the final scene of which a

Western woman goes out of the gates of an Oriental garden into the dark night of the desert. 'Members of the jury,' he said, 'I want you to open the gates where this Western woman can go out, not into the dark night of the desert, but back to her friends, who love her in spite of her weaknesses—back to her friends, who will be glad to receive her—back to her child who will be waiting for her with open arms. I ask you to open the gate and let this Western woman go back into the light of God's great Western sun.'

Marshall Hall pointed to the skylight where the bright English September sun was streaming in and suffusing the court with its warmth and brightness. With this final dramatic gesture, he sat down after one of the most moving speeches of his life.

In the face of this superb pleading, it took the jury little over an hour to reach their verdict—not guilty of murder, and not guilty of manslaughter. The cheering which greeted the result was so great that the judge immediately ordered the court to be cleared.

The prisoner broke down when she was discharged, the climax to an ordeal in which she had not been able to understand a single word of the concluding speeches and the judge's summing-up. 'Oh, I am so happy, I am so thankful,' she sobbed as she stumbled from the dock supported by two wardresses. 'It is terrible to have killed Ali, but I spoke the truth. I spoke the truth.'

Marshall Hall's oratory in defence of Marguerite Fahmy drew a strong protest to the British Attorney-General from the leader of the Egyptian Bar, who accused the advocate of 'allowing himself to generalise and to lash all Egypt and indeed the whole East'. This was unfair, as indeed Marshall Hall himself pointed out. 'Any attack I made was on express instructions, received through Egyptian sources on the man Ali Fahmy, and not on the Egyptians as a nation,' he wrote to the Attorney-General. 'If my instructions were, as I believe them to be, accurate, anything I said about that person was more than justified. The only thing that I remember saying that might be misunderstood was that it was a mistake for the Western woman to marry the Eastern man, and his idea of his rights towards a wife were those of possession instead of mutual alliance.'

It must be remembered that these were the days of plays like *The Sheik* and *The Garden of Allah* and stories which romanticised the sexual allure of the East. As the *Daily Mirror* wrote in an editorial at the time, the moral of the Fahmy trial for most people had little to do with the circumstances in which the fatal shot was fired, but bore chiefly if not solely upon the undesirability of marriage which united Oriental husbands and Western wives. The editorial continued:

> Too many of our women novelists, apparently under the spell of the East, have encouraged the belief that there is something specially romantic in such unions.
> They are not romantic.
> They are ridiculous and unseemly; and the sensational revelations of the trial which terminated on Saturday will not be without their use if they bring that fact home to the sentimental unsophisticated girl.

For Sir Edward Marshall Hall the Fahmy trial remained perhaps his most outstanding and widely known forensic triumph. Letters of congratulation poured in to him from all over the world. One of them was addressed simply to 'Marshall Hall, the Greatest Lawyer on Earth'. The Post Office delivered it safely to his chambers in the Temple.

# 11

# The Teapot Dome Scandal

The Teapot Dome Scandal with its revelations of corruption in high places of government shocked the American nation as it had not been shocked since the time of President Grant half a century before when similar disclosures took place. The nation was not to be shocked again to a comparable extent until the Watergate affair half a century later. Like Watergate, the public exposure of the Teapot Dome and associated transactions began with a United States Senate investigation. What the Senate committee, which began its hearings in October 1923, was called upon to inquire into was how the fabulously rich naval oil reserves at Teapot Dome in Wyoming and Elk Hills and Buena Vista in California were leased to Harry S. Sinclair's Mammouth Oil Company and Edward L. Doheny's Pan-American Petroleum & Transport Company respectively, in return for a royalty ranging from twelve and half to thirty-five per cent of the value of the crude oil extracted, and with no competitive bidding.

The committee's chairman was the sixty-two-year-old United States Democratic Senator from Montana, Thomas J. Walsh, who before he entered the Senate in 1913 had been Montana's ablest lawyer, practising largely in the field of mineral law. Personally incorruptible, Senator Walsh had the reputation of being a determined and relentless prosecutor. His committee's findings were to lead to the prosecution among others for conspiracy and bribery of a fellow US Senator, the Republican Albert B. Fall, from New Mexico, who as Secretary of the Interior in the Harding administration had authorised the grant of the leases to the two companies.

'America's present need is not heroics, but healing,' Harding had proclaimed at the outset of his Presidential campaign; 'not nostrums, but normalcy; not revolution, but restoration; not surgery, but serenity.' Thus the slogan, 'Back to Normalcy with Harding and Coolidge,' became the keynote of the campaign. Harding did not define the meaning of normalcy, but the electors knew what he meant when they went to the polls, since they voted overwhelmingly for Warren Gamaliel Harding and his Vice-Presidential running-mate Calvin Coolidge. In the words of one observer of the contemporary scene, 'getting away from the austerity of Wilson was as warming as a spring thaw after a winter of discontent'. It was particularly so for Harding's backers who had agreed to nominate him as the Republican Party's choice in the 'smoke-filled' room in the Congress Hotel in Chicago. Now they descended in strength on Washington for the pay-off. First in line was Harry M. Daugherty, a crooked lawyer from Harding's home state of Ohio, to whom the new President really owed his political existence. Harding offered him the Department of State, but Daugherty was content to settle for the office of Attorney-General, where he thought the pickings would be juicier. Scarcely less discreditable Cabinet appointments which Harding made were Edwin Denby as Secretary of the Navy and Albert B. Fall as Secretary of the Interior, though to be fair to the President he did send Charles Evans Hughes to the State Department, Herbert Hoover to the Department of Commerce, and Andrew Mellon to the Treasury, all respected men. Unfortunately the lower echelons included appointees as bad as Daugherty and Fall, notably Charles F. Forbes, head of the Veterans Bureau, and Colonel Thomas W. Miller, the Alien Property Custodian, who were to engage in looting on an appalling scale. Below them there was a disreputable collection of hangers-on and go-betweens against the unsavoury background of the notorious 'Little Green House on K Street', which served as the headquarters of Daugherty and his 'Ohio Gang' where a brisk trade went on in such commodities as Federal judgeships, pardons, and alien property, to the accompaniment of poker sessions, ladies of easy virtue, and cascades of bootleg liquor in an era of Prohibition and general graft. The gang was also in a position to blackmail Harding if necessary by threatening to expose his affair with his mistress Nan Britton, by whom he had a child.

Meanwhile the country's oilmen were rubbing their hands in

gleeful anticipation of a very rosy future. The phenomenal success
of the automobile—already seven million vehicles were on
American roads—made petroleum a most desirable commodity
for exploitation. In the words of one of Harry Sinclair's associates,
'oil was money, and the struggle for it was earnest and relentless'.
Senator Fall had been working hand in glove with the big oil
interests for some years and he had strongly urged US military
intervention in Mexico in order to safeguard the oil wells of his
friends Sinclair and Doheny, both of whom had contributed
heavily to Harding's campaign fund. Nevertheless nothing was
publicly known to Fall's discredit prior to his appointment as
Secretary of the Interior which he had sought from Harding, and
which the President, who had known him as a bluff Senatorial
colleague and fellow poker player, had cheerfully given him.
'There is more opportunity for graft and scandal connected with
the disposition of public lands, etc., than there could be in any
other department,' Fall told his wife at the time, 'and he [Harding]
wants a man who is thoroughly familiar with the business and one
he can rely upon as thoroughly honest.'

With his goatee beard, gambler's bow-tie, broad-brimmed
Stetson hat, and a thin cigar invariably clamped to his mouth,
Albert Bacon Fall, who was sixty-one at the time of his appointment as Secretary of the Interior, looked the incarnation of the
West. Although he had been born and raised in Kentucky, he had
struck out as a youngster in New Mexico, where he worked on
ranches and in mines before becoming a lawyer. He first entered
politics as a Democrat but switched to the Republicans shortly
before New Mexico became a state of the Union in 1912, when he
was elected to the United States Senate, in which he served until
becoming Secretary of the Interior. At heart he remained a
frontiersman and had been known to carry the six-shooter of his
frontier days even on the floor of the Senate. He believed that
northern Mexico should be annexed to the United States and that
public lands should be disposed of immediately and without
restrictions. As might be expected, he was a keen poker player.

Since 1912 the US Navy Department had been constructing
warships which used oil burners exclusively. Hence the con-
servation of oil became a vital element in national defence and it
was to ensure the Navy's oil supply that certain oil-bearing lands
in California and Wyoming were statutorily constituted as naval

petroleum reserves, revocable only by the President or Congress. The former, in Elk Hills and Buena Vista, consisted of approximately 69,000 acres, and the latter at Teapot Dome of 9,320 acres. Fall had no difficulty in persuading Navy Secretary Denby, a politically inept millionaire automobile manufacturer from Detroit, to transfer the oil reserves to the Department of the Interior. 'I suppose they know what they're doing,' said President Harding as he blithely signed the executive order for the transfer.

On 7 April 1922, secretly and without competitive bidding, Fall leased the entire Teapot Dome reserve to the Mammoth Oil Company, a subsidiary of the Sinclair Consolidated Oil Corporation which had been specifically formed to handle the lease and development of Teapot Dome. A few months later, he leased the Elk Hills and Buena Vista reserves to Doheny's Pan-American Petroleum & Transport Company. From Sinclair Fall received $26,000 in Liberty Bonds and from Doheny a 'loan' of $100,000 in cash. Fall was later to argue that these leases were fair to the Government and that no undue profits should have accrued to Sinclair and Doheny. However, Doheny went on record as saying that he 'figured that the Elk Hill Reserve ought to be worth a hundred million dollars to me'.

The transfers aroused the interest of the trouble-shooting Senator from Wisconsin, Robert M. LaFollette, on whose initiative the Senate voted to investigate the 'entire subject of leases of naval oil reserves' and 'compel the presentation before it of all documents and official data connected therewith'. Although President Harding wrote to the Senate expressing his unqualified approval of the actions of Secretaries Denby and Fall, the investigation went ahead under the chairmanship of Senator Walsh. However, by the time the committee was ready to begin public hearings eighteen months later, Fall had resigned as Secretary of the Interior and Harding was in his grave.

On his way to Alaska in the summer of 1923, Harding stopped at Kansas City, where Fall's wife dined with him at his hotel and afterwards was closeted with him alone. The President was said to have emerged 'scared and shaken' from this secret meeting, at which Mrs Emma Fall allegedly appeared 'veiled and furtive', having communicated disquieting news about Teapot Dome. Later in Alaska the President received a long coded message from Washington and for the next two days seemed on the verge of collapse. On his way back to the United States he was said to be suffering from ptomaine poisoning. He died suddenly in San Francisco on 2 August 1923 as the result of an embolism, so it was given out. But the newspaper accounts of his illness were confused and contradictory, and it has been suggested that he either took his own life or was murdered by his wife out of jealousy arising from his affair with Nan Britton. However that may be, there is little doubt that had he lived a few months longer President Harding would have been impeached, and that the scandal would, for a time at least, have destroyed the Republican Party.

On 22 October 1923, the Senate investigating committee held its first public hearing in the large caucus room of the Senate building, when two geologists testified that Teapot Dome contained thirty per cent less oil than was estimated and that the existing reserve was draining steadily into adjacent areas. This was corroborated next day by ex-Secretary Fall, when he was called as a witness and defended his action on the ground that there was grave danger of the reserves becoming exhausted and that in exercising the discretion which the President had vested in him, he had found what seemed to him a solution to the problem of the vanishing oil and he had no apologies to offer for what he had done. There was no sinister purpose in keeping the negotiations secret, he said. Nor had he asked for competitive bids because he knew he could get a better price through private negotiation, and he did not wish to draw international attention to the fact that contracts were being made for enormous storages of oil for use in a possible future crisis. Asked by the chairman about his business contacts with Sinclair and Doheny since he had left office, Fall replied that he had made a business trip to Europe for Sinclair for which Sinclair had paid his expenses amounting to $10,000. He said nothing about either the Liberty Bonds or the 'loan' from Doheny.

Fall's answers made a good impression on the committee and the Press representatives present, and if the matter had rested there all would have been well for the Senator from New Mexico. Unfortunately Fall had enemies; one of them was Carl C. Magee, editor of the *State Tribune* of Albuquerque. Magee offered to swear that in 1920, before his appointment to the Harding Cabinet, Fall had complained he was 'dead broke', that his New Mexico ranch was run down, and that his taxes on it were in arrears for the past ten years. In 1922, according to Magee and others, there was a remarkable change in Fall's financial condition. He paid up all his back taxes and made improvements on his ranch which must have cost at least $40,000. He bought the adjoining N. W. Harris ranch for $91,500 and Sinclair, who had visited his ranch, gave him a valuable addition of blood stock, cattle, hogs and a racehorse.

These facts were duly sworn to before the committee, and Fall was called upon for an explanation. After some delay, he came to Washington and registered in a hotel, saying he was too ill to attend the committee hearings. Instead he submitted a written statement in which he declared that he had obtained $100,000 in cash from Edward B. McLean, a rich Washington socialite, who had inherited an enormous fortune from his father and had married the Hope Diamond heiress, whose fortune was as great as his own. McLean was known as 'a soft touch' in Washington circles and at first Fall's statement surprised no one who knew the Federal capital. Naturally the committee wished to obtain verification from McLean. The latter duly testified that in November 1921 he had, at Fall's request, drawn three cheques totalling $100,000 on his personal bank accounts and given them to Fall. However, the cheques were never presented to the banks for payment and in fact were returned to McLean shortly afterwards by Fall who explained that he was getting the money from another source.

The day after McLean made this statement before the committee, Fall wrote to the chairman, endorsing its accuracy. 'It is absolutely true that I did not finally use the money from Mr McLean which he expressed himself willing to give me because I found that I could readily obtain it from other sources,' he told Senator Walsh. 'I wish it thoroughly understood that the source from which I obtained the money which I used was in no way connected with Mr Sinclair or in any way involved in the concession regarding the Teapot Dome or any other oil concession.'

It is difficult to see what Fall hoped to gain from this communication since it was an admission that his statement about getting the $100,000 from McLean was a lie. It was inevitable that he should now be asked to tell the committee where he did get the money. Doheny and his lawyer urged him to appear and make a clean breast of it. But Fall procrastinated, and eventually, unwilling to wait any longer, Doheny at his own request appeared before the committee, on 22 January 1924, to amplify his earlier testimony to the effect that Fall had never profited, directly or indirectly, from the Elk Hills leasing. 'I wish to inform the committee,' he now said, 'that on 30 November 1921 I loaned to Mr Fall $100,000 upon his promissory note to enable him to purchase a ranch in New Mexico. This sum was loaned to Mr Fall by me personally. It was my own money and did not belong in whole or in part to any oil company with which I am connected. In connection with this loan there was no discussion between Mr Fall and myself as to any contract whatever. It was a personal loan to a lifelong friend.'

Questioned by the committee about the details of the loan, Doheny said that Fall offered to put up the ranch as security, but the witness told him that he would give him the money on his note. When Fall later telephoned him to say he was ready for the money, Doheny got $100,000 in cash, put it in a satchel and gave it to his son to deliver to Fall.

'Was it not an extraordinary way of transmitting money?' the chairman asked.

'I do not know about that,' replied Doheny, adding that he had remitted more than a million dollars in that way over the past five years. 'In making the decision to lend this money to Mr Fall,' he went on, 'I was greatly affected by his extreme pecuniary circumstances. . . . I realised that the amount of money I was loaning him was a bagatelle to me, that it was no more than $25 or $30, perhaps, to the ordinary individual.'

'I can appreciate that on your side,' remarked the chairman, 'but looking at it from Mr Fall's side, it was quite a loan!'

Asked whether he saw any impropriety in loaning money to an officer of the government with whom he had very large business transactions, Doheny replied that he did not. 'And I do not now, Senator, with all due respect to your question.'

Asked whether he could produce the promissory note that Fall had given him, the witness was unable to do so, saying that he had searched for it and was still searching. This made the committee suspicious. However, Doheny returned six days later with the note, minus the signature, which he said he had torn off and given to his wife, since he did not wish to embarrass Fall in the event of his (Doheny's) death by his executors pressing Fall for payment.

He added that he hoped to find the missing portion of the note which he was sure was among his or his wife's papers.

Fall returned to Washington on the evening of the day that Doheny made his sensational disclosure. He was immediately served with a subpoena to appear before the committee once more. When he did so, on 2 February 1924, he was a broken man, having lost more than forty pounds in weight and his flesh hanging in wrinkled folds about his face and neck. In his trembling hand, he held a piece of paper from which he read the following statement: 'I decline to answer any questions on the ground that it may tend to incriminate me.'

Slowly and in shocked silence Fall rose from his seat and his lawyer led him out of the Senate caucus room by the arm. It was his last appearance before his old colleagues.

Sinclair, who was also recalled before the committee, likewise refused to answer any further questions, but not for the reason given by Fall, since (as he said) 'there is nothing in any of the facts or circumstances of the lease of Teapot Dome which does or can incriminate me.' He wished to reserve any further evidence he might be able to give, he said, for the legal proceedings which were bound to follow from the committee's investigation. The committee thereupon reported his action to the Senate which by an overwhelming majority declared him guilty of contempt and ordered his prosecution on this charge. He was promptly indicted.

Finally, one of Sinclair's lawyers testified that in June 1922 Fall told him he needed $25,000 and that the lawyer reported this to Sinclair who said, 'If he wants it, give it to him.' Sinclair's secretary thereupon deposited $25,000 in Liberty Bonds in an El Paso bank for Fall's account. According to this witness, the transaction was a loan and Fall gave Sinclair a note for the $25,000.

A series of lawsuits followed. First, the Government brought successful actions against the Doheny and Sinclair companies to set aside the leases on the ground of fraud. The companies were accordingly ordered to account for all oil removed from the reserves, and these were now restored to the Navy Department. At the same time, indictments were preferred against Fall and Doheny, and against Fall and Sinclair, charging them with conspiracy to defraud the United States; also against Fall, charging him with bribery, and against Doheny and his son, charging them with bribery. The evidence given before the Senate committee was substantially repeated with the addition of several new witnesses including Mrs Doheny who produced the torn piece of the promissory note and identified Fall's signature on it.

Verdicts of not guilty were returned by the jury on the first, third and fourth of the indictments. However, the trial judge found Sinclair guilty of contempt of court for having had most of the jurors placed under the surveillance of a detective agency, although Sinclair argued that he had not tried to intimidate or influence the jurors but merely to ensure that they were not improperly approached. He was sentenced to six months imprisonment which he served in addition to three months passed on him for having been in contempt of the Senate.

There remained the bribery indictment against Fall. Here the issues were simple, said the prosecutor. 'One is that Doheny wanted the lease of Elk Hills. The second is that Fall wanted money. The third is that Doheny got the lease. And the fourth is that Fall got the money.' On 25 October 1929, the jury found Fall guilty of accepting a bribe but added a recommendation to mercy. Fall was sentenced to a year in jail and to pay a fine of $100,000. His lawyer immediately gave notice of appeal on the ground that the evidence of Fall's transactions with Sinclair had been wrongly admitted.

While Fall's appeal was pending, Doheny was tried and acquitted of bribery. This may seem at first sight anomalous in the light of Fall's conviction, but it was the result of the judge directing the jury that because of their different situations a guilty intent might be attributed to Fall but not necessarily to Doheny.

On 7 April 1931, the Court of Appeals handed down a judgment in the Fall case agreeing with the trial judge that the evidence of Fall's transactions with Sinclair was relevant on the question of the defendant's intent and that it had been properly admitted. Fall's conviction and sentence were accordingly affirmed, and he became convict No 6991 in the New Mexico State Penitentiary at Santa Fe. He was found on admission to be suffering from chronic tuberculosis and he served the whole of his sentence undergoing treatment in the prison hospital. The $100,000 fine imposed upon him was never paid, since he filed a 'pauper's oath'. After his release he was to survive in obscurity and relative poverty until the Second World War.

With the conviction and imprisonment of ex-Senator Albert B. Fall, the decade of investigation and litigation arising out of the so-called Teapot Dome Scandal came to an end. Yet Fall showed very little regret for what he had done, and always hoped for some sort of vindication. 'My borrowing the money may have been unethical,' he said after his conviction. 'I certainly did not realise it at the time, and my employing a falsehood to prevent a volcano of political abuse pouring upon the administration that had honoured me deserves condemnation; but neither one nor the other justifies the charge that I was disloyal or dishonest as Secretary of the Interior and as a member of Harding's Cabinet.'

# 12

# The Amazing Crime of
# Leopold and Loeb

Murders are committed from a variety of motives, such as greed, passion, jealousy, revenge. Sometimes they are done in the heat of the moment when carrying out another crime. Occasionally they are the work of drunkards or epileptics or homicidal maniacs like Jack the Ripper. It is extremely rare for the killing to be deliberately planned and perpetrated solely for the sake of a thrill which the crime may give the criminal. In 1924 such a carefully premeditated and cold-blooded murder was carried out by two teenage members of wealthy Chicago families, Nathan Leopold, Jr and Richard Loeb. Their victim was another teenage youth named Robert Franks, whose father was a millionaire Jewish businessman in the same social and financial class as Leopold's and Loeb's in Chicago.

Young Leopold and Loeb thought they could get away with the 'perfect crime' in kidnapping and killing an acquaintance to whom Loeb was distantly related. They failed and were arrested and charged with murder. Their trial, which aroused worldwide interest, began on 21 July 1924 in the Criminal Court of Cook County, Illinois, before Judge John R. Calverly, the Chief Justice of that court. Apart from the bizarre circumstances of the crime, it was the first time in an American court of justice that an opportunity was provided by expert psychiatric evidence to determine the mental condition of the accused according to modern scientific principles rather than relying on the old arbitrary and unscientific test hitherto applied where the sanity of the accused was in issue as it was in this case. This test, embodied in England in the M'Naughten Rules and subsequently imported into

American law, was to the effect that to succeed in a plea of insanity the defence must prove either that the accused did not know what he was doing at the time of the killing, or if he did know that he did not know that it was wrong.

Leopold was nineteen years old, Loeb a year younger. Both had been educated at the University of Michigan in Ann Arbor and at the time of the murder they were studying law at Chicago University and living at home with their families. Both bore hitherto good characters. Loeb's was the stronger of the two, although he was not so able intellectually as Leopold, who had shown exceptional talent for learning languages and also for ornithology, having already achieved some distinction for his observations of a relatively rare bird called the Kirtland warbler. 'Dicky' Loeb, whose father was Vice-President of Sears, Roebuck & Co., the well-known mail order firm, had a personality which was sufficiently powerful to impose itself on his friend 'Babe' Leopold and to make the latter believe, on the strength of a half-baked study of the writings of the German philosopher Nietzsche, which incidentally were also exercising a baneful influence on the emerging Hitler at this time, that Loeb was an example of the characteristically Nietzschian type of 'strong' man or 'superman' which democracy was tending to produce by way of reaction and that Leopold was a fit associate for such a 'superman'. This they considered freed them from adherence to the conventional codes of law and ethics. In order to demonstrate the superman's contempt for such restrictions, they committed a number of petty thefts. Towards the end of 1923, they broke into Loeb's old fraternity house at Ann Arbor and stole among other articles a portable Underwood typewriter. On their way back to Chicago from this escapade they seem to have had doubts about each other's courage, and it was to put this to the test that they discussed the possibility of collaborating in a perfect crime. The project which they eventually decided upon was to kidnap someone whose disappearance would cause a sensation, then kill their victim and demand a ransom for the victim's return.

After further discussion, in the course of which they thought of kidnapping the father of one of themselves but dismissed this as too risky because as close relatives they would be too much involved in police inquiries, they decided to seize a boy belonging to another rich family. Their first choice was discarded because his father was notoriously mean. Finally they agreed to leave the victim to chance and began to lay their plans which could be adapted to any circumstances. To this end Leopold stayed in the Morrison Hotel in Chicago checking in under the name of Morton D. Ballard, in which name he received mail, opened a banking account and hired a car. He and his confederate also bought a chisel with which to knock their victim unconscious, a rope with which to strangle him, some cloth for covering the body, a bottle of chloroform in case of emergency, and a bottle of hydrochloric acid with which to mutilate the victim's features. At the same time Leopold used the stolen Underwood typewriter on which to write a letter informing the victim's father that his son had been kidnapped and demanding a ransom of $10,000 in old bills. ('Any attempt to include new or marked bills will render the whole venture futile.') The money was to be placed in a large cigar box or a heavy cardboard box and to be delivered according to the kidnappers' subsequent telephoned instructions. If these were carefully followed and the police were not alerted 'we can assure you that your son will be safely returned to you within six hours after our receipt of the money'.

On the afternoon of 21 May 1924, Leopold left his home in the hired car with Loeb in the passenger seat in search of a victim. At Loeb's suggestion they made for Lake Park, where the son of a wealthy lawyer named Levinson lived and who might be expected to be at home around that time. Fortunately for young Levinson they never reached his home, since before they could get there Loeb espied young Franks near the corner of 49th Street and Ellis Avenue. They stopped and Loeb spoke to Franks. 'Come in a minute,' he said, 'I want to ask you about a certain tennis raquet.' Franks did as he was asked and got into the car. He was also asked if he minded driving round the block, and he said no.

Leopold then 'stepped on the gas', as he afterwards put it. During the next few minutes Franks was hit on the head with the chisel and the cloth was forced into his mouth, as a result of which he died almost immediately. According to Leopold, it was Loeb who struck the fatal blow, but Loeb denied this and stated that it was Leopold who did so. But there was no doubt as to what happened then. The car was driven to a piece of waste land known as Hegewich to the south of the city, where Leopold used to go for bird-watching. There the unfortunate Franks's body was stripped, disfigured with acid and thrust into a drain where the murderers thought that it would be submerged and washed away. They then buried their victim's shoes and leather belt, threw away the chisel, destroyed the cloth and burned the rest of the boy's clothes in the cellar of the Loeb house. After that they mailed the ransom letter which was signed 'George Johnson' to Mr Jacob Franks, Robert's father.

Next morning Leopold and Loeb met at the University and together went to the Leopold house where the hired car had been left in the driveway. Finding some bloodstains inside the car, they set to work to remove them with a mixture of soap and water and petrol, at the same time assuring the Leopold chauffeur who was standing by and offered to help that some red wine had been spilled inside the vehicle. They then telephoned Mr Franks and told him to take the money to a certain drug store where he would find a letter waiting for him. The letter in question instructed Mr Franks to board a south-bound train and throw the box with the money out of the window opposite a particular building where Leopold and Loeb intended to wait and pick it up. However, before Mr Franks could leave the house he received a call from the police to say that his son's naked body had been found at Hegewich by some workmen who had spotted a pair of feet protruding from an open culvert.

The city's crime squad immediately got busy, together with a host of other detectives both professional and amateur. Judging by the relatively small amount demanded as ransom money, the police felt that the crime was the work of amateurs. Experts who examined the letter to Mr Franks declared that it had been written on a portable Underwood by an unskilled typist, although apart from the mispelling of one word—'kidnaped' for 'kidnapped'—it seemed to be the work of an educated person and possibly one with a smattering of legal knowledge. The police thereupon arrested three masters who taught at young Franks's school and endeavoured by rigorous questioning to get a confession from them—but without any success.

It was an amateur detective who produced the first clue. This was a reporter on the *Chicago Daily News*, who had been out to Hegewich where he found a pair of horn-rimmed spectacles near the spot where the body was discovered. He then visited the leading opticians in the city in the hope of tracing the owner of the spectacles. A week after the murder, the reporter ascertained that a pair of spectacles of this type had been sold to Nathan Leopold. The police proceeded to question Leopold and the latter agreed that the spectacles resembled his own which were at home, so he said.

When a search of his home failed to reveal the spectacles, Leopold was questioned further. He admitted that he knew the Hegewich marsh well from his bird-watching expeditions, which could be confirmed by numerous witnesses, who could also speak to his respectable character. Asked by the police to account for his movements on 21 May, he said that he had spent the afternoon with Loeb, that they had picked up a couple of girls in his car, driven them to a park, and finding that they were unwilling to have sexual relations with them, had turned the girls out of the car and told them to walk home. Questioned about the kind of typewriter he used, Leopold denied that he ever owned a portable Underwood. However, the same reporter who had been instrumental in tracing the spectacles now succeeded in tracking down some theses which had been typed a few weeks before at Leopold's house, clearly on the same machine as the letter to Mr Franks. The machine could not be found in the house, since the confederates had thrown it into a lake, from which incidentally it was later recovered. Both youths were now under considerable suspicion.

The Leopolds' chauffeur was next questioned and he told the police that young Nathan Leopold's car had not left the family garage on the day of the murder. He also mentioned the hired car and the stains he had seen in the interior. Confronted with this statement, Richard Loeb broke down and confessed to having participated in the murder. When his confederate, in an adjoining room, heard that Loeb had confessed he too gave in and made a confession. The only discrepancy in the two confessions, which in other respects were broadly identical, was that each accused the other of striking young Franks with the chisel. They then proceeded to show, apart from this discrepancy, exactly how the crime had been committed and where they had disposed of the various accessories which had been used in the course of its commission.

Meanwhile the parents of the two boys, who were generally expected to spare no expense in their endeavours to save their sons from the gallows, secured the services of Clarence Darrow, the best-known Chicago advocate of his day, to lead the defence. Darrow, who had been appearing in sensational trials for many years, was now sixty-seven; but his remarkable powers in court showed no signs of diminishing—indeed his most widely publicised court appearance, in the celebrated Tennessee 'Monkeyville' trial, was still ahead of him. At the trial of Leopold and Loeb he was to be assisted by Benjamin and Walter Bachrach, both criminal lawyers of much skill and experience.

In view of the public interest in the case, not to mention popular prejudice against the prisoners on account of their wealth and their race, the prosecution hurried on the trial with unusual speed. On 6 June 1924, Leopold and Loeb were indicted by a grand jury for the murder of Robert Franks. On their arraignment five weeks later, they formally pleaded not guilty. The State's Attorney for Cook County, Robert E. Crowe, who was in charge of the prosecution, anticipated that Darrow would run a defence of insanity. Accordingly Mr Crowe had the two prisoners examined by several of the most distinguished psychiatrists in Chicago, each of whom assured him that Leopold and Loeb were sane by every known legal standard. But the State's Attorney had reckoned without the leading counsel for the defence, who proceeded to counter Crowe's move with masterly skill. To the general amazement Darrow announced at the outset of the trial that his clients had changed their plea from not guilty to one of guilty.

Most taken aback was the State's Attorney, for the custom in American courts is that a plea of guilty on a capital charge is only entered as the result of an agreement with the prosecution that, in consideration of the saving of trouble and expense, the State will not demand the death penalty but will be satisfied with a sentence of imprisonment. In this case no such agreement had been concluded—indeed the prosecution neither needed it nor was willing to make such a concession to the defence in view of public opinion which had been greatly incensed by the brutality of the crime. Of course, Clarence Darrow was well aware of this. His tactics were much more subtle and depended upon current court procedures in the State of Illinois.

Darrow realised that if he attempted to argue that his clients were insane, a plea of not guilty must automatically be entered, since by the state law an insane person cannot be guilty of any crime, and in this case the two prisoners would stand trial before a jury, which would have to decide whether or not they were insane. If the jury found that they were sane in law—as was practically certain to happen in view of the psychiatrists' reports—the prisoners were equally certain to be sent to the gallows because in Illinois it is the function of the jury, after having found the accused guilty, to decide upon the appropriate sentence. It is safe to assume that in such circumstances no jury in Chicago would have passed any other sentence but death. On the other hand, if a plea of guilty was entered, the subsequent proceedings would take place without a jury, and the sentence would be left to the discretion of the judge, who would also have to take into account any mitigating evidence offered by the defence. Thus Darrow's tactics were dictated by the knowledge that he could not prevent Leopold and Loeb from being convicted of murder but that if the case were tried by a judge alone, rather than by a judge sitting with a jury, at least he would have a good chance of saving his clients' lives.

By Illinois law the prosecution must prove its case even when the defence pleads guilty, and this the State's Attorney, Robert E. Crowe, and his principal assistant, Joseph P. Savage, proceeded to do with ponderous precision. Thus the trial proceeded day by day for over a week during which time the State produced some eighty witnesses to prove every detail of the crime, about which there was no dispute. Darrow cross-examined little and without heat. Indeed the only witness he seriously challenged was a policeman who deposed that Leopold had said that with his father's millions to help him, and before a friendly judge, he would escape punishment. Darrow forced this witness to admit that he had not reported this remark to his superiors until several weeks after it was supposed to have been uttered.

On 30 July the State rested its case and Darrow opened the defence. The first witness he called to the stand was Dr William A. White, the Superintendent of St Elizabeth's Hospital for Mental Diseases in Washington, DC. As soon as Dr White had declared his position and qualifications, the State's Attorney objected on the ground that it was apparent that the purpose of this witness's testimony was to prove the mental condition of the defendants at the time of the commission of the crime, and that all such testimony was precluded by their plea of guilty. 'There is no such thing as degrees of responsibility,' said the State's Attorney.

Either the prisoners were sane—as their plea of guilty admitted them to be—or they were insane, in which case they must revert to their original plea of not guilty and be tried before a jury.

The question had been argued before in other cases with reference to degrees of crime, but never upon a plea of guilty to the crime of murder in the first degree. The legal battle which followed lasted for three days, at the end of which the judge ruled that it was his duty to hear any evidence that the defence might present in mitigation of the crime, irrespective of its nature. Clarence Darrow had won the first round, and Dr White was allowed to testify, along with four other psychiatrists, as to the allegedly abnormal minds of the prisoners.

In the case of Loeb, they deposed that he had been a weakly child until his tonsils were removed; that he had been dominated by his governess; that he was a glib liar as a child; that at the age of twelve he stammered; that he suffered from a repressed feeling of inferiority; that he was addicted to day-dreams in which he pictured himself as a master criminal or a sharpshooting frontiersman; that he still possessed three milk teeth; that he had to shave only two or three times a week; that he repented of the murder only because he had been found out; and that, in short, his emotional reactions were not and never had been normal and that his day-dreams were primarily responsible for his share in the murder. As for Leopold, it was stated that he too was a weakly child until his tonsils had been removed; that he also suffered under a dominating governess; that he like Loeb was peculiarly subject to day-dreams; and that he believed that social conventions were not binding on people of superior intelligence like himself and Loeb.

The prosecution then called a number of other psychiatrists to rebut this testimony. In their opinion neither Leopold nor Loeb was suffering from any mental disease at the time. 'The reasons for that opinion are these,' said the State's leading psychiatrist Dr Patrick. 'Unless we assume that every man who commits a deliberate, cold-blooded, planned murder must by that fact be mentally diseased, there was no evidence of any mental disease in any of this communication or in any of the statements the boys made regarding it or their earlier experiences. There was nothing in the examination. There were no mental obliquities or peculiarities shown except their lack of appreciation of the enormity of the deed which they had committed.' Dr Church, another psychiatrist called by the prosecution, stated that everyone had day-dreams and everyone knew they were dreams. 'They have an interest in relation to character and conduct, but they do not compel conduct or excuse it. Those additional facts would imply a slowly developing criminal character, but would not furnish the basis for an opinion that there was any mental disease in that individual.'

Immediately on the conclusion of this conflicting testimony, almost invariably in the case of expert witnesses, Clarence Darrow rose to make his concluding speech for the defence. It was a remarkable example of the great trial lawyer's advocacy, which lasted for many hours and which would have been quite inappropriate in an English court. But Darrow was not appearing in an English court. What he now set out to do was to convince an American judge in an American court to defy both the prosecution and public opinion by not sending two rich young prisoners, who had pleaded guilty to what the defence lawyer called a 'most distressing and unfortunate homicide', to the gallows. (At that date electrocution had not been introduced as the official method of carrying out the death sentence in the State of Illinois.)

Darrow began by denying that vast sums of money had been spent on the defence. On the contrary, he said, money 'has been the most serious handicap we have met', because of the public prejudice against the prisoners as the sons of millionaires. If they had been poor boys, their plea of guilty would have been met by the prosecution with an undertaking to demand not the death sentence but life imprisonment. After all, he went on, no boy under the age of twenty-one had ever been sentenced to death in Chicago on a plea of guilty. Why did the prosecution demand the extreme penalty in this case? The only conceivable reason for sentencing these boys to death, in Darrow's submission, was that the people in the streets of Chicago wanted it. Out of 340 murderers in ten years who had pleaded guilty in Chicago courts, only one—a man of forty—had been hanged! 'And yet they say we come here with a preposterous plea for mercy. When did any plea for mercy become preposterous in any tribunal in all the universe?' The judge, he urged in conclusion, stood between the past and the future, between blindness and progress, between ignorance and understanding, between hate and love. 'If I can succeed in saving these boys' lives, my greatest reward and my greatest hope will be that I have done something for the tens of thousands of other boys, for the countless unfortunates who must tread the same road in blind childhood that these poor boys have trod—that I have done something to help human understanding, to temper justice with mercy, to overcome hate with love.'

It might be expected that the State's Attorney, when it was his turn to wind up for the prosecution, would have countered the defence lawyer's eloquence with a sober repetition of the facts and calmly pointed out the weaknesses in his opponent's plea in mitigation. Instead Mr Crowe attempted to rival Darrow's rhetorical extravagances in language which, however well it might have gone down with a jury, was quite unsuitable when addressing a judge. Indeed he got so far carried away in his concluding remarks that he made a most unfortunate statement to the effect that if any sentence short of death were passed on the prisoners, it would be regarded by the general public as proof that the court had been bribed. Not unnaturally Judge Calverly took the strongest possible exception to this observation 'as being a cowardly and dastardly assault upon the integrity of this court' and ordered it to be stricken from the record.

Mr Crowe's folly added to Clarence Darrow's brilliant summation had their effect upon the judicial bench. When it came to the final moments in this extraordinary court-room drama, Judge Calverly announced that chiefly because of the prisoners' youth he did not intend to sentence them to death. Instead they would both be imprisoned for life in the Joliet Penitentiary on the murder charge, with a recommendation to the authorities not to admit them to parole. On the kidnapping charge they were both sentenced to 99 years, this sentence to operate even if contrary to the judge's recommendation they were eventually paroled on the murder conviction. The kidnapping sentence caused some surprise, since it meant that neither Leopold nor Loeb could ever be released except as the result of a special amnesty.

The trial requires a footnote. While Clarence Darrow added another triumph of advocacy to his already impressive list, Judge Calverly became the best abused judge in Chicago and had to be accorded police protection for long afterwards. Richard Loeb, who developed homosexual tendencies in Joliet, was killed as the result of a homosexual brawl with another inmate in the prison baths on 28 January 1936. On the other hand, Nathan Leopold served thirty-three and a half years of his sentence, during which time he organised the library of the penitentiary, learned thirty-seven languages and became an authority on many subjects, finally offering himself as a guinea pig for medical research into a new anti-malaria drug. His excellent prison record ultimately earned him his freedom.

Leopold was released from Joliet in 1958 and went to Puerto Rico where he became a laboratory technician in a missionary hospital at a salary of ten dollars a month. He later entered the University of Puerto Rico and took a master's degree. He then worked for the San Juan Health Department, and in 1961 he married a doctor's widow. After a dozen years of useful service to the local community, he died on 19 August 1971. Thus, as Judge Calverly had endeavoured to make sure in passing sentence, were the ends of justice satisfied and the interests of society safeguarded.

# 13

# The Minister
# and the Choir Singer

One of the juiciest scandals in the New York commuter belt reached its climax in a most horrible murder in 1922 for which three persons stood trial four years later in the Court of Oyer and Terminer in Somerville, New Jersey. They were Frances Noel Hall, the widow of one of the two murder victims, and her brothers Henry and William Stevens. The presiding judges at the trial, which opened on 3 November 1926 and lasted a month, were Charles W. Parker, Supreme Court justice of New Jersey, and Frank L. Cleary, Somerset county judge. New Jersey State Senator Alexander Simpson acted as special prosecutor, while the chief defence counsel was Robert J. McCarter. The background to the trial had already received extensive treatment in the Press and had aroused the greatest public interest which went far beyond the territorial limits of New Jersey, since it possessed all the features of an exciting movie drama—sex, passion, jealousy, and illicit love between a pastor in a well-to-do rural community and a woman who sang in the choir and was the wife of the church sexton.

Mrs Frances Hall was a dignified middle-aged woman with greying hair. On the first day of the trial she appeared dressed in a black corded silk coat with a squirrel collar and a black ribbon hat, and she sat with her two brothers, who had been indicted with her, in a row of seats directly in front of the rail in the court-room, a concession to the defendants which obviated the more usual requirements for them to be physically placed in the dock. After the all-male jury had been chosen in a remarkably short time,

just over an hour—notwithstanding the fact that one of the jurors
delayed the proceedings by explaining at prodigious length his
views on circumstantial evidence—State Senator Simpson opened
the case for the prosecution.

Although the murders with which Mrs Hall and her brothers
were charged had taken place four years previously, the case had
not come to trial earlier, because the grand jury which had
initially examined the matter were not satisfied that there was
sufficient evidence to indict the defendants. The Governor of New
Jersey had ordered the case to be reopened following a newspaper
story that a woman named Louise Geist, who had been employed
as a parlour maid in the Hall household and had subsequently
married, was having trouble with her husband who was trying to
get the marriage annulled. In his petition for annulment, he stated
that she had been bribed by Mrs Hall and her brother Willie
Stevens to give false evidence before the original grand jury, that
Louise had accompanied Mrs Hall and her brother to the scene of
the murders on the evening that they were committed, and that
she had either participated in the crime or been an accessory to it.
The murders had taken place on 14 September 1922, off a quiet
road much favoured by courting couples called De Russey's Lane,
on the outskirts of New Brunswick, a small New Jersey town about
thirty-five miles from New York.

The prosecutor made it clear from the outset that he blamed the
tragedy on Mrs Hall's desire to catch her husband in a compromising position with Eleanor Mills, the sexton's wife. There
were few people in New Brunswick, at least among those who
worshipped at the Church of St John the Evangelist, who had not
heard gossip linking the names of the handsome Rev. Edward
Wheeler Hall and the pretty young choir singer. Indeed there are
some grounds for supposing that they were planning to elope
together. According to the prosecution, Mrs Hall overheard her
husband making a date to meet Eleanor Mills in De Russey's Lane
on the evening of 14 September and she had asked her two
brothers to accompany her there. Unfortunately for the defendants,
Senator Alexander went on, their crime had been witnessed by a
certain Mrs Jane Gibson, who kept pigs and for that reason was
nicknamed the 'Pig Woman' by the newspapers.

The bodies of the Rev. Edward Hall and Mrs Eleanor Mills
were discovered by another courting couple, who had gone for a

walk on the morning of 16 September and made their gruesome find when the minister and the choir singer had been dead for about thirty-six hours. The bodies were lying side by side on their backs beneath a crab-apple tree, with Eleanor Mills's head resting on the minister's right arm and her left hand on his right knee, as if this shocking tableau had been deliberately arranged. His head was covered with a Panama hat, while a brown scarf concealed the lower portion of her throat which had been slit from ear to ear right down to her chin and when the scarf was removed revealed a mass of maggots. She was wearing a cheap spotted muslin dress, while the minister wore an ordinary double-breasted suit. His pockets were empty and his gold watch was missing. Propped up against the dead man's left foot was one of his visiting cards inscribed in Gothic lettering with his name and that of his church. Also lying on the grass was his wallet containing his driving licence and Masonic and YMCA cards, some passionate love letters in Mrs Mills's handwriting, and two spent cartridge cases. Mrs Mills had been shot between the eyes as well as having had her throat cut and her tongue and vocal chords removed. The minister had also been fatally shot. Any notion of a suicide pact was ruled out by the nature of the wounds, by the disappearance of the minister's money and his watch, and by the absence of weapons beside the bodies. There was a rumour which persisted for long afterwards that the minister's penis had been amputated and placed in the choir singer's mouth, but such a mutilation is not borne out by the autopsy report.

The love letters found scattered about the grass were scrawled in pencil on cheap writing paper. They betrayed a most ardent passion on the writer's part. 'There isn't a man who could make me smile as you did today,' wrote Eleanor Mills in one of them. 'I know there are girls with more shapely bodies, but I do not care what they have. I have the greatest of all blessings, a noble man, deep, true, and eternal love. My heart is his, my life is his, all I have is his, poor as my body is, scrawny as they say my skin may be, but I am his for ever.'

The first two witnesses called by the prosecution were John S. Dickson, an accountant with a Wall Street brokerage firm, and his wife; they lived in North Plainfield, a small community about ten miles north of New Brunswick. Mr Dickson testified that at 8.30 on the night of the murders a man he said was Willie Stevens

6

called at his house and asked to be directed to Parker House, an old people's home, where he said he had relatives. At first the witness thought he was drunk. ('He was agitated. He was anxious to get out of the neighbourhood.') Mr and Mrs Dickson accompanied him to the trolley bus stop and on the way their visitor said he was an epileptic. According to Mr Dickson, he pulled out 'an open faced' gold watch, presumably resembling the Rev. Hall's, to see the time. Mr Dickson also said he had taken his hand. 'It was a very soft hand. I would say one that is not in the habit of doing hard work.' Mrs Dickson bore out her husband's testimony in this respect, describing the man's hand as 'soft, but very cold and clammy'. She caused an outburst of laughter when she went on to state that she had never felt a man's hand before.

Judge Parker banged his gavel on the bench to restore order. 'I want to say to this audience that this is a murder trial that is being tried,' the judge warned, 'and if there is going to be any hilarity the court-room will be cleared, and cleared without compunction.'

In cross-examination both the Dicksons stated that their visitor was not wearing glasses. Thus, whoever he was, he was certainly not Willie Stevens, who could not move a yard without his special lenses.

Charlotte Mills, the murdered woman's twenty-year-old daughter, who was now a newspaper reporter, identified a number of her mother's letters to the Rev. Hall. It had been her habit, said Charlotte, to leave notes for the minister in a large book in his study.

'Where was the large book?' asked Senator Simpson.

'The second shelf from the bottom of the bookcase.'

After dinner on 14 September, according to Charlotte, Mrs Mills had cut out an article by a well-known Episcopal clergyman, who had long advocated liberalisation of the church's divorce canons, from that day's New York *World* and taken it to the Rev. Hall's study. She returned home at 7.15 and told her daughter that she had met Miss Opie, a dressmaker who lived next door to Mr and Mrs Mills, and Miss Opie had told her that a telephone message had come from Mr Hall for her. Mrs Mills then told her daughter that she was going up the street to phone the minister—apparently there was no phone in the Mills house—and see if there was anything Mr Hall wanted. Her mother then left the house, said Charlotte, and that was the last she saw of her alive.

The prosecutor thereupon handed Charlotte a second package of letters. She identified these as being in the Rev. Hall's handwriting and said that her mother kept them in a crocheted bag which used to hang on the back of their living-room door. In addition the bag contained a diary kept by the minister. Charlotte also stated in cross-examination that her father James Mills had been given $500 for the letters and diary by a newspaper company, but she said she did not know whether her father had ever read them.

Charlotte Mills was followed on the witness stand by Anna Hoag who lived close to the scene of the crime: she was a woman of uncertain age with a pale complexion accentuated by brown curls which peeped out from the brim of a modish turban. She said she heard four shots about ten o'clock on the night of the murder. She went on to say that one afternoon in August 1923 a man whom she identified as Henry Stevens had visited her home. He was immaculately dressed in a dark suit and Panama hat, and he called to ask the way to Raritan.

'I asked him to sit down, and he sat on the porch,' said Mrs Hoag. 'I thought the man was sick because he trembled so. And then he got talking that he had been in Florida that winter and he talked on Florida for a while. Then all at once he said, "Wasn't there a tragedy on this place?" and I said "I know nothing about any tragedy." And with that I ran into the house because I was frightened.'

After she left the porch, it appeared that Mrs Hoag's unexpected visitor walked to the pump for a drink of water. 'Then I came out to watch him,' she went on. 'I had my dog with me, and I watched him up the lane and the man nearly collapsed—when he passed the place where the bodies were found, he nearly collapsed.' Although, according to her, Henry Stevens told her he was out for a walk, Mrs Hoag was convinced that there was a car waiting for him in De Russey's Lane. 'He must have had a car, because he was so immaculate,' she said.

The prosecution now produced the Rev. Hall's visiting card which had been found beside the bodies, and claimed that it bore an unmistakable thumbprint of Willie Stevens. While fingerprint experts were giving evidence, Senator Simpson was handed a note informing him that the Pig Woman had been taken ill and would be unable to testify. At the Senator's suggestion the judges

left the bench and hurriedly visited the hospital where Mrs
Gibson was a patient. They returned half an hour later to announce
that the state of the Pig Woman's kidneys was indeed serious. The
trial thereupon continued and the defence was able to show
without much difficulty that the thumbprint on the visiting card
had been fraudulently superimposed. Thus another prop in the
prosecution structure was knocked away.

The sexton James Mills duly took the stand and stated that Mrs
Hall had called on him before the bodies were found. He suggested to her that her husband and his wife had eloped, whereupon, according to the witness, Mrs Hall bluntly replied that they
were dead. He was severely cross-examined by the defence counsel,
who extracted some unexpected admissions, including one to the
effect that, despite his original denials, he had read 'a good part' of
the affectionate letters sent to his wife by her clergyman lover.
But when he was asked if he had told a detective four years
previously that he had quarrelled with his wife because of her
affection for the Rev. Hall, the sexton said that he could not
remember. The love letters of the unfortunate pair were then read
out in court and provided a tasty dish for the spectators and
newspaper readers.

After this the prosecution called Louise Geist, the former
parlour maid, whose matrimonial troubles had precipitated the
reopening of the case. It was confidently expected that her
evidence would restore the shaken fortunes of the prosecution,
but again the Senator was disappointed. She declared that her
husband's affidavit was nonsense; he had married her, she said,
only in order to learn from her the secret of the murders, and,
discovering too late that she did not know it, was revenging himself by bringing these charges against her.

The Pig Woman was then brought into court on a stretcher and
placed in a hospital bed, attended by a nurse and a doctor who
kept feeling her pulse. Speaking in a weak voice, she said that a
few nights before the murders a thief had robbed her of two rows
of Indian corn. Hoping to catch him as he returned for more, she
tied her dog to a tree between her shanty and the scene of the
crime. Roused by the dog's barking on the night of the murders,
she went to the scene but saw nothing. However, she lost a slipper
and returning to recover it she saw two women and two men
quarrelling in the lane. One of the couples, a white-haired woman

and a bushy-haired man were standing beneath the crab-apple tree. 'Explain these letters!' the white-haired woman had cried, after which there was a struggle, something gleamed in the moonlight, and the man shouted, 'Let's go!' Then the other woman screamed, four shots were fired, and the Pig Woman decided that she had better retire.

Handed photographs of Mrs Hall and Willie Stevens by the prosecutor, the witness had no hesitation in identifying them as the white-haired woman and the bushy-haired man whom she saw by the crab-apple tree. Meanwhile the Pig Woman's aged mother, who had been tracked down by the defence and provided with a seat near her daughter's bed in court, kept remarking loudly, 'She's a liar, a liar, a liar! That's what she is, and what she's always been.' There is no doubt the mother was right and that the Pig Woman had deliberately made up her story for the sake of the accompanying newspaper publicity. Indeed she claimed she would be 'the Babe Ruth of the trial', referring to the popular baseball player of the day.

It was not difficult for the defence to put up a convincing answer to the prosecution's case. When Mrs Hall took the stand, she disputed the Pig Woman's account and swore that she (the witness) had played no part in the tragedy. As far as she knew, her husband was devoted to her and his conduct had never given her any cause to suspect his morals. On the other hand, she had known Eleanor Mills as an active church worker and in fact she had helped her with hospital and medical expenses when she was ill. Mrs Hall went on to say that she knew that her husband had received some letters from Eleanor because he had shown them to her. 'They were, as near as I remember,' she said, 'descriptions of evening services at church.'

Mrs Hall proceeded to describe how her husband left home on the night of the murders, as the result of a telephone call from Mrs Mills, saying that he must go and see the sexton about his wife's hospital bill. The minister had fifty dollars in his pocket and also his gold watch. Surprised by her husband's long absence, she woke her brother Willie who lived with them and together they went to the church to see if the Rev. Hall had fallen asleep there. They found the church shut up and in darkness. They then walked on to the sexton's house and finding no light there either they returned home, entering by the back door.

Asked why she had not alerted the police sooner about her husband's disappearance, she replied that she had in fact telephoned them early next morning, without giving her name, and had asked whether there were any accidents in the area which had been reported. She was told that there were none. She then got in touch with several members of her husband's family and instructed her lawyer to carry on with the investigation from there.

Willie Stevens corroborated his sister's account of how she had wakened him in the dead of night and they had gone together to the church and to the Mills's house. He was quite unshaken under cross-examination. Indeed he scored neatly off the prosecutor who had badgered him with questions as to where he was at a certain time. 'If a person sees me go upstairs and doesn't see me come downstairs,' he asked Senator Simpson, 'isn't that a conclusion that I was in my room?'

'Certainly,' the Senator agreed.

'Well,' said Willie Stevens, 'that's all there was to it.'

In the middle of the fifth week, Senator Simpson appealed to the judges to order a new trial on the ground that the jurymen were not paying proper attention to his arguments. His motion was refused. Counsel's final speeches on both sides matched each other in extravagance. The defence went so far as to suggest that the Pig Woman might have shot the Rev. Hall and Mrs Mills and cut the latter's throat under the erroneous impression that they were the thieves who had stolen her corn. Not to be outdone, Senator Simpson declared that Mrs Hall's lack of emotion at the death of her husband showed that she was a Messalina, a Lucretia Borgia and a Queen ('Bloody') Mary. 'Has she ever batted an eyelid?' he asked the jury with some heat.

On 3 December 1926, the jury returned a verdict of not guilty, after deliberating for five hours, though they never revealed what they found to discuss in the time. Mrs Hall, her two brothers, and her cousin Henry Carpender, who had taken care of the Rev. Hall's funeral arrangements and was being held on a charge of complicity in the murders pending separate trial, were all immediately released. James Mills, the sexton, remarked that he was not surprised by the result—money, he said, could buy anything. This innuendo, it is hardly necessary to say, was quite unfounded. However, it is certain that the defendants spent many thousands of dollars in clearing themselves of the baseless charges brought against them. The expenses of the prosecution were still greater, as the taxpayers of New Jersey were soon to discover.

The killer or killers of the Rev. Hall and Mrs Mills were never brought to justice, and to this day the case remains one of America's unsolved crime mysteries. The most plausible solution has been put forward by William Kunstler, a New York lawyer, who has made a profound study of the crime. It is that it was the work of the Ku Klux Klan, which organised the slaying of the clergyman and his mistress for their flagrant violation of the order's rigid standards of sexual morality. There were many New Jersey branches of the Klan at the time and Klansmen were particularly active in the state. The killing bore all the signs of a ritual Klan murder, the deliberate juxtaposition of the bodies to emphasise their adulterous relationship, and the severing of the soprano singer's vocal chords to make the same point as forcefully as the emasculation of a southern negro for raping a white woman. There was also the persistent rumour referred to above but admittedly unsubstantiated, of the treatment of the minister's genitalia. At all events, if the Kunstler theory is true, the admitted circumstances of the murders indeed formed a most terrible warning to other would-be violators of the Seventh Commandment.

# 14

# A Matter of Official Secrets

In the autumn of 1932 the English literary world was astonished to learn that a well-known writer and successful novelist was to be prosecuted for a breach of the Official Secrets Act. The writer was Mr (later Sir) Compton Mackenzie, whose publishers had been obliged to withdraw his recent book *Greek Memories* on the same day as its publication, following action by the British Foreign Office. It was on account of certain disclosures of confidential and secret matter which the author was alleged to have made in this work that the authorities had decided to prosecute him.

Although he was a man of unorthodox opinions on many subjects and was no favourite with the governing Establishment, Edward Montague Compton Mackenzie—known to his friends as 'Monty' from his second name—had by this time, when he was rising fifty, become an established figure in the world of English letters. His recent novel *Extraordinary Women* on the theme of lesbian relationships had shocked many people when it appeared, as had his use of such wicked words as 'tart' and 'bitch' in his earlier novels, which incidentally his American publishers had deleted from their editions, and he was attacked for corrupting youth. Nevertheless, novels like *Carnival* and *Sinister Street*, which he had written twenty years earlier, still sold well, having been acclaimed by such a distinguished critic as Henry James.

The offence specifically alleged against Compton Mackenzie under the Official Secrets Act was that in July 1932, having in his possession information which he had obtained owing to his position as an officer in the Royal Marines during the First World War, he had unlawfully communicated the information to his publishers, Cassell & Co., contrary to the Act. On 16 November

1932, Mr Mackenzie appeared at the Guildhall magistrate's court in the City of London to answer to the charge. The presiding magistrate was seventy-five-year-old Alderman Sir George Truscott, a former Lord Mayor of London, whose appearance in the blue fur-trimmed robes of his civic office reminded the defendant of the stock opening in many Dick Whittington pantomimes. He treated the defendant throughout the preliminary proceedings with studied old-world courtesy and indeed appeared to sympathise with him as the case went on. The prosecution was in the hands of Mr Eustace Fulton, the Senior Old Bailey Prosecutor, while for his defence counsel Mackenzie had chosen his Oxford college contemporary Mr St John Hutchinson. The hearing took place in the Old Court at the Guildhall, employed by Charles Dickens as the setting for the famous action of Bardell *versus* Pickwick, but latterly little used except as an adjunct to City banquets where the wine would be uncorked.

In opening the case for the prosecution, Eustace Fulton explained that the words of the statute were exceedingly wide. They prohibited a person from publishing any matter which came to his knowledge by reason of his employment under the Crown. 'When you have heard the evidence in this case, a substantial part of which I shall have to ask you to hear *in camera*,' Mr Fulton told the magistrate, 'I think you will come to the conclusion that the legislature acted wisely.' While occupying an official position during the war, the defendant had become aware of various facts and, in spite of his having pledged himself never to communicate such facts either orally or in writing to any unauthorised person, he had done so.

St John Hutchinson immediately intervened to say that his client had never been asked to give such a pledge, which in fact was never demanded at the time Mr Mackenzie had been seconded for intelligence work. The prosecutor accepted this correction but pointed out that he had nevertheless committed an offence under the Official Secrets Act whether or not he had given any such pledge.

The defendant, Mr Fulton continued, had joined the Royal Marines in the first year of the war and in July 1916 he had been promoted to the rank of Captain and detailed for duty with the Allied Intelligence Staff in Athens. Having returned to civilian life after the war, he decided to write his war memoirs, of which

the first volume (*Gallipoli Memories*) appeared in 1929 and the
second (*First Athenian Memories*) in 1931. Shortly after the
second volume came out, Sir Basil Thomson, who had been
Director of Intelligence at Scotland Yard from 1919 to 1921 and
for some years previously had been closely involved in official
counter-espionage activities, published a book entitled *The Allied
Secret Service in Greece*. According to the prosecutor, Mr
Mackenzie held the view that Sir Basil had made statements in his
book which were inaccurate. In fact Mr Mackenzie went further
than this, stigmatising Thomson's book as 'scurrilous and
mendacious', and asserting that he had been paid to write it for
propaganda purposes from funds available to the exiled Greek
Royal Family.

It was to correct what Mr Mackenzie called the 'untrust-
worthiness' of Sir Basil Thomson's narrative that he had written
the third volume of his war memoirs (*Greek Memories*), which was
suppressed on the day of publication at the instigation of the
authorities. In endeavouring to do that, said the prosecutor, Mr
Mackenzie had 'completely ignored the provisions of the Act of
Parliament, and used for the purpose of establishing his own
records or to impress the world with his knowledge of official
documents to which he had access.' These documents included
the texts of letters and despatches from Sir Edward Grey, the
Foreign Secretary, and Sir Arthur Nicolson, the permanent head
of the Foreign Office, to Sir Francis Elliot, the British minister in
Athens, and also a number of telegrams passing between London
and Athens, which had been paraphrased. Mr Mackenzie took
care to see that all his statements controverting Sir Basil Thomson
were fully documented. 'All this, of course, might have been done
by inadvertence or stupidity,' the prosecutor concluded, 'or it
may have been that the narrow field of his own employment did
not make him realise what he was doing.'

Evidence was then called. A member of Compton Mackenzie's
firm of literary agents, J. B. Pinker & Son, gave details of the
author's contract to write the three volumes of memoirs.

'You would know,' St John Hutchinson asked him in cross-
examination, 'that hundreds of books of memoirs dealing with
the war and with the Secret Service are published every
year?'

'Yes.'

'And these were personal memories of what the writer saw during certain operations?'

'Yes.'

'Many of them are or claim to be documentary?'

'I gather that.'

Questioned about Compton Mackenzie's literary earnings, the literary agent said that the author's advance for *Greek Memories* was to be £500 and nothing more. For a novel Mr Mackenzie received for Great Britain and the British dominions £1,500 and for America £750 on account of royalties. If the royalties exceeded those sums he got more.

'I am only asking these questions,' Mr St John Hutchinson informed the magistrate, 'to show that as a matter of fact Mr Mackenzie was making a very large sacrifice in writing these books of memoirs; that he did not do it for the purpose of gain, and that he could have made much more by writing an ordinary novel.'

The prosecution went on to call a young clerk who worked in the library of the Foreign Office to testify about the official and confidential papers kept in his department, and to produce the originals or official copies of correspondence of Sir Edward Grey and others which were in his custody for purposes of comparison with the texts quoted in *Greek Memories*. Of course, this was long before the fifty-year rule or even the thirty-year rule relating to official departmental records available in the Public Record Office, and at this date the Foreign Office had not released or declassified any papers later than the year 1885.

After the prosecutor had taken the library clerk through various texts and telegrams, which in the case of the latter he agreed had been paraphrased, Mr Fulton asked him: 'These documents are all secret and confidential, and Mr Mackenzie has no authority from the Foreign Office to publish them?' The witness agreed that this was so.

Rising to cross-examine, Mr St John Hutchinson asked whether all these documents dealt with matters in 1916. The witness said they did. 'And we are now in 1932,' counsel commented.

'As far as you can see,' Mr Hutchinson went on, 'is there anything in them which at the present moment is in any degree secret?'

The witness appeared momentarily nonplussed and looked appealingly at the prosecutor. 'I do not think it would be in the public interest to answer that question,' said Mr Fulton to the magistrate.

'This gentleman is a representative of the Foreign Office,' said St John Hutchinson, 'and he is the only person of whom I can ask this question.'

'I do not think the witness should answer it,' the magistrate ruled.

'Someone must be produced who can answer that question,' defence counsel protested.

'I will get someone from the War Office of greater authority than the witness,' said the prosecutor. Thereupon the embarrassed young Foreign Office library clerk left the witness box with a sigh of relief.

The hearing had not been concluded when the court rose for the day. At the adjourned hearing, on 24 November, the prosecution called a more senior member of the Foreign Office library staff than the clerk who had previously testified. This witness confirmed that the latest date for the unrestricted publication of Foreign Office documents was 1885, but he added that the Secretary of State could and in practice did give leave for documents to be published after that date. So far as he was aware the defendant had not obtained the necessary permission.

In cross-examination, St John Hutchinson put it to the witness that this discretion on the part of the Foreign Secretary was entirely *ultra vires*. 'Do you suggest that there is anything in the Official Secrets Act that, if rigorously enforced, would allow such permission to be given?'

'I am afraid I am not sufficiently conversant with the Act to answer that.'

'Now you have looked at these documents which have been published—documents referring to 1916,' the defendant's counsel went on. 'Is there anything in them that, from the public point of view, it would be dangerous to publish in 1932?'

'I don't think that in this case the public interest has been prejudiced,' the witness replied cautiously.

'That is all I want,' said Mr Hutchinson.

'No detriment has been suffered,' added the witness by way of explanation.

The prosecutor then asked the magistrate to exercise his powers under the relevant statute and order that the proceedings should now be heard *in camera*. The magistrate agreed, with the result that everyone was directed to leave the court, except those directly concerned with the case. This included the Press.

When the court had been cleared, Mr Fulton proceeded to enumerate a list of more than a dozen names of people who had been connected with the Secret Intelligence Service and whom the defendant had mentioned in his book. There were other reasons for the damage which the publication of *Greek Memories* had allegedly done. One was that the author had revealed that the Passport Department in British embassies and consulates abroad was used as cover for intelligence work and that the Passport Control Officer in these missions could easily be identified as the person in charge of secret service activities in the country or area concerned.

'I am now going to call as a witness a present member of the Secret Service,' Mr Fulton continued. 'And, although we are *in camera*, Sir George, I am going to ask you if he may keep his name secret and that he be alluded to as Major X?'

The magistrate agreed and Major X went into the witness box. He confirmed the alleged damage done by revealing the names which the prosecutor had already read out, and which the witness had apparently drawn up.

'Major X,' Mr Hutchinson began his cross-examination, 'you have told my learned friend that by publishing in his book the names of these gentlemen who worked on intelligence duties in the war Mr Mackenzie has jeopardised their future. Why?'

'Because when war comes——'

'When war comes?' defence counsel interrupted. 'Are we to feel indebted to our Intelligence Service for knowing when war will come?'

'I meant if another war comes,' the witness corrected himself.

'Ah! Please go on, Major X.'

'If another war comes, we may want to call upon their services again.'

'I see,' said defence counsel. 'So that you must know where all these gentlemen are and what they are doing now?'

Major X hesitated for a moment or two and gulped some water from the large tumblerful beside him. 'I have no doubt we know,' he replied at last.

'Then shall we go through the list? The first name is Mr C. E. Heathcote-Smith. Do you know where he is now?'

'I don't myself know, but I've no doubt it is known.'

'Perhaps you don't know that he is now His Britannic Majesty's Consul-General in Alexandria?'

'I hear you say so.'

'You can trust your ears, Major X,' counsel assured the witness. He went on: 'Have you read Mr Mackenzie's two previous volumes of war memories?'

'I have,' replied the anonymous major, 'and if I may say so with very much pleasure.'

'I'm sure Mr Mackenzie and his publishers will appreciate that unsolicited testimonial.'

Counsel went on to ask the witness whether he did not remember that in *Gallipoli Memories* the defendant had written at some length about Mr Heathcote-Smith's intelligence work when he was Vice-Consul at Mytilene. 'And perhaps you are not aware, Major X, that in the entry in *Who's Who* under his name Mr Heathcote-Smith says he was working in Intelligence from 1915 to 1916?'

Major X took another gulp of water. 'I hear you say so,' he repeated.

'You can take it from me, Major X,' said Mr Hutchinson with a distinct note of sarcasm in his voice, 'that *I* am not indulging in fantasy.'

'Well, so much for the Consul-General in Alexandria,' counsel resumed, when Major X had recovered from this verbal blow. 'Let us take the next name on the list—Mr A. J. B. Wace. Do you know where Mr Wace is now?'

'I do not know myself.'

'Then perhaps you do not know that he is the Deputy-Keeper of the Victoria and Albert Museum?'

'I hear you say so,' the witness repeated once more.

'Perhaps you do not know that Mr Wace was never in the Secret Service?'

This question completely floored Major X, who was unable to reply. In fact, Mr Wace was an archaeologist who had been Director of the British School in Athens. His name seems to have been put on the list in error owing to the fact that during the war he had been seconded from the School to the staff of the British Legation in Athens.

So the questions went on, and each time the witness looked more and more embarrassed and miserable; indeed he drained no less than five glasses of water during this protracted and painful interrogation. Finally, counsel came to the last name on the list, that of a certain Captain Christmas.

'Surely, Major X, the page in Mr Mackenzie's book shows that Captain Christmas was nothing more than a figure of fun?' The gentleman in question had been described by the author as 'a fantastic half-pay Danish sea-captain' who turned up in Athens with credentials from the British Secret Service man in Alexandria and a request for him to be maintained at government expense and allowed to communicate with London by the intelligence cypher under the pseudonym of Brutus. This was done, and Captain Christmas disseminated a series of telegrams about imaginary enemy submarine bases and other nonsense, much to the annoyance of the British Minister.

Major X now looked acutely uncomfortable. 'Well, as a matter of fact, Mr Hutchinson,' he said, 'we do not wish to press that name?'

'No? Why not?'

'Because we have found out that Captain Christmas is dead. '

'Indeed? When did he die?'

'I believe it was about ten years ago.'

'Indeed!' commented counsel, this time in a tone of withering sarcasm. 'So that not even the Secret Service will be able to call on Captain Christmas when war comes—I should say if another war comes. Thank you, Major X. I have nothing more to ask you.'

There was no re-examination, since the prosecutor evidently did not care to risk looking as ridiculous as his witness, whose testimony he had originally announced so portentously. The unfortunate Major X thereupon hurried from the witness box and out of the Guildhall, so it seemed to Compton Mackenzie at the time, 'as fast as Mr Winkle after his examination by Serjeant Buzfuz'.

After the prosecution had closed its case there was a further adjournment to enable the defendant to call witnesses, if he wished, and to testify on his own behalf. At the same time the magistrate intimated that he must commit the defendant for trial at the next Old Bailey Sessions in January. Any disposition which Sir George Truscott may have felt to throw the case out, after Mr Hutchinson had submitted that this should be done, was checked by the Clerk of the Court, who whispered loudly in the magistrate's ear, 'The Attorney-General has issued his fiat.' This meant that the case must be sent for trial.

Asked to plead to the charge, the defendant read the following brief statement:

> My object in writing *Greek Memories* was not financial gain but to tell the truth about Mr Venizelos and the patriots who followed his lead sixteen years ago; and, being the only person in possession of the facts of the situation in Athens, I thought it my duty to answer the propaganda which for many years has been carried on against the Allies and the Venizelist Greeks.
>
> I plead 'Not Guilty' and reserve my defence.

The magistrate thereupon released the defendant on bail in his own recognisance of £100, pending the trial. 'I have absolute confidence in Mr Mackenzie,' he added.

For the trial Compton Mackenzie's solicitor decided to brief a senior counsel to lead St John Hutchinson in the person of Sir Henry Curtis-Bennett, KC. Before the case came on, there was a consultation in Sir Henry's chambers in the Temple, at which the leader told Compton Mackenzie that he must change his plea to 'Guilty'. If he persisted in pleading 'Not Guilty', said Curtis-Bennett, and witnesses in his defence were brought from places like Athens and Constantinople, the case might go on for weeks and cost him several thousands of pounds. In the end the judge would tell the jury that it was not their business to say whether any harm had been done by his book but merely whether the author had used unauthorised information by reason of his official position contrary to the Official Secrets Act. In the result he would no doubt go to prison for nine months, and as the trial would be held *in camera* the public would conclude that he had done something dreadful, which of course he could not publicly deny in any detail under pain of incurring a further penalty for contempt of court due to the proceedings having been conducted *in camera*.

Curtis-Bennett went on to say that he had spoken to the Attorney-General, who would represent the Crown at the Old Bailey, and it now appeared that a letter which Mr Eric Holt-Wilson, a senior officer in the British counter-espionage service

(MI5), had written to Compton Mackenzie was not a warning against publication, as the prosecution had originally suggested, but more like an encouragement to go on. In these circumstances the Attorney-General had been in touch with Mr Justice Hawke, the trial judge, and there was an understanding that if the defendant pleaded guilty he would be fined a sum not exceeding £500 with £500 costs.

'Well, you have destroyed almost my last illusion,' said Compton Mackenzie. 'I hadn't many left. But I did believe that the judicature in this country was incapable of being influenced by the executive.' However, he agreed to plead guilty and pay any fine which the judge inflicted.

When the defendant took his place in the dock at the Old Bailey on 12 January 1933, he thought that since he was pleading guilty his case would be quickly disposed of. But he was again disillusioned. The Attorney-General, Sir Thomas Inskip, asked for the court-room to be cleared, and as soon as this had been done he proceeded to address the court at considerable length just as if the defendant had pleaded not guilty, much to the exasperation of Mr Justice Hawke.

One point which the Attorney-General made the most of was that the defendant had revealed the mysterious consonant ('C') by which the Chief of the Secret Intelligence Service was known. This was alleged to be particularly dangerous, since those army officers connected with the SIS still had MI1 (c) after their names to show what they were engaged upon.

'But, Mr Attorney,' the judge broke in, 'if "C" is such a dangerous consonant, why is it still being used nearly fifteen years after the war?'

'That I couldn't say, m'lud,' answered Inskip.

'No, I shouldn't think you could,' commented the judge. 'That consonant should surely have been changed by now.'

The Attorney-General went on to state that not only had Mr Mackenzie revealed the mysterious consonant, but he had also indicated that at the period in question it stood for the late Captain Sir Mansfield Cumming, RN.

'But surely this officer's name was perfectly well known during the war?' asked Mr Justice Hawke.

'I think not, m'lud.'

'Come, come, Mr Attorney, in clubs you and I both belong to?'

(Inskip belonged to the Athenaeum, and Hawke to the Garrick, of which Sir Mansfield had also been a member.)

'No, m'lud, with great respect, I think not.'

'Oh, well, have it your own way, Mr Attorney, but please be quicker. I'm growing excessively tired of this case.'

A minute or two later, the judge again broke in on Inskip's laboured explanation of the danger of telling the world who 'C' was. 'When did the officer die?' he asked sharply.

The Attorney-General admitted he did not know. Neither did his junior counsel Mr Eustace Fulton. Nor did Sir Henry Curtis-Bennett or Mr St John Hutchinson.

'It may seem a little irregular, m'lud,' said Inskip, 'but as we are *in camera* perhaps I might ask Sir Vernon Kell to tell us.'

Major-General Sir Vernon Kell, who was sitting in court, was the chief of the equally secret Security Service (MI5) and was known as 'K', although he described himself in *Who's Who* as 'Commandant War Department Constabulary'. He was responsible for counter-espionage in British territory at home and overseas. On the other hand, 'C' as head of MI6 was responsible for espionage and counter-espionage abroad outside the British Empire in addition to his other intelligence work.

Sir Vernon Kell, who made a fetish of secrecy, was embarrassed at being referred to by name even *in camera*, the more so as he was obliged to admit that he did not know when Sir Mansfield Cumming had died. Thereupon Compton Mackenzie asked one of the court officials beside the dock to give him a piece of paper, as he intended to write down the information and pass it up to the bench. But the judge quickly anticipated him.

'Do you wish to tell me something?'

'Yes, my lord, with great respect,' the defendant answered, 'the officer in question died in June or July 1923.' He was quite right. Mansfield Cumming, the first letter of whose surname had caused him to be known throughout the service and in the top government echelons as 'C', had died on 14 June 1923.

'Thank you,' said the judge, glaring round the court and fixing with his irate gaze the row of black-coated secret service men in the gallery. 'I accept that.'

The court remained *in camera* until the lunch break, after which the public were again admitted, and Sir Henry Curtis-Bennett rose to make his plea in mitigation. He began by calling two witnesses to testify as to the defendant's good character. The first of these witnesses was the veteran General Sir Ian Hamilton, then a few days short of his eightieth birthday. He was Lord Rector of Edinburgh University, and to speak as he did on behalf of a neighbouring Lord Rector—Compton Mackenzie was Lord Rector of Glasgow—must have been unique. He had known the defendant since May 1915, when he had come out to Gallipoli and joined his staff as an intelligence officer. 'During the time he was out there,' said Sir Ian, 'Mr Compton Mackenzie's conduct was in every sense of the word excellent. He acted in every way as a thoroughly honourable and efficient officer.' Replying to the judge, who asked him about the defendant's 'attitude to this country,' Sir Ian described it as 'patriotic'.

This witness's testimony was confirmed by Rear-Admiral William Sells, who had been Naval Attaché in Athens from 1915 to 1917. He said he constantly saw Mr Compton Mackenzie during that time and agreed that he was 'in every sense of the word a man of honour and a loyal subject'. He added that he had seen him with his back arched with pain and within four or five minutes he was carrying on dictating and giving directions and doing his work. 'Every member of his organisation would have laid down his life for him,' the Admiral added.

Then the gallant old sea-dog turned towards the bench and asked, 'Anything more you want to know, my lord?'

'No thank you, Admiral,' replied the judge. 'Your evidence has been of the greatest help to me and to Mr Mackenzie.'

Sir Henry Curtis-Bennett then addressed the court in mitigation, stressing his client's loyalty to the state and the fact that his motive in writing the book was not financial gain but to tell the truth about Mr Venizelos and his followers when Venizelos raised the standard of revolt against the pro-German King Constantine, subsequently heading the provisional government in Athens after the king had lost his throne and fled abroad. When Curtis-Bennett had finished, Compton Mackenzie stood up in the dock to hear the judge pass sentence.

'I have thought deeply over the matter,' said Mr Justice Hawke, 'and hesitated very much whether I ought to send you to prison. But I say at once, because I do not want you to have any anxiety about it, that I have come to the conclusion that I can do justice without sending you to prison. But you must be punished. You have already suffered a very great pecuniary loss, which to some extent I will consider, although these losses were inflicted on yourself by yourself.' No harm had possibly come from the documents he had published except perhaps in one instance, the judge went on, and of course the defendant should have sought official permission to use them as he did in his book. 'No testimony to your character could have been stronger than that given today,' the judge concluded, 'but I cannot pass this over. In these circumstances you must pay a fine of £100 and a further £100 towards the costs of the prosecution.'

Anticipating a heavier penalty, Compton Mackenzie's solicitor had brought more than ample funds with him into court, and he was consequently able to secure his client's immediate release by paying the £200 at once.

Compton Mackenzie got his own back on the official bumbledom which had brought him to the Old Bailey dock, when losing no time after the trial he sat down and wrote *Water on the Brain*, a novel which is a hilarious caricature of the British Secret Service and its methods. As a result there was more weeping and gnashing of teeth in the respective headquarters of 'C' and 'K'. But this time the outraged mandarins could do nothing to silence the object of their wrath, since the author had taken care to point out in a prefatory note that all the characters in his story were imaginary and none of the incidents was built upon even the thinnest substratum of fact. 'However, the burnt child fears the fire,' he added. 'Hence this fireproof disclaimer.' He was wise to make it.

# 15

# The Eight Saboteurs who Failed

In democratic countries such as Britain and the United States, whose legal systems stem from the English common law, it is generally accepted that not only must justice be done but it must be *seen to be done*—also that every accused person is presumed to be innocent until proved guilty, instead of the other way round. However, occasionally in times of war or other grave national emergency, when the accused are tried by a military court, it is necessary to dispense with these traditional safeguards of civil liberty. Such a trial took place in secret in Washington, DC, during the Second World War, when the accused were eight Nazi saboteurs who had been put ashore from a German submarine at two separate points on the American mainland with instructions to carry out specific acts of sabotage against American war industries and other strategic targets. The shorthand transcript of this extraordinary trial was kept locked up in the US Justice Department for eighteen years, and it was not until 1960 that it was declassified and the details became generally known. All that the public were able to gather at the time was that eight named enemy saboteurs had been captured, that they had been tried and convicted by a special military commission and that the death sentences passed upon them by the court had been confirmed by President Roosevelt in the case of six of the prisoners and immediately carried out, while in the case of the other two prisoners the sentences had been commuted to long terms of imprisonment.

The court sat in a large room on the fifth floor of the Justice Department Building, normally used by the Federal Bureau of Investigation for lectures and motion pictures in the training

courses which the Bureau ran for its agents. The windows were
covered with heavy black curtains which completely excluded the
daylight, while the motion picture screen was draped in green
velvet forming a somewhat bizarre backdrop to the sombre scene.
There were seven military judges, four major-generals and three
brigadier-generals. The presiding judge was Major-General
Frank R. McCoy, a veteran who had commanded an infantry
brigade in France during the First World War and had served on
various important boards and commissions since his retirement
from active service. Behind the President's chair an American flag
hung loosely. It was the first time a military court had sat to try
civilians since seven men and one woman had been charged with
conspiring with John Wilkes Booth to assassinate Abraham
Lincoln in 1865.

To the left of the judges was a dark mahogany chair for the use
of the witnesses. Further to the left, at right angles to the judges'
bench, was a long table for the prosecution team which was led by
the Attorney-General Francis Biddle. A special place at the
prosecutor's table was provided for Mr J. Edgar Hoover, the
FBI chief. Behind this table were the eight prisoners, seated
alphabetically and guarded by soldiers. For convenience here they
may be divided into two groups corresponding to the groups in
which they landed. The first group, led by George John Dasch,
included Peter Burger, Heinrich Harm Heinck, and Richard
Quirin. The second group consisted of Herbert Hans Haupt,
Hermann Otto Neubauer, Werner Thiel, and Edward Kerling,
who was in overall charge of both groups. Dasch was defended
by Colonel Carl Ristine and the others by Colonel Cassius Dowell
and Colonel Kenneth Royall, counsel assigned by the court for the
purpose. The defence counsel occupied a table to the right of the
judges' bench, facing the prosecution team.

At the outset of the trial, which began on 8 July 1942, General
McCoy announced that he would preside according to President
Roosevelt's order constituting the commission. Under this the
court would have the right to admit evidence which in the opinion
of the judges had 'probative value to a reasonable man'. This was
a legal device, often employed in hearings before special tribunals,
to permit the admission of evidence which might not be admitted
in civil courts where the rules of evidence were strictly applied.

The commission was then sworn and the oath of secrecy was

administered to all present. The Press was excluded from the proceedings and was only to be admitted for a very short time on one occasion when the court recessed; this was to allow the newspapermen to satisfy themselves as to the existence of the prisoners and the composition of the court. They were also allowed to inspect the clothing, explosives, boxes and other exhibits in the trial.

The prisoners were formally charged with violating, and with conspiracy to violate, the law of war, in that they were enemies of the United States, 'acting for and on behalf of the German Reich', who had 'secretly and covertly', while in civilian dress, passed through American military lines for the purpose of committing sabotage and other hostile acts in order 'to destroy certain war industries, war utilities and war materials'. They were also accused of spying. When all the accused had pleaded not guilty, the Attorney-General opened the case for the prosecution. It was an amazing story he had to tell the court.

On 13 June 1942, the first group of saboteurs under the command of George Dasch, who had been a waiter in New York and San Francisco before the war, landed on Amagansett beach, at the southern tip of Long Island, from a rubber dinghy dropped under cover of night from a U-boat, which managed to elude local US destroyer patrols and also to escape the vigilance of the local coast guards. The saboteurs wore German naval fatigue uniforms which they buried in the beach along with boxes of explosives and other equipment. The second group was similarly transported and landed four days later on Ponte Vedra beach, Florida, some twenty-five miles south of Jacksonville.

Each group possessed a substantial supply of TNT and other high explosives and fuses, timing devices and detonators, which in the hold of a boat or in the baggage room of a crowded railroad station would be capable of causing untold damage and loss of life. The saboteurs also carried with them plans of key railroad centres and bridges and of the locks on the Ohio River from Pittsburgh to Louisville. Besides all this, they had the layouts of three plants of the Aluminum Company of America, of the Niagara Falls hydro-electric plant, of the New York water supply system, and of a number of key industries. The men in the second group were to concentrate on railroads. They all possessed forged birth certificates, automobile driving licences, and selective service and social security cards. They also had plenty of cash, each man carrying $4,000 in a money belt and $400 in small denominations in his wallet, while in addition Kerling and Dasch each carried a reserve of $70,000. They had all undergone a rigorous training in a sabotage school at Quentz, near Berlin, in the use of explosives; they had also been taught how to communicate with their Nazi masters in secret writing.

Although six of the sabotage team were loyal Nazis, the other two were not. Dasch and Burger both detested Hitler and it is remarkable that the Nazis did not check their bona fides before they embarked on the U-boat. Burger, in particular, had no love for the Fuehrer, since he had spent seventeen months in a concentration camp and been tortured for having been a supporter of Ernst Roehm, the SS leader whom Hitler had had murdered in the abortive *putsch* of June 1934. At all events they quickly combined to give their comrades away to the American authorities. Five days after wading ashore at Amagansett beach, Dasch took the train from New York to Washington, checked into the May-flower Hotel, and next morning put through a telephone call to FBI headquarters. He was interviewed at length, signed a long, rambling confession—the prison psychiatrist who later examined him considered that he was suffering from an 'obsessive, compulsive, neurotic, hysterical personality disorder'—and as the result of the information he gave all the saboteurs were rounded up and in custody by 27 June. Brief details of the landings and arrests were then released by Mr Hoover, who was warmly congratulated on all sides for the success of the coup, and later given a 'medal of honour' by President Roosevelt.

The first witness called to testify for the prosecution was twenty-two-year-old Coast Guardsman second class John C. Cullen, who had surprised Dasch and his three companions when they were burying their uniforms and explosives in the sand at Amagansett beach. He was patrolling the foggy beach at the time and he described how he saw the shadowy silhouettes of the saboteurs. 'I hollered out,' he said, and as he hollered one of the men walked towards him. According to Coast Guardsman Cullen the man said he and his companions were fishermen who had come from nearby Southampton, Long Island, and run ashore. A voice in the fog—it was Burger—shouted out something in a foreign language and this made the guard nervous and suspicious. The man he had hollered at approached closer and said, 'Forget about this and I'll give you some money and you can have a good time,' having previously told him that he would not like to kill him. He held out two fifty-dollar bills. The coast guard refused to accept them but after the man had reached for more money and said 'Here's three hundred dollars,' he took the proffered bills. Coast Guardsman Cullen then went off into the fog and reported his experience to his superior, Warren Barnes, the chief of the Amagansett Coast Guard Station, handing over the money which was found to total $260. The young guard then took a party of other guards back to the beach and pointed out the spot where the suspicious encounter had taken place. It was still too foggy to make a search, so station chief Barnes returned with some of his men, not including Cullen, when it was light. Soon they dug up the boxes with the explosives, uniforms and other paraphernalia which the saboteurs had buried.

'Do you recognise the man in the court who walked towards you?' the Attorney-General asked the witness.

'I think so, sir,' replied Coast Guardsman Cullen.

'Will you stand up and identify him, if you see him in court?'

The witness did so and pointed towards Dasch in the row of prisoners. He then asked Dasch to say something so that he could identify him by voice as well as by sight. Dasch's counsel had no objection, so the prisoner asked the witness, 'What is your name?' Coast Guardsman Cullen then turned towards the Attorney-General and said, 'That's the man.' Asked about what Dasch had suggested to him if he did not go away, he replied, 'He said he would not want to have to kill me.' But when he went on to refer to the boxes of explosives as 'this equipment they had dug up', Colonel Royall objected for the defence that this was hearsay, and the President was obliged to sustain the objection and strike out the reference from the record after the Attorney-General had agreed with the objection. 'Since the witness did not see the boxes dug up,' said Biddle, 'he cannot testify with respect to their being dug up. We shall later show that they were dug up and put the witnesses on.' It was a small point, but it shows how the niceties of 'due process' were observed in a wartime secret trial.

Cullen's evidence was confirmed by his chief who also identified the various articles found on the beach. He was followed by various FBI agents and explosives experts, after which the

articles themselves were put in evidence and finally the statements made by the accused after they had been arrested. This led
to a legal argument between the opposing counsel, the defence
lawyers arguing that under the rules of common law evidence the
confession of one was not evidence against another except on the
point of conspiracy, since otherwise hearsay would prevail.

To Biddle it was a simple issue which involved incontrovertible
facts. To deny them because of a technicality in common law was
preposterous, he submitted. 'Those men, not having an opportunity to confer or talk it over, on the whole made confessions
entirely bearing out what each other said,' the Attorney-General
declared. 'Dasch supports Burger, Burger supports Kerling, and
so on, right down the line. . . . The defendants say that in spite of
that close interlocking of all those statements, all alike, all bearing
the obvious marks of truthfulness, all comparable to each other,
all showing this essential common intent . . . you must in some
curious way take out of your mind with respect to some defendants the confessions of the others.' In the event the commission
upheld Biddle and ruled that it would 'admit the confessions and
admissions for all purposes'. With that the prosecution rested its
case, and the prisoners' fate was virtually sealed.

Briefly the case for the defence was that the eight men had no
intention of going through with their instructions, there was no
indication that they were spies, and there was the patent fact that
they had committed no act of sabotage by the time they were
arrested. Broadly speaking this was borne out by the prisoners
themselves who all testified in their own defence, though some of
them were more convincing than others. Kerling, for instance, did
not plead a change of heart about Germany or the Nazis; his
doubts of the success of the sabotage assignment were due to his
profound disrespect for the quality of the others as effective
saboteurs—if they had only been more like himself, he felt, they
would not have been caught and somehow would have succeeded
in carrying out their orders. On the other hand, Neubauer and
Thiel felt they had been trapped. 'As a soldier you are not supposed to think,' the former said in reply to his counsel. 'I just got
the order and I didn't know what for.' Even when he was told that
it was for sabotage, what could he do about it? Kappe, his superior
in the sabotage school was a lieutenant, 'which in Germany is
quite a high superior above me,' he explained. 'There was nothing

I could do. I had the order from my regiment to report to him.'
But he was relieved, he added, that Kappe's instructions specifically ruled out killing or harming Americans.

The seventh man to be called to the witness chair was George
Dasch. His defence was based on the single undeniable fact that
he had voluntarily gone to the FBI and revealed the sabotage plot.
Unlike the six previous witnesses, who may have intended to do so,
Dasch had acted. Asked by Biddle in cross-examination why he
had delayed for a week, Dasch replied: 'First of all I was a mental
and nervous wreck. I was so glad I was here. Second, I had to be
human. . . . To be a real decent person I had to wait. I had to give
every person a chance to say what I had to say. That's the
reason.'

Perhaps the most effective and forthright of the eight prisoners
was Burger, who had become an American citizen of his own
choice but who had lost his citizenship when he was drafted into
the German army in 1941. Ever since the attempted *putsch* of
1934 he had been anxious to leave Germany, but an illegal escape
would have meant serious trouble for his family. The only way
out was when he joined the sabotage group.

General McCoy asked him whether he knew Hitler. Yes,
Burger replied, he knew Hitler intimately at one time and had
taken part in his first grab for power. But his loyalty to the
Fuehrer had died during the purge in which his friend Roehm
had been killed.

'Do you remember,' McCoy finally asked him, 'whether or not
Kappe told you to confess in case one or all of you were caught?'

'No, sir,' said Burger. 'On the contrary, in case anyone got
caught we were not to tell anything. That was understood from
the beginning.'

In the circumstances a verdict of guilty was inevitable. The
court convicted all eight prisoners and sentenced them to death by
electrocution. However, the judges recommended that in the cases
of Dasch and Burger, the sentence should be commuted to life
imprisonment because of the assistance they had given the
Government in the apprehension and conviction of the others—
Burger had given particularly valuable information about the
operations of the sabotage school where the men had been trained.
As a result President Roosevelt commuted the death sentence to
life imprisonment for Burger and thirty years for Dasch.

If he could, President Roosevelt would have gladly added to the punishment in a rather old-fashioned way. When told by the Attorney-General that a total of $175,000 had been collected from the prisoners, he remarked with a chuckle: 'Not enough, Francis. Let's make real money out of them. Sell the rights to Barnum and Bailey [the circus showmen] for a million and a half—the rights to take them round the country in lion cages at so much a head!'

There was no appeal against the sentences. Nevertheless the defence tried to get them quashed by applying to the Supreme Court for a writ of *habeas corpus* on the ground that a military court had no right to try civilians when the civil courts were open and properly functioning. Colonel Royall, who argued the matter, based his argument on the precedent of the case of a man called Milligan who had been condemned to death during the American Civil War for sending military supplies to the Confederates and his sentence had been confirmed by President Lincoln, but whose release was ordered by the Supreme Court which held that the law of war 'can never be applied to citizens where the courts are open and their process unobstructed'. However, in the case of the saboteurs the court now held that the earlier decision had reference to the particular facts of Milligan's case which were different from that of the saboteurs and that as a general rule individual offenders against the law of war like the saboteurs could be tried and punished by a special military court since they were not entitled to be treated as prisoners-of-war. Thus the defence motion failed and justice duly took its course.

About 3 a.m. on Saturday 8 August 1942, three American soldiers and a British sailor arrived at the entrance to the District Jail where the condemned men were being held, saying they had come to volunteer as a firing squad 'to save the government some money on electricity'. They were firmly turned away by the guard on duty, but not before their pictures were taken by waiting news photographers. Later the same day the executions were carried out in the electric chair, a proceeding which lasted from 12 noon to 1.20 p.m. The six bodies were afterwards taken to Blue Plains, the District Potters's Field and buried in nameless graves, surmounted by six unpainted wooden boards numbered 276 to 281, to correspond with US Health Department records. The six graves were in a new plot which by a grim touch of irony was separated from the bodies of the other unclaimed dead in Blue

Plains by a five-foot wire fence of a type called 'anti-sabotage' by its manufacturer.

In 1948, Roosevelt's successor in the White House, President Truman, commuted the remainder of the prison terms being served by Burger and Dasch, and both men were deported to Germany. Nothing more was heard of Burger, but Dasch eventually erupted into print with the result that Francis Biddle had anticipated. 'I have no doubt,' wrote Biddle, 'that Dasch, one of the most unhaltingly voluble men I have ever encountered, has by now generously embellished the strange story of his capture and release as he keeps recounting it to a younger generation.' Indeed the saboteur's account, which appeared in 1959, is much more fanciful than trustworthy. It was entitled *Eight Spies Against America.*

# 16

# Who Killed Sir Harry Oakes?

For hours people waited outside the yellow colonial building in Nassau for the Supreme Court of the Bahamas to open on the morning of 18 October 1943. For it was on this date that thirty-three-year-old Count Marie Alfred Fouquereau de Marigny was to stand trial for the murder of his father-in-law Sir Harry Oakes, American-born self-made millionaire who had made his fortune in Canada and had become a naturalised British subject, being subsequently created a baronet by King George VI for his philanthropic benefactions. Nevertheless, Oakes, who was sixty-seven at the time of his death, had always been a rough diamond and there remained something of the prospector about him which went back to the time of his incredibly lucky gold strike in Ontario thirty years before.

The trial was one which had aroused widespread interest in the British colony of which King George VI's elder brother the Duke of Windsor was Governor. When the doors were eventually opened over a hundred spectators, many of them coloured Bahamians, crowded into the small court-room, as the Irish Chief Justice Sir Oscar Daly, in full-bottomed wig and fur-trimmed scarlet robes, took his seat on the bench and the court usher called for silence and intoned the customary, 'Oyez! Oyez! God save the King.'

The prisoner, who had been in custody for the past three months, was tall, thin and muscular, with dark hair and hard green eyes. He wore a light blue suit and a bright tie, but he looked pale as he thoughtfully chewed on a match. Those who knew him thought he had lost some weight, but otherwise he appeared cheerful, grinning and winking at his friends. He was a native of Mauritius and still spoke with a marked French accent, which was noticeable when he answered the question put to him by the clerk of the court as to how he pleaded. In this instance he replied confidently, 'Not guilty.'

The jury sworn to try the case was an all-male one and was quickly empanelled without any of its members being challenged. The prosecution was led by the Attorney-General, Eric Hallinan, an Irishman and a graduate of Dublin University like the Chief Justice. With him at the prosecutor's table was an eminent Bahamian Negro barrister, Alfred Adderley, whom the prisoner had tried to brief but who had been pre-empted by the Crown. Thus Alfred de Marigny had to make do with the services of a local white barrister Godfrey Higgs, not in the same class as Adderley but able and straightforward, who only undertook the defence when his client had assured him that he was innocent. As his junior Higgs had a witty young lawyer of mixed white and Negro blood named Ernest Callender; he had the reputation of being utterly indifferent about whose toes he might tread on.

The newspapers both in the Bahamas and the United States had been full of the case for weeks past, so that everyone in court was familiar with the prisoner's background which Mr Adderley, who opened for the prosecution, proceeded to elaborate. Although he was in his early thirties, Alfred de Marigny had been twice married and divorced before he wed Nancy Oakes, the dead man's nineteen-year-old daughter and the eldest of his five children by his Australian wife Eunice. De Marigny's second wife was a well-known New York socialite Ruth Fahnestock, whom de Marigny had met while doing business with the American brokerage house of Fahnestock & Co. when he was operating as a stockbroker in London. Some newspapers made him out as a playboy and an adventurer, but this was far from the truth. In fact he made a lot of money, working hard and playing hard; indeed he became a champion yachtsman and his Star-class yacht *Concubine* was renowned from Nassau to Long Island and collected many trophies. His closest friend in the Bahamas was a fellow Mauritian Georges Marquis de Visdelou Guimbeau, who occupied an apartment in his house. However, the fact was that Fred de Marigny was not popular with the whites in the colony apart from a few Nassau sportsmen. He did not care for the Government House circle, and it sometimes seemed that he went out of his way to annoy the Duke of Windsor, in whose hearing he once remarked, 'He is not my favourite ex-King of England.' On the other hand, he liked the Bahamian natives and they responded to his affection.

Admittedly de Marigny was most attractive to women, although like most men who find them easy to possess he had a basic contempt for them and generally speaking he preferred the company of men. In May 1942 he had gone off to New York and married Nancy Oakes, a small, shy girl with red hair and freckles, who had become infatuated with him a couple of years earlier when she saw him winning race after race with *Concubine*. It was a secret wedding contracted more or less on the spur of the moment in the Bronx County Court House, where they waited their turn in a line of GIs and their prospective brides. At this time Nancy's parents were staying at their place in Bar Harbour, Maine. 'So you're married,' said her father when she broke the news to him over the telephone. 'How much money do you want?'

'Nothing,' said Nancy.

Nancy and her husband went to Bar Harbour and at first the atmosphere was cordial. 'Frenchie,' Sir Harry said as he slapped his son-in-law on the back. 'You are the son-of-a-bitch for marrying my daughter, but I like you!' But their amicable relations soon cooled and gradually turned to dislike, which was mutual. The millionaire offered his son-in-law a directorship in his profitable Lake Shore Mine in Canada, but de Marigny declined. Their relations deteriorated and early in 1943 Sir Harry made a new will, wording it so that his son-in-law should get no part of Nancy's money.

The Hon. Harold (later Sir Harold) Christie, the leading real estate man in the colony and a member of the Legislative Assembly, who had done more than anyone else to develop the islands on the right lines, was friendly with both parties and what he saw plainly worried him. 'You know, Fred,' he said to de Marigny, 'Harry can't understand anybody who isn't trying to get something out of him. He is funny that way. If he sees you are, it makes him mad, but when he sees you are not, it makes him madder.'

Matters came to a head one night when Oakes and his eldest son Sydney, aged fifteen, dined with Fred and Nancy. Georges de Visdelou was also there with a friend, Betty Roberts, who worked as a cashier in a local cinema. Fred and Nancy had been invited, along with Oakes and his son to cocktails at Government House earlier the same evening, but Fred had ignored the invitation. When he was twitted by his father-in-law for not turning up, he laughed and said, 'To hell with the Duke!' This infuriated Harry Oakes, and the two had a blazing row.

'You've been doing that sort of thing too long around here, God damn you!' screamed Oakes. 'As far as I'm concerned you are out, do you understand?'

'Too bad, too bad,' de Marigny retorted. 'I don't give a damn. I've never asked anything from you and I never will. As far as Nancy is concerned, if she ever gets anything from you she will be no worse off. Everything she's got, every stitch of clothing, I bought for her.'

By this time Oakes was beside himself with fury. 'I'll have you horsewhipped,' he yelled. 'I'll have you thrown into the gutter to rot!'

'Will you indeed,' answered his son-in-law calmly. 'Don't forget I have a big foot and if you are coming here to insult me I shall apply it to your behind!'

With that Oakes stormed out of the house, taking his son with him. They were to meet again a few nights later, when young Sydney Oakes was spending the night with his sister- and brother-in-law. Sir Harry pounded at the front door at five o'clock in the morning, shouting to de Marigny to open up, and when he did so in pyjamas his father-in-law rushed into Sydney's room, ordered the youth to put on his clothes and took him away. According to de Marigny, it was the last time he saw Sir Harry Oakes.

About five o'clock in the afternoon of 7 July 1943, Oakes called for Harold Christie in Nassau and together they drove out to the Oakes house, Westbourne, now part of the Nassau Country Club, and played a set of tennis. After their game the two men adjourned to the house for cocktails where they were joined by several others whom Oakes had invited for drinks, Lady Oakes and the rest of the family being away at Bar Harbour. They were Charles Hubbard, a retired Woolworth's executive from London, Mrs Heneage, who was also English, Sally Sawyer, a niece of Christie's, and a girl friend of hers. It looked as if a storm might be brewing.

The girls left early, and Hubbard, who knew Oakes only slightly and was anxious to cultivate his friendship, invited his

7

host and the others to dine with him at the Prince George Hotel. 'No, no,' said Sir Harry, 'we'll have dinner here.' This they did, and after dinner the party sat down to play Chinese checkers. Meanwhile the storm blew up and the waves pounded on the rocks outside the house. At eleven Hubbard excused himself and drove Mrs Heneage home. Christie, who was a bachelor and liked to sleep where he dined, decided to spend the night at Westbourne. He borrowed a pair of pyjamas, and the servants made up one of the guest bedrooms which was two rooms away from Sir Harry's with an empty bedroom and bathroom in between. It was about eleven-thirty when Christie said good night to his friend and climbed under the mosquito netting above his bed. He was soon asleep.

However, Harold Christie did not sleep well, what with the storm and thunder outside and the mosquitoes in his room which he would get up from time to time and squash. Finally he rose about seven and went into his host's bedroom. He could scarcely believe the horrible sight which met his eyes. The place was a shambles. Sir Harry Oakes had been brutally battered to death and as his body lay on the bed his murderer had poured petrol over it, particularly the genitals, and set fire to this macabre pyre. Curiously enough he did not switch off the electric fan which continued to whirr and added to the wind from the storm had the effect of extinguishing the flames so that the body and the bed-clothes were merely scorched.

As soon as Christie had raised the alarm and the police came on the scene, the Governor was informed and told that unless expert investigative action was taken immediately the evidence of finger prints and other clues was likely to evaporate into nothing due to the humidity. The Duke of Windsor did not call in Scotland Yard or the FBI, as some thought he should have done, but instead he summoned two detectives from Miami, who had been assigned to him as a bodyguard when he visited Florida. They were Captain Edward Melchen of the Homicide Bureau of the Miami Police and Captain James Barker, supervisor of the Police Criminal Laboratories at Miami—in other words, a couple of routine cops.

In accusing de Marigny of the crime, Adderley permitted himself a touch of Shakespeare when he called the murder 'as black as hell and as dark as night in its foul construction'. Briefly the case against the prisoner rested on his admission that he had driven two women back to where they were staying next door to Westbourne after entertaining them at his own home, so that he was in the neighbourhood during the night the murder was committed. Also, when physically examined by Melchen and Barker for incriminating traces, burned hairs were found on his hands and arms and his beard was singed. Furthermore, he was unable to produce the shirt he wore that night. 'I don't know where the maids keep the laundry,' he had said. 'I never ask them.' Also the suit he wore had been newly pressed, though de Marigny stated that his manservant invariably did this to his clothes every morning.

The first material witness was Harold Christie. He looked exhausted as he stepped into the box, but he told his story quietly and convincingly—how he had swatted the mosquitoes which had penetrated the netting in his room, and how he had been awakened intermittently by the storm and the rain and what he had seen when he went to call his host. 'I went into the room and saw some smoke,' he said. 'Then I rushed to the bed and found Sir Harry with his clothing burned off and raw spots on his body. I shouted. The body was still warm. I lifted his head and put a pillow under it, took a glass of water and put some in his mouth. I got a towel and wet it, wiped his face, hoping to revive him. I thought he was still alive. Then I went to a porch and called for help. I telephoned the doctor and others. I rushed into my own room and wiped the blood off my hands with a towel.'

Adderley was aware that the defence witnesses included an experienced officer of the Bahamas Police Force named Edward Sears, who had been driving along Bay Street into George Street about midnight on the date of the murder and that a station wagon had passed him. The officer was sure he recognised a man sitting in the front seat beside the driver as Harold Christie, though he could not identify the driver nor say whether he was black or white. The prosecuting counsel therefore decided to anticipate this witness's evidence by questioning Christie about it. Asked how long he had known Sears, Christie replied that he had known him since childhood.

'What would you say if Captain Sears said he saw you out that night?' Adderley went on.

'I would say he was very seriously mistaken,' replied Christie with a hint of anger in his voice, 'and that he should be more careful in his observations.'

Asked by Godfrey Higgs in cross-examination whether Sears was not a reputable person, Christie agreed that he was, 'but,' he added, 'reputable people can be mistaken.'

Higgs at first appeared nervous and repetitive in his questions. At one point he exasperated the witness by asking him which end of the towel he had used to wipe the dead man's face. 'For heaven's sake, Higgs, be reasonable!' Christie exploded.

Another local police officer, Superintendent John Douglas, who was a friend of de Marigny's, testified that he had heard the prisoner say, 'That guy, Sir Henry, the old bastard should have been killed anyway.' He said that de Marigny had questioned him about whether a man could be convicted in a British court if the murder weapon could not be found. 'Don't worry about it, Freddie,' he had told the prisoner, who had also asked him if a man could be convicted on circumstantial evidence. The witness had told de Marigny that he thought so.

These admissions were effectively disposed of in cross-examination when the witness declared: 'I know French law is different from English law, and I know the accused came from Mauritius. I paid no attention to these statements or questions at the time.'

Captain Melchen was next questioned by the prosecutor, and he told about the burns on de Marigny's arms and de Marigny's inability to produce his shirt. He was asked by Callender in cross-examination about a visit he had made with his colleague Captain Barker to Bar Harbour where they interviewed Nancy de Marigny and her mother the day before the funeral. The witness went on to say how Captain Barker had told them about fingerprints or a fingerprint of the accused having been found in Sir Harry's room. Asked whether he had discussed the case with his colleague during the flight to Bar Harbour, Melchen said he had, but added somewhat surprisingly that he had not discussed the question of the fingerprints.

'Barker must have known that the fingerprint found at the scene of the crime was the accused's. When would you say he knew that?'

'He must have known it before we left Miami.'

'He claims he knew it on July 9th when the accused was arrested,' remarked defence counsel. 'He gave out an interview to the Press to that effect. And yet you are now willing to swear on your oath that you travelled with him from Nassau to Miami and from Miami to Bar Harbour—arriving there on the 16th—and yet in all this time Barker never mentioned this important fact to you?' 'Yes.'

'Captain Melchen,' the judge asked the witness, 'do you not now consider it strange that Captain Barker did not tell you about the fingerprint on your journey to Bar Harbour?'

'Yes, I do now,' said the witness, looking distinctly uncomfortable.

Captain Barker was the next witness. Questioned about a fingerprint on the screen in Sir Harry's bedroom which he swore was de Marigny's, he said it had been 'lifted' from the screen; but the original had not been photographed as he did not bring a fingerprint camera with him, relying on the one at Nassau which turned out to be broken. 'You could have telegraphed for one,' remarked the judge acidly.

'Prints left on the screen by others were destroyed by the humidity,' Higgs went on with his cross-examination. 'If the accused were there that night, wouldn't his be destroyed too?'

'We were fortunate to have found it,' said Barker.

'I don't believe "fortunate" is the word,' counsel retorted sharply. 'Let us say, "It was a coincidence we found it".'

The judge leaned forward. 'Does the defence mean to infer that the fingerprint may be a forgery?'

'I do, sir,' said counsel. However, after a protest from the Attorney-General the judge ruled that the evidence was admissible and that it was up to the jury to accept it or reject it.

The last witness for the prosecution was Lady Oakes. Sadly she described the strained relations with her son-in-law who, she said, was not accepted into the family because he was irresponsible. 'As a result,' she added, 'Sir Harry and I changed our wills to protect the children as far as possible until they had attained the age of discretion.'

The defence opened with the prisoner taking the witness stand. He described his meeting and marrying Nancy, how he had between £7,000 and £8,000 in cash at the bank, and property in the colony worth another £5,000. He went on to relate how he had first been friendly with the dead man and how their relations had deteriorated. But he strongly denied having said, 'That guy, Sir Harry, the old bastard should have been killed anyway.'

Questioned by his counsel about his movements on the night of the murder, he related how he had given a dinner party at his house, to which among others he had invited two girls he had met at the Prince George Hotel, and at which Georges de Visdelou and Betty Roberts were also present in addition to six or seven others. Because of the weather, he had lit some hurricane lamps and candles for the dinner table, singeing his hands and beard in the process. He went on to describe how he took the two girls back to where they were staying next door to Westbourne, which was in darkness as he passed it. On his return, he said, he went up to his friend Georges de Visdelou's apartment and asked whether he should take Betty Roberts home. Georges replied that he would do so himself.

The prisoner stated that he then went to bed and awoke about three to hear Georges's Maltese cat mewing in his room— apparently it had got caught up between the Venetian blind and the mosquito net. Shortly afterwards he heard Georges talking to Betty, driving off, and returning a few minutes later. 'Georges,' he shouted in the darkness from his bed. 'Come and take your damned cat out of here.' His friend did so, moving uncertainly through the darkness into the room and out again.

De Marigny was cross-examined by the Attorney-General, who asked him about his quarrels with Sir Harry Oakes. 'I was not humiliated by what Sir Harry said,' the prisoner declared. 'He was a man of violent temper and might forget the whole thing the next day. Sir Harry disapproved of our refusing the invitation to Government House and said we should meet people. Personally I don't go out with the society crowd in Nassau. I stay with my friends.' His credibility remained unshaken by the Attorney-General's questions.

Several of his dinner guests including Betty Roberts testified about his lighting the lamps and candles and burning himself. They were followed by the Nassau police officer Captain Sears, who doggedly stuck to his story that he had seen Harold Christie in a station wagon around midnight. The doctor then testified that he had examined de Marigny in prison and found no burns on him, though he admitted that he had made the examination with the naked eye and not through a magnifying glass.

Georges de Visdelou was the next witness. He confirmed that he had spoken to de Marigny about 1.30 a.m. and again about 3 a.m. when his friend had asked him to get the cat away.

'Did you go into the accused's room for the cat?' asked Adderley in cross-examination.

'I may have done,' replied the witness, 'but I can't recall if I did.'

Prosecuting counsel then held up several sheets of paper which turned out to be a statement which the witness had signed when he was first questioned by the police. It read in part: 'I did not see de Marigny from eleven p.m. until ten a.m. the following morning.'

'How do you explain the discrepancy in your statement in this court and your written statement?' Adderley pressed the witness.

'Do you not think it strange that you now contradict the statement you made when the facts were fresh in your mind?'

'I can't understand it,' the witness stammered.

It looked as if Georges de Visdelou's testimony was completely discredited. However, the situation was retrieved by Callender in re-examination, when it was brought out that de Visdelou's statement included an account of how de Marigny had come to the door of his apartment and asked if he could take Betty Roberts home, and that the witness had said no.

'Mr Adderley,' the judge looked stern, 'you gave me and the jury to understand that Mr de Visdelou's statement was a contradiction of his evidence. What we have here puts a completely different light on the matter.'

Prosecuting counsel coughed nervously as he addressed the bench. 'If you will pardon me, my lord,' he said, 'I was showing that the witness stated that he did not *see* de Marigny from midnight on. The statement just read by my learned friend Mr Callender does not contradict that. The statement merely says that the witness *talked* to the accused.'

The judge was understandably angry. 'I don't appreciate the fineness of the distinction when a man's life is at stake, Mr Adderley,' he admonished the prosecuting counsel. 'The impression you tried to convey in your cross-examination was that the witness had said in that statement that he had *neither seen nor talked* to the accused from midnight until ten the next morning.'

The last defence witness was the prisoner's wife. It was a considerable physical effort for her to take the stand at all, as she was seriously ill and running a temperature of 102°.

'Mrs de Marigny,' Higgs asked her, 'has your husband ever asked you for money?'

'No.'

'Has he ever made any offers for the use of your money?'

'No,' the witness repeated. 'I did invest £3,000 in his chicken farm, but that was at the suggestion of my mother.'

It was not what Nancy Oakes de Marigny said that mattered so much as the fact that she was prepared to go into the witness box in defence of the man charged with her father's murder that impressed the court.

In his final speech to the jury Higgs called the prosecution's case 'a combination of statements of an irrelevant nature and deliberate lying by police officers whose duty it is to protect the public'.

In his speech the Attorney-General declared that 'with a rising crescendo of enmity between de Marigny and the Oakes family, he finally was in such a predicament that in an attempt to get control of the family fortune he was willing to resort to murder.' The Chief Justice then summed up largely in favour of de Marigny. 'As for the clothing,' he pointed out, 'if it were bloodstained the accused would be expected to get rid of it, but no evidence has been produced that the clothing has been burned or destroyed. . . . It remains for you to decide whether the alleged threats were made in all seriousness or were merely the aroused statements of the moment.' He went on to describe Barker's statements as incredible for an expert. 'One would think an expert would be more careful.'

It took the jury just over an hour to return their verdict by a majority of nine to three—Not Guilty. The prisoner was immediately discharged and borne along and out of the court-room on the shoulders of a great throng of blacks and whites singing, 'For he's a jolly good fellow!'

Asked by a reporter who had killed Sir Harry Oakes, Alfred de Marigny replied that he did not know. 'I was tried ten per cent for killing Sir Harry,' he added, 'and ninety per cent for marrying Sir Harry's daughter.'

Next day the acquitted man took a lie detector test in front of his wife, counsel, a score of friends and reporters. A lie would set the detector wobbling. The needle never flickered as it traced its way along the graph.

The question remains, who did kill Sir Harry Oakes? It was certainly not Alfred de Marigny who was rightly acquitted.

Nor was it Harold Christie, upon whom suspicion rested for a time.

Some fifteen years after the murder, the present writer happened to be having tea with the late Lord Astor at Westbourne, which by then had been taken over by the Nassau Country Club. Our talk turned to the Oakes affair, which interested me, especially since I had once met Sir Harry, having been introduced to him by the Duke of Windsor when he was Governor of the Bahamas. Since I knew that Lord Astor owned considerable property in the islands and had for long been familiar with local affairs, I asked him what he thought about the crime. His theory was that Sir Harry Oakes had been killed out of revenge by the father of a native girl whom he had seduced, which accounted for the victim's genitals having received particular attention from the killer.

Another theory which I have heard put forward is that Harry Oakes was murdered by a syndicate of financial adventurers involved in an intricate plot to get their hands on the Oakes fortune.

Christie was one of the largest and wealthiest landowners in the Bahamas, having been a pioneer of real estate development there. He was also one of the colony's leading citizens, being a member of both the Bahamas House of Assembly and the Governor's Executive Council. What possible motive could the forty-seven-year-old landowner have for killing a man with whom he was known to be on very friendly terms and whose guest he was on the night in question? Nevertheless, tongues wagged in the colony. From the state of Oakes's bedroom when Christie discovered his friend's body, allegedly still warm, it was obvious that Oakes had put up a tremendous struggle. Although there was a bathroom and another bedroom between Christie's room and that of the murdered man, the struggle must have caused a considerable noise. Why then, people asked, didn't Christie hear it? Yet at the trial Christie had sworn that he had slept through it all, although one witness, a police officer, thought he had seen him in a car in Nassau during the night.

Harold Christie died in 1973, and now that he is dead there would appear to be no objection to stating why he heard nothing of the fracas which went on in his host's bedroom. The answer is simple. Christie was not in his own room at the time Oakes was killed and he did not return to it until afterwards. What happened

was this. Some time after midnight the storm which had been
raging, and which had resulted in Christie accepting his host's
invitation to stay the night, abated somewhat. Christie, who had
been unable to sleep owing to the mosquitoes in his room, got up,
dressed and slipped quietly out of the house to where he had left
his car. He then got into the vehicle and drove to the house of a
lady friend with whom he was having an affair. Whether he stayed
with her or drove her to his own house is not clear—if the latter,
this may explain why police officer Sears at the trial claimed to
have seen him in Nassau. At all events Christie and the lady spent
several hours together, after which Christie left her and returned
to Westbourne, by which time Oakes was already dead. If Christie
had given a true account of his movements on the night of 7–8
July 1943, he would have compromised the lady and this for
understandably chivalrous motives he was unwilling to do. Hence
his decision to give his testimony as he did.

Whatever may be the truth of the matter, there are undoubtedly
people still alive in the Bahamas who are aware of the murderer's
identity. No doubt, too, they are wise to keep silent.

# 17

# The Cleft Chin Murder

During the last months of the Second World War, the headline news of a sensational murder near London, and the trial which followed, vied with the accounts of continued allied victories in Western Europe in attracting and holding public attention. One of the two persons accused of the murder was an eighteen-year-old striptease dancer, who imagined herself in the role of a 'gun moll'. The other was a deserter from the American armed forces who had recently gone 'over the hill'. Their victim was a private-hire car driver, aged thirty-four, named George Heath, who was reputed to be concerned in 'Black Market' operations. The fact that he had a hollow in his chin led to the crime being popularly known as 'the cleft chin murder'.

The girl and her companion who entered the dock at the Old Bailey on 16 January 1945 and pleaded not guilty to the murder were named as Elizabeth Marina Jones and Karl Gustav Hulten. Mr L. A. Byrne, later Mr Justice Byrne, led the prosecution, while Jones was represented by Mr J. D. Casswell, KC, and Hulten by Mr John Maude, KC, later Judge Maude. Mr Casswell's junior, who had also appeared for the dancer at the preliminary police court proceedings, was Mrs Lloyd Lane, later Mrs Justice Lane: it was the first time in English history that a woman barrister had appeared in a case of such gravity. The trial judge was Mr Justice Charles, the senior judge of the King's Bench. The jury was composed of nine men and three women.

The two prisoners were quite unlike what the spectators in court, who had read accounts of the case in the newspapers, anticipated. Elizabeth Jones, known to her family and friends as Betty, looked deathly pale and bore little traces of glamorous beauty; in fact she seemed a wretched drab. In deference to war-time clothes rationing, she was allowed to enter the dock without a hat, the first time, so it was said, that a female prisoner had appeared hatless in a murder trial. Hitherto ecclesiastical pre-judice had ordained that women should cover their heads in court, as they were usually required to do in church. As for Hulten, he did not seem at all like the 'gangster' type that the papers had made him out to be; he looked an ordinary, stocky, youth with dark hair who wore an army uniform and greatcoat. Although an American citizen, he was in fact a Swede by birth, who had been taken to the United States as a baby. He was also a Roman Catholic, an unusual combination with dark hair in Sweden.

In opening the case for the prosecution, Mr Byrne began by explaining why a member of the US Army was being tried in an English court, since legislation existed enabling American service men charged with crimes in England to be dealt with by American courts unless the US Government requested otherwise. In this instance there had been such a request which resulted in the unusual sight of an American serving soldier standing in the dock of an English criminal court. Although he had posed as 'Second Lieutenant Richard Allen', he was really Private Karl G. Hulten, and at the time of his arrest he had been absent without leave from his unit for several weeks.

The prosecutor went on to describe the finding of Heath's body in a ditch just off the Great West Road at Staines. No articles of any value were found on the dead man's person. The subsequent post-mortem examination showed that a bullet had passed through his body from back to front. In the opinion of the pathologist Dr Teare, who carried out the autopsy, Heath must have been paralysed within about half a minute of the firing of the bullet, and in his view he could not have lived longer than a quarter of an hour after the fatal shot was fired.

'The next question is—who killed George Heath? And it therefore becomes necessary for me to tell you one or two things about the prisoners.' With these words the prosecutor prefaced his description of the events which led up to the foul and cold-blooded murder of a harmless car driver only a few days after the two prisoners first met each other.

One evening—it was 3 October 1944—Betty Jones went into a café in Hammersmith Broadway. A man named Leonard Bexley, whose daughter worked as a waitress in the café, was talking to Betty when Hulten came in dressed in the uniform of a lieutenant. Hulten had met Bexley in the same café a few days previously and he told them that his unit was in Holland and that he could not draw any pay. On the occasion of his second visit, Hulten asked Bexley if he knew the girl. 'I said yes,' Bexley afterwards stated in evidence, 'and I sort of fixed up an acquaintance there and then.' At that time Betty was living in a room she rented in the name of Miss Georgina Grayson in King Street, Hammersmith. Later the same evening they again met and she had gone for a ride with 'Ricky Allen', as she knew Hulten, in a ten-wheeled American army truck, which he told her was stolen; she had previously told Mrs Evans, her landlady, that she thought he was a deserter and Mrs Evans had tried without success to dissuade her from keeping the appointment. 'I told him in the truck that I would like to do something dangerous, meaning to go over Germany in a bomber,' said Betty afterwards. 'But he got me wrong.' According to Hulten's version of the conversation, 'she said she would like to do something exciting like becoming a gun moll like they do back in the States'. Consequently he told her, untruthfully, that he was a gangster in Chicago.

In spite of her landlady's advice, they continued to meet during the following days and he spent one night in bed with her at her lodgings. On the night of 6 October, Jones told the landlady that 'Ricky' was calling for her. At 11.20 p.m. Mrs Evans heard someone whistling outside the house, and she heard her tenant run down the stairs and go out. She did not hear her return that night.

Next morning, Saturday 7 October, Hulten went in to a barber's shop in Hammersmith, where he had been a customer for some months. The barber, a man named Levene, had asked Hulten to buy a watch for him through the American canteen. When he was being shaved, Hulten told the barber that he had a watch for him, which he proceeded to hand to Levene who paid him £5 for it. The barber, who was busy, put the watch in his pocket and did not look at it until later, when he found that it was not an American watch as he had expected. In fact the watch had belonged to the dead car driver and had been taken from him after he had been shot.

Two evenings later, a policeman was on his beat in the Fulham

Palace Road and noticed a Ford V-8 bearing a registration number which had been circulated to the police. In fact it was the murdered man's vehicle and the policeman accordingly kept it under observation. In due course Hulten came out of a house nearby where he had been visiting another girl friend and got into the driving seat of the car. He was pulled out by the policeman and asked if the car belonged to him. He said no, after which he was searched. The search revealed he was carrying a Remington automatic pistol together with six cartridges. He was taken to the police station for questioning, where he gave his name as Lieutenant Richard John Allen, 501st Parachute Infantry, US Army. He was later questioned by a real US army lieutenant, Robert E. De Mott, to whom he had admitted that he was Private Karl G. Hulten of the 501st Infantry Regiment.

Asked to explain his possession of the Ford car, Hulten said he had found it in a wood near his base. Further asked how to account for his movements since the previous Friday night, he said that he had slept that night in a truck outside Newbury and had hitchhiked to London, sleeping the following night in a hotel and on the Sunday night with a prostitute. He later admitted that he had spent the Friday night with a girl he knew as Georgina Grayson in the Hammersmith area; he now stated that he did not find the car at Newbury but in Hammersmith. 'I do not know George Heath and I have never seen him,' Hulten went on to state. 'I only saw his picture in the newspapers. I swear that I did not shoot him, and I never saw the Ford I had when I was apprehended until I found it in the car park on Monday afternoon 9 October.'

Meanwhile the police had interviewed 'Georgina Grayson', who told them that this was her professional name as a striptease artist and that her real name was Elizabeth Jones. She went on to say that she was eighteen, Welsh, and married, but did not live with her husband, who was on active service with the army. She confirmed that 'Ricky Allen' had spent the night of 6–7 October with her, and there being no reason to detain her she was released. The police then had an extraordinary piece of luck which was to save them a lot of further investigation into the murder.

The same afternoon Betty Jones happened to encounter a casual acquaintance, a War Reserve policeman, who remarked how ill she was looking. She replied that she had just come from the police station where she had made a statement in connection with Heath's murder. 'I know the man they've got inside,' she went on, 'but it would have been impossible for him to do it, as he was with me all Friday night.' Then, after a pause, she added, 'If you had seen somebody do what I have seen done, *you* wouldn't be able to sleep at night.'

This remark so impressed the policeman that he at once reported it to Inspector Tansill, who had previously interviewed the girl, and he hurried to her house. There she confessed that she had lied to him earlier in the day and would now like to tell the whole truth. They drove back to the police station, and Betty said, 'I was in the car when Heath was shot. I didn't do it.' She was immediately cautioned and elected to make another statement, in which she gave a detailed description of Heath's death.

When Hulten called for her shortly before midnight on the Friday, she said, he said, 'Come on, let's go and get a cab', which she knew meant robbing a cab driver. They walked into the Hammersmith Road, where she stopped a car and they both got in, telling the driver (who was Heath) to take them to the top of King Street where she lived. The driver agreed to do this for ten shillings. This was an expensive fare for such a short journey, but the car was a private-hire one and not a taxi and the driver was not supposed to pick up casual passengers under penalty of being fined. They did not stop where she lived, Mrs Jones went on, as Hulten told the man to drive on. When they reached the beginning of the Great West Road, Hulten asked the driver to stop, and as he leaned over to open the passenger door, Hulten shot him. Then the American climbed into the driving seat, 'ordering Heath to move over or I'll give you another dose of the same.' He then told the girl to go through the dying man's pockets and take off his wrist watch, which she did. Then he stopped the car, 'got out and dragged Heath's body from the car and rolled it into the ditch', after which they drove back to Hammersmith, wiped the car clean of fingerprints and went up to her room where they spent the rest of the night. There, she said, she rebuked Hulten for the cold-blooded murder, but he replied, 'People in my profession haven't the time to think what they do.'

Hulten now admitted the general truth of Betty's statement, but he turned against her vindictively, seeking to show that she was responsible with him for the killing. However, he denied that the shooting was deliberate. They had decided to rob the car driver, and when the car stopped Hulten intended to fire the pistol through it (so he said), but at the crucial moment Heath leaned back to open the door and the pistol went off. He added that the girl afterwards helped him to place the body in the ditch, she taking it by the feet and he by the arms. 'I wanted to go for a walk, but she didn't want to,' he added. 'We went into a shop doorway and she started yelling for a cab. The first one was a naval car; it had a small anchor on it. The next one was Heath's car and he stopped. If it had not been for her, I wouldn't have shot Heath.'

After the prosecutor had concluded his opening speech to the jury, the latter were sent out while Mr Casswell for Mrs Jones submitted that his client's name which appeared first on the indictment should come after that of Hulten. He did this because he wished to have the last word with the jury. Hulten was the prime mover in the affair and he had confessed to the actual shooting of Heath, Mrs Jones's counsel argued; also she was only eighteen while Hulten was of full age and in addition he had been arrested first. In reply Mr Byrne submitted that the prosecution had the undoubted right to choose the order in which the prisoners should be indicted, and in the event the judge ruled against Mr Casswell.

The first material witness called for the prosecution was Leonard Bexley, a coach trimmer, who had introduced the two prisoners to each other in the Hammersmith café and had spent some time in their company during the fateful six days of their acquaintanceship. When he first saw Hulten, he said, the American was wearing a private's uniform. A day or two later, he was dressed as an officer, but, explained the witness, 'I didn't go into it all that much.' Hulten, he went on, had shown him his revolver and even taken him for a ride in the truck. On the Saturday, 7 October, Hulten had sold him a fountain pen and a revolving pencil for the modest sum of eight shillings. (In fact, as the prosecution proved, they had been taken from the dead man.)

Mr Maude's cross-examination was directed towards showing that even on the afternoon after the murder, when they went to the dog races together, Mrs Jones showed no signs of distress, nor did she seem at all afraid of Hulten, although she looked very ill.

'What was her attitude towards him?'

'I should say intimate.'

'Very fond of each other?'

'Yes.'

'Was there any sign at all of fear of him?'

'None whatever.'

'What was his behaviour towards her throughout the afternoon?'

'Absolutely as a gentleman, quite decent.'

The point of this line of cross-examination became clear when a subsequent police witness, Inspector Tarr, testified how he had gone to see Mrs Jones in Holloway Prison in response to a letter from her asking him to do so, and she told him that she had acted throughout 'because Ricky had threatened her with violence'.

The next witness gave her name as Mrs Violet Fleisig. She identified a fountain pen she had lent Heath, also his pencil and wrist watch, all of which Hulten had sold to the barber Levene. She also recognised his empty wallet which had been found near the scene of the crime. She was not cross-examined.

Mrs Fleisig was followed in the witness box by Mrs Jones's landlady Mrs Evans, who said that her tenant had given her name as Georgie Grayson. She repeated what had passed between them on the night of the murder. Georgie had told her why she thought Hulten was a deserter, adding that she was going to meet him at twelve o'clock that night. 'I said it was very foolish and that Hammersmith Broadway was a very silly place to be at twelve o'clock at night, and quite a few other things.'

Cross-examined by Mr Casswell for Jones, Mrs Evans said she was positive that her lodger had told her she thought Hulten was a deserter. 'She gave me all the technical reasons why she thought so, which conveyed nothing to me,' the witness added. 'To tell you the truth, I thought, if he was so patently a deserter to somebody so young as her, the police would have had the sense to pick him up earlier.'

'When you met him, what did you think of him then?'

'I thought he was a very decent chap. He seemed a bit excited, and I thought it was because he was very keen on her.'

Again Hulten's counsel emphasised Mrs Jones's attitude to the American both before and after the murder. 'Did she seem frightened of him at all?' asked Mr Maude.

'No.'

'What was her manner towards him?'

'Just an ordinary manner.'

'Nothing abnormal at all?'

'No.'

In reply to further questions, Mrs Evans told how after Mrs Jones and Hulten had come back from the dog races, her lodger had asked her to 'mind' some money for her. Jones then produced £7, which Mrs Evans told her to put in the oven, which she did.

'What happened to the £7?'

'Well, she kept taking a little bit at a time until it had all gone, as far as I know. I gave her the run of my kitchen.'

Morris Levene, the Hammersmith barber, was then called to say that he had bought Heath's wrist watch from Hulten for £5 the day after the murder, under the impression that it had been honestly obtained by his customer from the American canteen. Asked by Mr Maude whether he thought this was a 'quite normal, straightforward business transaction', the witness said that he thought it was.

'Do you still think so?'

'Yes.'

'Are you going to try to get somebody else to get you one?'

'No,' the barber replied emphatically.

More or less formal evidence was then given by the police and the pathologist who had carried out the post-mortem on Heath's body, and also by Lieutenant De Mott, the American officer who had taken statements from Hulten. When he came to cross-examine De Mott, Mr Maude clearly indicated the line that Hulten's defence would take. 'What he was saying to you was that it was an accident? That he had not intended to shoot Heath, but Heath had moved across and had been in the way?' The witness admitted that this was so.

The prosecution closed its case on the third day of the trial, and after the luncheon adjournment Mr Casswell put his client in the witness box. Although she looked a drab, miserable creature in the dock, Betty Jones gradually perked up in the witness box, the colour returned to her cheeks, and her voice, at first practically inaudible, became stronger, until at moments she showed traces of the vitality and good looks that she undoubtedly possessed.

She was first asked how old she was, and said she was eighteen. 'Eighteen and seven months, isn't it?' queried the judge signifi-

cantly and made a note. The point, which was not lost on most
people in court, was that at that date persons convicted of a
capital charge in England could not be hanged unless they had
attained the full age of eighteen.

The prisoner went on to describe her upbringing partly in
Wales and partly in Canada, how as a young girl she had always
been interested in dancing, and how she had later obtained
engagements in nightclubs. She described her marriage but said
that she never lived with her husband, 'because he struck me on
the first night we were married,' and only saw him a few times
thereafter when he was on leave from the army, but she received
the usual army wife's allowance.

'Is there any truth in the suggestion which has appeared
unfortunately in the Press that you were a prostitute and lived in
that way at any time?'

'No, sir.'

'You did live with other people?' the judge broke in.

'There was only one man,' the girl replied.

Answering further questions from her counsel, she went on to
tell how she first met Hulten whom she knew as 'Ricky' on
3 October. 'I thought he was a gentleman,' she said, and added
that he told her he had just come back from Holland. She had no
reason to suppose he was a deserter, and the first she knew about
it was from the police. When he told her on their ride in the
army truck that he was a gunman in Chicago and was the leader of
a gang operating in London, 'he said it in a way that I believed
him.' She added that this had frightened her very much. He also
showed her his revolver and two daggers, with which he threatened
her, she said.

On the night of the murder, she went on, he told her to stop a
taxi-cab. She did not know why he wanted one, but supposed it
was to take her home. When they passed near her house without
stopping, she guessed that 'Ricky' meant to rob the driver but she
was afraid to ask any questions. Then at the beginning of the
Great West Road he had shot Heath and told her to search his
pockets. At first she had refused, but then 'Ricky' picked up the
revolver which was lying on the seat and told her, 'You heard
what I said—I will do the same to you.' She then went through
Heath's pockets and removed their contents. 'Ricky' was 'very
touchy' at the time.

She denied that she helped him to put the body in the ditch. 'I was terrified and I was dazed,' she said. 'I just couldn't believe it had happened.' When she reproached him with the murder after they had got back to her place, he replied simply, 'People in my profession are used to things like that.' According to her, he warned her what would happen if she betrayed him to the police. He said he knew how to deal with informers: 'he always got them first and asked questions after.'

Finally her counsel brought her to the weakest part of her story. Why had she not told the police, either before or immediately after her arrest, that Hulten had terrorised her?

'I just gave the police the facts—that was all,' she replied.

The judge then took a hand in the questioning. 'Now,' he said, turning towards the prisoner in the witness box, 'the greater part of your evidence is that step by step you were terrified, dazed, frightened, ordered to do this, ordered to do that. Why didn't you say a word of that to the police?'

'Because I didn't think it concerned me, that I would be drawn into it.'

'You didn't think it concerned you?' asked Mr Justice Charles. 'Why do you think it concerns you today?'

'Because it has all been explained to me now,' said the witness. It was a damning reply.

After Mr Maude for Hulten had destroyed in cross-examination what little credibility attached to her story, there was little left for Mr Byrne to do for the prosecution with this witness. His questions were mainly directed to emphasising the fact that both she and Hulten were very short of money on the Friday night—they had, by her account, less than thirty shillings between them—at a time when, as she now claimed, they were ready to spend ten shillings on a short car-ride home.

Hulten then took her place in the witness box and told his story in a thoroughly self-possessed manner.

'Is there any truth whatever,' his counsel asked him, 'in the story about your having been a Chicago gunman?'

'No, there is not.'

'Have you ever been to Chicago in your life?'

'I have been there, yes,' Hulten replied unexpectedly. Mr Maude did not pursue the point, but went on to question his client about his meetings with Jones and her alleged wish to be a gun moll. 'I thought she was kidding at first and I didn't take her serious,' he said, 'but she did say she was serious about it.' He denied having told her any stories about being a gangster; but he was later to admit in cross-examination that he told her he had been one in Chicago. He added that he had never threatened her in any way. It was her idea, not his, that they should rob a cab.

Coming to the night of the fatal car drive, Hulten said that it was only when they were standing in Hammersmith Broadway that they decided to rob a cab, and even then he had no intention of shooting the driver. He did not know the pistol was loaded, and he had the gun in his lap when they reached the Great West Road because it had fallen out of his belt 'on the jauncing around of the car.' ('Jaunce' is an old English word used by Shakespeare and meaning to prance like a horse, but it has long since been obsolete in England, though it appears to have survived in America.) The shooting happened accidentally as he started to get out of the car, Hulten went on. 'My right sleeve caught in something on the right-hand side of the door. What it was I don't know and, as I went to go, the door just jerked me and the gun went off.'

Hulten stuck to his story that the shooting was accidental when he was cross-examined by Mr Byrne for the prosecution.

'Did you trouble to look when, by accident, you shot the man?'

'I did not.'

'Did you care whether or not he was dead or alive?'

'I really don't know.'

Prosecuting counsel repeated the question. 'I am sorry, but I can't answer that,' said Hulten. 'I don't know what you mean by it.'

'It's a simple question,' the judge pointed out.

'But it carries a lot of meanings, sir,' Hulten replied. It certainly did.

In spite of powerful pleas by both defence counsel to the jury to return verdicts of manslaughter if they did not acquit the prisoners, it took the jury little over an hour to find Elizabeth Jones and Karl Hulten guilty. But in the case of Mrs Jones they added a recommendation to mercy.

Both prisoners were then sentenced to death. After Mrs Jones had been taken below to the cells, hysterically weeping and screaming, and her companion had followed her impassively, the judge did something unusual, although it was not unprecedented. 'I think you should know,' he told the jury, 'that the statements of both of them show that these two people had been engaged in murderous or near-murderous assaults on other people on their expeditions, and that upon one occasion Hulten with a revolver held up another car, but, finding that an American officer was in it, desisted from his attempt to stop it. I thought that perhaps it would interest you to know that which, by the rules of law in this country, it was impossible to disclose to you at an earlier time.' Mr Justice Charles added that he would of course forward the jury's recommendation to mercy in the case of Mrs Jones to the 'proper authority'.

Both prisoners appealed and, as was generally anticipated, the Court of Criminal Appeal dismissed both applications. 'The crime which Hulten committed was by the Common Law of England plain murder,' said Mr Justice Macnaughten in delivering the judgment of the court, 'and there was no evidence on which the jury could have arrived at a verdict of manslaughter.' As for Mrs Jones, the jury had been satisfied that she was a willing actor in the matter and had rejected her suggestion that she acted through fear of Hulten.

Three days before the date set for the execution, Mr Bernard Shaw, the world-famous dramatist and critic, then aged ninety, wrote an extraordinary letter to *The Times* on the subject of Mrs Elizabeth Jones:

> She has earned her living as a striptease girl, which I, never having seen a striptease act, take to be a performance as near to indecent exposure as the police will allow. Clearly we have to put such a character to death or to re-educate her. Having no technique of re-education immediately available, we have decided to put her to death. The decision is a sensible one.

Mr Shaw went on to observe that a long term of imprisonment was 'far crueller and wickeder than burning at the stake'. As for hanging this was out-moded as a method of execution, in his opinion, and he suggested that it should be replaced 'by State-contrived euthanasia for all idiots and intolerable nuisances', of whom he considered that the striptease girl was one.

His argument did not carry any weight with the Home Secretary, then Mr Herbert Morrison, who traditionally exercises the prerogative of mercy on the Queen's behalf. Next day it was officially announced that Elizabeth Jones had been reprieved and her sentence commuted to life imprisonment. Why the 'proper authority' should have left it to within two days of the appointed date for her execution to act on the jury's recommendation in her case is difficult to understand, in view of the fact that the appeal court's decision had been given a fortnight previously. Possibly there had been a sharp difference of opinion in the Home Office.

Hulten was hanged on 8 March 1945, five days after his twenty-third birthday, despite last-minute pleas from his wife and others in the United States for his reprieve. Jones served a little more than nine years of her sentence, and having obtained full remission for good conduct was released in May 1954 to begin a new life.

# [18]

# Van Meegeren, the Master Forger

As dawn broke on 29 October 1947, there was already a queue of would-be spectators outside the Fourth Chamber of the District Court in Amsterdam's Prinsengracht. By the time the court sat at ten o'clock the court-room was filled with two hundred onlookers, swelled by Press representatives from all over the world who had come to see the trial of the man who can claim to be the greatest art forger of all time. The man in question was a fifty-eight-year-old artist and confirmed morphia addict, who suffered from angina. Dressed in a pale blue shirt, dark blue tie and an elegant dark blue suit, but looking gaunt and hollow cheeked, he did his best to exude an air of jaunty confidence, waving to his friends, his son and daughter and his divorced second wife Jo, as he entered the court. Round the walls of the crowded court-room hung some of the pictures he was alleged to have forged—*Christ at Emmaus*, *Head of Christ*, *The Last Supper*, and *Isaac Blessing Jacob*, all of which were attributed to the great seventeenth-century Dutch artist Vermeer, although in fact the signatures on the canvases had all been cleverly faked, as had the entire paintings, by the man in the dock.

As soon as the presiding judge had taken his seat on the bench, the clerk of the court asked the prisoner: 'Are you Henricus Antonius van Meegeren?' The clerk used the Latin style of nomenclature which was customary on formal occasions, although the prisoner's two first names were often contracted to Han, by which he was generally known. The defendant acknowledged his identity with a curt nod, after which the Public Prosecutor read the indictment. The defendant was charged under two counts—first, that he had obtained money by fraud, and secondly, that he had put false names or signatures 'on certain paintings' contrary to Articles 326 and 326B of the Netherlands Penal Code.

'Accused, do you admit the charges?' the judge addressed the man in the dock.

'I do,' answered van Meegeren.

The fact that Han van Meegeren was in the dock at all had been the result of a chance happening two years previously, when the Allied Military Government Art Commission had discovered a large collection of pictures in a disused salt mine near Salzburg. The pictures had been mostly looted by the Nazis from museums and private collections in Europe. It was the task of the Commission to return such finds to their owners where they could be traced and also to seek out and punish 'collaborators' who were known to have disposed of them. One of the pictures found in the salt mine was listed as *Christ with the Woman taken in Adultery* and bore the prominent Vermeer signature—the usual 'I. V. Meer'—in the top left-hand corner. The accompanying particulars revealed that this painting belonged to Field-Marshal Goering, who had acquired it from a Bavarian banker named Aloys Miedl, who had an office in Amsterdam. Although the price was the absurdly large one of 1,650,000 guilders, the equivalent of half a million pounds, Goering had paid not in cash but in kind, and had handed over in exchange for the *Woman taken in Adultery* more than two hundred paintings which had been stolen from Holland by the occupying Nazis. Further inquiries showed that Miedl had got the picture from an intermediary called Dr Hofer, who made a business of supplying leading Nazis with art treasures for their own collections and that Hofer had in turn got it from a Dutch art dealer named Rienstra van Strijvesande, to whom it had been entrusted by van Meegeren to sell on commission and whom the authorities later failed to trace.

When two uniformed officers of the Netherlands Field Security Service called at van Meegeren's large house on the Keizergracht one day in May 1945 and told him they were investigating the circumstances of the sale of an important painting by Vermeer, van Meegeren received a shock. He admitted that he had sold the *Woman taken in Adultery* to van Strijvesande during the war but that the dealer had assured him that it would not fall into any German hands. Therefore, as van Meegeren assured his callers, the eventual fate of the painting was not his responsibility and thus he could not be accused of trading with the enemy.

The security men were prepared to accept this explanation, but they told van Meegeren that in view of the work's undoubted importance, the high price paid for it and the identity of the buyer, they would have to know where he had obtained it. Such information, they assured him, would be treated as strictly confidential. However, all van Meegeren would tell them was that he had bought the picture from 'an old Italian family' who had fallen on hard times and been forced to sell their family treasures. When pressed for further details he angrily refused to say anything more.

Van Meegeren's choice of an Italian provenance for the painting may have made the authorities suspect—quite wrongly—that he had been acting as a middleman between the Fascists and the Nazis for the disposal of looted works of art. At all events he was arrested four days later and charged with being a collaborator.

For the next six weeks Han van Meegeren persisted in his refusal to supply any further information about the picture. Then, perhaps because he was depressed and suffering from the effect of the lack of his accustomed drugs, he broke down before his astonished interrogators. 'You are fools like the rest of them!' he exclaimed. 'I sold no great national treasure—I painted it myself!'

If he had stopped there, all might have been well and no doubt he would have been lauded as a wartime hero who duped the Nazis. But his innate conceit made him go on and declare that he had likewise painted three more supposed Vermeers and a de Hoogh—*Christ at Emmaus*, *Head of Christ*, *The Washing of Christ's Feet*, all signed 'I. V. Meer', and *Interior with Drinkers*, signed 'P.D.H. 1658' and ascribed to de Hoogh. Incidentally, the latter painting, like *Christ at Emmaus*, had been bought by Dr D. G. Van Beuningen, a well-known private collector in Rotterdam, and at the time it was remarked that it bore a strong resemblance to de Hoogh's undoubted work *The Cardplayers*, which is in the Royal Collection at Buckingham Palace. For *Christ at Emmaus*, which was the first of van Meegeren's forgeries to come on the market—at Rotterdam in 1937—and was later presented to the Boymans Museum, van Beuningen paid the equivalent of £180,000. At the time it was hailed by the eminent art historian Dr Abraham Bredius as the most important example of the known work of Jan Vermeer of Delft.

At first the police thought that van Meegeren was either mad or else had invented a far-fetched story in order to escape conviction on a more serious charge. They began to change their minds when they subjected the *Woman taken in Adultery* to an X-ray test which revealed that it had been painted over an earlier picture on a genuine old canvas as van Meegeren told them he had done.

The police thereupon put it to van Meegeren that, if he had really painted *Christ at Emmaus*, he should be able to make a copy without much difficulty. Since this was within the capability of any skilled artist, van Meegeren dismissed such a naïve proposal with contempt. He then made the police an alternative proposal, namely that he should be given his freedom and allowed to work in his studio with the materials, including drugs, that he needed. He would then create another Vermeer before their eyes. This novel proposal was agreed to and van Meegeren accordingly set to work on a large canvas, $58\frac{3}{4} \times 75\frac{1}{2}$ inches, to produce the work known as *Young Christ Teaching in the Temple*. All his requirements were met and he was supplied with pigments, oil of lilacs, phenol and formaldehyde as well as morphia and Bols gin. Although two members of the security or police were always present in the studio and he painted under some difficulty, nevertheless he finished his last masterpiece in two months. Meanwhile the story of his fakes had become known to the outside world and the Press eagerly seized upon his latest studio activity, headlined by one newspaper as HE PAINTS FOR HIS LIFE.

The authorities now dropped the accusation of collaboration with the wartime enemy and substituted charges of fraud and forgery. At the same time the Minister of Justice appointed a commission of experts led by Dr P. B. Coremans, Director of the Central Laboratory of Belgian Museums, to pronounce upon the supposed forgeries, eight in all, which were believed to be the work of van Meegeren. The experts, consisting of two art historians and three scientists, were the principal witnesses for the prosecution when, after considerable delay, the case of Han van Meegeren came to trial. Indeed they found the defendant artist most co-operative since he supplied them with all the details of his technique and the materials he had used. Meanwhile van Meegeren had been declared bankrupt following the claims made upon him by the Boymans Museum and other purchasers of the faked works.

Each member of the Coremans Commission was asked two
questions at the trial—whether in his opinion all the paintings
were modern and whether they could be the work of van Meegeren.
All replied to both questions in the affirmative. Then the curtains
in court were drawn and Dr Coremans on behalf of the Commission showed with the aid of slides how these conclusions had
been reached. There was the 'crackle' in the paint, the cross
sections of the layers, the presence of artificial resin, and finally a
fragment of the original canvas on which he had overpainted
*Christ at Emmaus*, mounted on its original wooden stretcher, and
from which van Meegeren had cut a vertical strip thirty to fifty
centimetres wide. He had shortened the horizontal arms of the
stretcher by the same amount, and he had left the sawn-off pieces
together with the strip of canvas at the Villa Primavera in
Rocquebrune where he had painted *Christ at Emmaus*.

From time to time the judge would interrupt to ask van
Meegeren whether he agreed with the witness's statements and he
invariably answered that he did. 'That is perfectly correct,' he
would reply. Asked for his comment on the defendant's work
when he had finished his lecture, Dr Coremans said: 'I find this
work excellent. Indeed it is phenomenal. It will never be possible
to get away with forgery again.'

The next witness was another member of the Commission,
Dr A. M. de Wild, who had advised the Netherlands Government
to buy the least good of van Meegeren's pseudo-Vermeers, *The
Washing of Christ's Feet*, which it had done in 1943 for 1,300,000
guilders (about £320,000). Since the witness had subsequently
served on the Commission which had declared it to be false, he
was asked to explain the apparent discrepancy. Dr de Wild tried to
excuse himself by saying that the dealer with whom he had
negotiated twice refused to allow the picture to be X-rayed.
'Later on I was able to do so myself,' he said. 'This brought about
my change of opinion.' But he did not say how much later. In
fact it was not until after van Meegeren's confession.

When the pompous Dr de Wild went so far as to claim personal
credit, the court laughed outright. 'It soon became clear to me
that the accused had borrowed a formula for the composition of
his quasi-old paints from my treatise on the methods of Vermeer
and de Hoogh,' declared the witness. 'Even certain impurities that
I mention as being found in Vermeer's paint are also found in van

Meegeren's.' Dr de Wild was not asked why he had failed to notice this until after van Meegeren had confessed.

When the experts had finished their testimony, the judge leaned forward and asked the defendant at what stage in each work he had added the signature.

'I did that last of all and it was much the hardest job,' replied van Meegeren with a sigh as he remembered just how difficult the operation was. 'It had to be done in a single stroke,' he explained. 'Once I had begun it, there could be no going back.'

The next witness was a house agent named Strijbis, who had acted as agent for van Meegeren in disposing of his fakes. 'I was already acquainted with the accused when he asked me, in 1941, if I would sell a painting for him,' he stated in answer to the Public Prosecutor. 'I knew nothing about art but he offered me a handsome commission—one sixth of whatever price I got. I took the work, a *Head of Christ*, to Hoogendijk.' Hoogendijk was the leading Amsterdam art dealer at that time and had been concerned with the negotiations for the sale of *Christ at Emmaus*.

'Did you know it was a fake?' the Public Prosecutor rapped out the question.

'Certainly not,' said the witness, obviously nettled. 'The accused said it was a Vermeer. He never told me where he obtained it. Later I sold three others for him, all to Hoogendijk: the *Last Supper*, a Pieter de Hoogh and the *Blessing of Jacob*. They were supposed to be all from the same collection.'

'What were the prices paid?'

'I no longer remember,' replied Strijbis. 'I kept no record.'

In fact the total paid for the four forgeries sold by Strijbis was about three and a half million guilders, of which the witness's share was over half a million, on which sum incidentally he had paid no tax, a fact which was to get him into trouble later, although it was not mentioned at this stage. Strijbis added that Hoogendijk was as mysterious about his clients as he had been to Hoogendijk. 'He never told me who got the pictures,' he said.

The next witness was the dealer himself. 'I walked into the trap,' Hoogendijk admitted. 'When I saw the *Head of Christ*, it made me think of the *Emmaus*.'

'Did you not think it strange that more and more Vermeers were being discovered?' the Public Prosecutor asked.

'No,' replied Hoogendijk. 'The art historians agree that there should be more, that the *Emmaus* could not be the only one of its kind. I sold the *Head of Christ* to Dr van Beuningen. That was in 1941, in Rotterdam. It was a much finer painting then than it is now.'

Asked how he accounted for the acceptance of the *Blessing of Jacob*, the witness turned to have another look at it where it hung on the wall of the court-room before replying.

'Yes, it's difficult to explain,' he said after studying the painting for a minute or two. 'It is unbelievable that it fooled me. But we all slid downwards—from the *Emmaus* to the *Last Supper*, from the *Last Supper* to the *Blessing of Jacob*. When I look at them now, I don't understand how it could possibly have happened. A psychologist could explain it better than I can. But it should be remembered that the war-time atmosphere contributed to our blindness, and in particular the *Emmaus* had been declared authentic by experts of world-wide reputation. There was also the desire to keep the paintings in Holland.'

In fact a psychologist, or properly speaking a psychiatrist, did take the stand, and testified in professional jargon. 'The character of the defendant leads to sensitiveness to criticism, fed by a revenge complex which explains his anti-social attitude,' this witness stated. 'I would describe him as disequilibriated but fully responsible for his actions.' The psychiatrist went on to say that in his opinion a man of van Meegeren's personality 'would be greatly hurt by being kept in isolation', and he consequently would not advise a prison sentence in his case.

Dr Hannema, the Director of the Boymans Museum, was then called to the witness stand. He described how *The Washing of Christ's Feet* had been bought by the Government, though it was never hung. 'I immediately got the impression that it was a Vermeer,' said the museum director. 'It was examined by a Government committee which decided to advise its purchase. None of us liked it much, but we were afraid it would go to Germany.'

'But you also bought it for its artistic value?' queried the Public Prosecutor.

'Of course,' Dr Hannema agreed. 'After all, Vermeers are scarce.'

'Did no one inquire about the origin of the work?'

'Yes, but it was all very vague.'

The museum director was followed on the stand by Dr van Beuningen. He said he had always been convinced of the authenticity of his three purchases, the two Vermeers and the de Hoogh. 'I never had any doubts,' he declared.

When the evidence was concluded, the presiding judge asked the man in the dock, 'You still admit that you painted all these fakes?'

'Yes, Mr President,' answered van Meegeren.

'And also that you sold them, at a very high price?'

'I had no alternative. If I had sold them at a low price, it would have been an indication that they were false.'

'Why did you continue after the *Emmaus*?' the judge persisted.

'I found the process so beautiful,' van Meegeren replied blandly. 'I came to a condition in which I was no longer my own master. I became without will, powerless. I was forced to continue.'

'That's all very well,' said the judge with more than a hint of sarcasm. 'At least you made a nice little profit.'

'I had to, Mr President,' said the prisoner. 'I had been so belittled by the critics that I could no longer exhibit my own work under my own signature.'

'Perhaps the financial side had *some* influence on your actions?'

'It made little difference,' answered van Meegeren. 'The millions I earned from the later pictures were added to the millions I had earned already. I didn't do it for the money, which brought me nothing but trouble and unhappiness.'

'So you acted from no desire for financial gain?'

'Only from a desire to paint. I decided to carry on, not primarily from a desire to paint forgeries but to make the best use of the technique I had developed. I intend to continue using that technique. It's an excellent one. But I will never again offer my paintings as Old Masters.'

In his closing speech the Public Prosecutor, who was well aware of the considerable public sympathy expressed for van Meegeren for having so successfully fooled the art world, did not press the case against the defendant with any noticeable enthusiasm. He asked for a two-year prison sentence, half the maximum under the relevant article in the Penal Code.

It was then the turn of Meester Heldring, van Meegeren's defence counsel. His speech was witty and persuasive and at times anecdotal. For instance, he told how his client visited the Boymans Museum in 1938 to view the acquisition of the latest Vermeer and was reproved by the attendant on duty for coming too close to it. Counsel went on to analyse each of the sales and argued that in none of them was there any element of fraud or false pretences. It was true, he said, that certain 'clever artifices' had been used in the painting, but there had been 'no tricks' in the selling. It had never been said (except possibly to Strijbis) that a canvas *was* a Vermeer or a de Hoogh, or even that it might be—in each case this had been left to the expert or the dealer or the buyer to decide. Of course, he continued, there was the little matter of the signatures, but 'really a signature was not so very important as a guide to authenticity'. On the fraud charge Meester Heldring submitted that his client was not guilty and asked for an acquittal. On the forgery charge he asked the court to exercise the 'utmost leniency' and pass a suspended sentence.

Asked by the presiding judge whether he had anything to say, van Meegeren replied 'No'. The court then adjourned for a fortnight to consider its verdict and van Meegeren, who had been granted bail, went home. On 12 November he was brought up again to hear the judge's verdict: guilty on both counts, for which he was sentenced to one year in prison, the minimum possible. The court also ordered that the forged paintings should be returned to their owners, with the exception of *The Young Christ* which van Meegeren had painted at the instigation of the police. This was to be sold for the benefit of his creditors in his bankruptcy. It was duly put up for auction and bought by a dealer in The Hague for 3,000 guilders (about £300). It was later sold to the South African diamond magnate Sir Ernest Oppenheimer and is now in a church in Johannesburg.

Van Meegeren's counsel drafted a petition for a free pardon which was forwarded to Queen Juliana. Since the Public Prosecutor stated that he would not oppose it, there is little doubt that it would have been granted if the master forger had lived. But before the Queen's decision could be announced, van Meegeren suffered a fatal heart attack. He died at the Valerium Clinic in Amsterdam on 29 December 1947.

# 19

# Death in Cabin 126

The scene in the Assize Court in Winchester Castle on the morning of 18 March 1948 when stocky, thirty-one-year-old James Camb appeared in the dock on the charge of murdering a woman passenger on board the vessel where he worked as a deck steward, was an unusual one. For one thing, the court was unable to sit in the chamber it customarily occupied owing to the subsidence of a wall of the castle, and had to make do with temporary accommodation formed by plywood partitions. The bizarre appearance of the makeshift court was heightened by a large array of exhibits which had been introduced by the prosecution. They included a cabin bed, pillows, sheets and towels, a bell push and a porthole mounted on a wooden frame and a collection of miscellaneous objects ranging from women's cosmetics to a female contraceptive appliance.

The trial judge, Mr Justice Hilbery, was accompanied on the bench by the High Sheriff and his chaplain. The prosecution was led by Mr G. D. Roberts, KC, a former international rugby footballer of renown, known affectionately throughout the legal profession as 'Khaki Roberts', a nickname he had received from an early appearance on the rugger field. Mr J. D. Casswell, KC, another athletic barrister who had represented Oxford three times in the Long Jump, led for the defence. Both men were leading counsel on the Western Circuit and well matched in forensic skill as well as athletic prowess.

When the prisoner was asked to plead to the indictment by the Clerk of the Court, he answered 'Not guilty, sir' in a clear and confident voice. His confident and even jaunty demeanour throughout the four days of the trial was to contrast strongly with the story he was to tell of losing his head and becoming panic-stricken on the night of the previous 18 October. As a result, James Camb was charged with murdering a young actress named Eileen Isabella Ronnie Gibson, professionally known as Gay Gibson, on the high seas in the Union Castle liner *Durban Castle* on the night in question. The accused steward was married with one daughter, and inclined to promiscuous behaviour with other women.

In opening the case for the prosecution to the jury, 'Khaki' Roberts drew their attention to two peculiar features of the case. The first was that a crime committed on a British ship wherever committed—and this one was stated to have been committed about ninety miles off the West African coast when the *Durban Castle* was sailing through a shark-infested sea—is subject to the jurisdiction of the British courts. Secondly, Gay Gibson's mortal remains were never recovered. 'There is no body here, no *corpus delicti* as the lawyers say,' observed the prosecutor, adding that though this was unusual it was by no means unprecedented. According to the prosecution, the ship's steward had disposed of her body by pushing it through her cabin porthole, either after he had strangled her or after he had overcome her resistance when she was still alive.

Mr Roberts went on to outline the dead woman's background and the events leading up to her disappearance from the *Durban Castle* on her homeward-bound voyage to Southampton. Although born in India, where her father was a businessman, she had been educated in England and had served during the war in the Auxiliary Territorial Service (ATS); she later transferred to a theatrical touring company of service personnel known as 'Stars in Battledress', since she had always hankered for a career on the stage. Early in 1947, she and her mother left England for South Africa to join her father who was employed near Durban. Feeling that there was more scope for her as an actress in Johannesburg she went there shortly after her twenty-first birthday, and there happened to meet an actor-producer named Henry Gilbert, who was so impressed by her performance in a radio show that he immediately cast her as leading lady in *The Man with a Load of Mischief*. In this she played opposite Eric Boon, ex-lightweight British boxing champion. Unfortunately the successful run of this play was unexpectedly terminated by the discovery that the theatre did not comply with existing fire regulations, and before the producer could arrange for it to go on at another theatre Gay Gibson decided to return to England and try her fortune on the West End stage. It was with this end in view that she hopefully embarked on the *Durban Castle* at Cape Town on 10 October 1947, in the prosecution's words, 'to all appearances a healthy girl, bright and cheerful, and looking forward to continuing her theatrical career in this country'.

Miss Gibson occupied Cabin 126 on B deck on the port side of the ship. There was not a great deal of activity among the passengers since the ship was less than half full, and one day passed very much like another as it does on shipboard, uneventful and to most people probably rather boring. Gay Gibson usually had her meals in the saloon with a Mr Hopwood, an official of the Union Castle line, and a Wing-Commander Bray, and she would go to bed about eleven-thirty, when Mr Hopwood made a habit of seeing her to the door of her cabin where he would bid her good night. From the outset of the voyage James Camb, who was the promenade deck steward, took an interest in Miss Gibson and when they were a few days out from Cape Town he suddenly asked Miss Field, Gay Gibson's cabin stewardess, if she knew that Miss Gibson was three months' pregnant, adding that Miss Gibson had told him so herself. The stewardess replied that if true it was a dangerous thing to say, and the conversation finished.

About five o'clock in the evening of 17 October, Miss Field saw Camb near Miss Gibson's cabin, and suspecting that he might be going there she told him that if he did so she would report it, since the deck steward's duties were confined to the promenade deck and the gallery leading off it and he was not permitted to go to any of the passengers' cabins. About two hours later the stewardess saw Gay Gibson dressed in a black evening gown and silver shoes, ready for dinner and the dance which was to take place afterwards. She seemed to be very happy and cheerful. As usual she sat at the same table as Mr Hopwood and Wing-Commander Bray, and later she danced with the Wing-Commander and two other passengers. She had two or three drinks in the course of the evening and smoked very little. About eleven o'clock there was some talk of having a swim in the ship's pool, since it was a hot night, and Gay Gibson left the others, saying she was going to her cabin to look for a swim suit. Half an hour later she returned, saying she could not find it. She remained for some time with the other two leaning over the ship's rail and chatting until 12.40 a.m. when Mr Hopwood escorted her to her cabin as was his custom and said good night to her—as it happened, for the last time.

Several curious things occurred in the course of the evening and night hours. During the time that Gay Gibson left her two table companions to look for her swim suit, the ship's senior night-watchman, James Murray, observed her and Camb talking together in the long gallery which led off the promenade deck. He overheard the deck steward say, 'I have a bone to pick with you, and a big one at that.' He was unable to hear any more. Later it appeared that after Hopwood had said good night to her, she did not go to bed immediately, since about one o'clock the boatswain's mate, whose name was Conway, saw her on the after end of the deck on the port side, leaning against the rail and smoking a cigarette. She was still wearing her black evening dress and silver shoes. Conway was in charge of a working party engaged in washing down the promenade deck and told her that she would get wet if she stayed where she was. She thanked him and said she had found it 'too hot down below'. That was the last time he saw her. It was indeed a fine, hot night, as one might expect in the tropics. The bow wave was curling back and hitting the ship's sides, while the steady roar of the dynamos came from the engine-room behind the bridge.

Suddenly, a few minutes before 3 a.m., the nightwatchman, who was sitting with his assistant, Frederick Steer, in the first-class galley on A deck, heard a cabin bell ring above their heads. It was the nightwatchman's duty to answer any of the cabin bells which at that time were all switched through to the galley.

Accordingly Steer made his way to B deck, where the indicator showed that the bell had been rung in Cabin 126. On reaching this cabin he saw that two lights were showing outside, green and red, indicating that both the steward and the stewardess had been rung for. This struck Steer as odd, since normally a passenger would ring for either one or the other.

The light was on in the cabin and shone through the grille in the door. Steer knocked and tried to enter. The door was opened a few inches and then suddenly shut in his face, but not before the nightwatchman was able to see a man's face, right hand and body, clad in a sleeveless singlet and dark trousers held up by a belt. It was Camb, the deck steward. As he shut the door, Camb said, 'It's all right!'

Steer immediately returned to the galley to report to Murray, and together they went back to Cabin 126. The lights were still on, but no sound came from within. After listening for some minutes and hearing nothing, Murray went up to the bridge and reported the matter to the officer of the watch. But not wishing to get a fellow member of the crew into trouble he did not tell the officer that it was Camb whom his mate had seen. The officer thereupon dismissed him, saying that the morals of the passengers were their own affair.

At about seven-thirty the same morning, Miss Field, the stewardess, went to Cabin 126 and, receiving no answer to her knock, tried the door. It was open, which she considered unusual, since she knew that Miss Gibson was in the habit of locking her cabin at night and unlocking it when the stewardess called her in the morning. At first she did not attach much importance to the fact that the cabin was empty, since she thought that Miss Gibson might have gone to the bathroom. However, she noticed that the bed was rather more disarranged than usual, and she also noted that there were one or two stains on the sheet and pillow case. When Miss Gibson did not return, the stewardess became anxious and eventually reported her absence to the Captain, whose name was Patey. After the ship had been thoroughly searched without result, the Captain concluded that she must have gone overboard and ordered the ship to reverse course, at the same time alerting all other ships in the neighbourhood by radio. But Captain Patey soon realised that a search for a missing passenger in such a vast expanse of shark-infested sea was hopeless, and he ordered the ship to resume her normal course.

Soon afterwards Steer told the Captain that it was Camb whom he had seen in Cabin 126. The Captain then sent for the deck steward and told him that he was suspected of having been there. Camb at once denied it, and said that he had not been near any passenger cabin since he had gone to bed at twelve-forty-five. Next day Camb agreed to submit to a medical examination, since Captain Patey told him that it was in his own interest to do so. He was accordingly seen by the ship's surgeon, Dr Griffiths, who found scratches on his shoulders and wrists. Camb explained them

by saying that they were self-inflicted, since he had felt itchy due
to the heat some days previously and had scratched himself.

Meanwhile the police in Southampton were informed by ship's
radio of what had happened, and in the circumstances Camb was
held for questioning when the *Durban Castle* docked. At first the
steward repeated his previous denial to Captain Patey that he
knew anything about Gay Gibson's disappearance. But on being
further questioned he made a statement to the effect that he had
been in her cabin, sexual intercourse had taken place between
them with her consent, and that while still in the act of copulation
she had clutched at him and foamed at the mouth, after which she
was suddenly still and he could hear no sound of her heart beating. He then tried artificial respiration without success, after which
he lifted her body to the porthole and pushed it through. He was
fairly certain she was dead, but he felt 'terribly frightened'.

Camb was told that he would be detained and was then charged
with murder. 'I did not think it would be as serious as this,' he
told another police officer who came to his cell to arrange for his
fingerprints and photograph to be taken. 'I can't understand why
the officer of the watch did not hear something. It was the hell of
a splash when she hit the water. She struggled. I had my hands
around her neck, and when I was trying to get them away she
scratched me. I panicked and threw her out of the porthole.'

However, the inference which the prosecuting counsel invited
the jury to draw was that Miss Gibson objected to the prisoner's
advances, and she pressed both bells for outside help. She
scratched the prisoner and then for his self-preservation he
strangled her. Alternatively Mr Roberts suggested to the jury that
they might think that in order to destroy the evidence of rape or
attempted rape which might be proved against him Camb had
thrown her out of the porthole into the sea.

The most significant exhibits put in by the prosecution were the
two sheets on the bed in Cabin 126, which revealed traces of
human blood belonging to 'Group O'. These smears also showed
traces of saliva and lipstick. Camb's blood group was 'A', so that
it would appear that the blood came from the body of Gay
Gibson. In addition, a contraceptive appliance was found in a
suitcase in the cabin which belonged to the dead woman. It was
unused and its existence was to throw grave doubts on Camb's
story that there had been sexual intercourse with her consent.

Captain Patey and various members of the ship's company, including boatswain's mate Conway, the nightwatchmen Murray and Steer, and Gay Gibson's stewardess Miss Field, as well as her table companion Mr Hopwood, all confirmed their recollections of Miss Gibson during the time she was on board the *Durban Castle*. Dr Griffiths and other medical witnesses also testified, but Griffiths was the only one to see Camb within a few hours of Gay Gibson's disappearance, when the scratches on his body were still fresh, whereas the rest of the medical experts had to depend on photographs taken a week later after many of the scratches had healed. Dr Donald Teare, the well-known pathologist, testified for the prosecution as well. While agreeing that the bloodstains on the bedclothes were consistent with strangulation, he would have expected that there would also have been traces of urine. In fact, he was unaware that an examination conducted by another expert witness, who was to be called for the defence, Dr Frederick Hocking, showed that urine had in fact been passed by Miss Gibson 'as a terminal act', although this had not been revealed by the police laboratory findings which Dr Teare was bound to accept. Evidence was also given by the doctor who had examined Gay Gibson on her release from the ATS that her general physical condition was good.

Since the defence was that the prisoner was a welcome visitor to Gay Gibson's cabin and that her death was due to natural causes during the performance of the sexual act with him, it was inevitable that Camb's counsel should seek to prove in cross-examination that she was a young woman of easy morals. It is never pleasant to have to attack the character of a dead person, particularly when she is a girl, and Mr Casswell's tactics brought a dignified protest from his opponent. The suggestion that Gay Gibson was not averse to jumping into bed with casual male acquaintances was also indignantly denied by her mother, who was also called by the prosecution and would not hear anything against her child. She was one of the finest types of English womanhood, said Mrs Gibson, physically, mentally and morally. 'My daughter was not pregnant,' she declared with emphasis.

'Did you know your daughter was going about with several men in Johannesburg?' Mr Casswell asked her.

This Mrs Gibson again denied. 'She told me everything and I know she was not interested in men. Her career was her life.'

'Can you explain the contraceptive which was found in her cabin?'

The witness brushed this question aside. 'You know university students and others often carry them about with them,' she said. 'That is nothing to go by.'

While denying that her daughter had misconducted herself with several men whose names were put to her, Mrs Gibson admitted that a man named Charles Sventonski had paid her passage to England and had given her £500. 'It was a business proposition,' the witness explained. 'He was ready to back her in her career as a business proposition.'

'You say you see nothing wrong in your daughter accepting £500 from a man she had only known for a short time?'

'She said she would very soon pay him back. She was a hard-working conscientious girl, and she was hoping to become successful in her career.'

Mr Casswell then opened the defence and called the prisoner to the witness box. He appeared calm and self-possessed, showing no visible signs of emotion, as his counsel took him through his story and later when subjected to a most probing cross-examination by the prosecutor. He confirmed that the second or third day out of Cape Town Gay Gibson ordered a drink and they fell into conversation. She told him that she was in love with a man named Charles in Johannesburg and thought she might be going to have a baby, though it was too soon to tell yet. Camb later brought afternoon tea to her cabin and she gave him a standing order for a supper tray to be left outside her cabin at night. He explained the words he had been overheard using, 'I have a bone to pick with you, and a big one at that', as referring to the fact that she had not used her supper tray the night before or her tea tray that day.

About eleven o'clock that evening he had followed her down to her cabin after he had overheard her saying that she was going to look for a swim suit. A glass of rum had been left on her supper tray and Camb, according to his story, said he had a good mind to bring down a drink later and join her. She replied something like, 'Please yourself—it's up to you.' In fact, he did join her in her cabin shortly before 1 a.m. She was lying on the bed in a dressing-gown but wore no pyjamas underneath and appeared naked when she removed it and Camb got into bed with her.

'What happened after that?'

'There was a certain amount of preliminary love play, and then sexual intercourse took place.'

'When sexual intercourse took place, what were your relative positions?'

'I was lying on top of Miss Gibson. I was face down.'

'What happened in the end?'

'She suddenly heaved under me as though she was gasping for breath.'

'What happened to her body?'

'It stiffened for a fraction of a second and then relaxed completely limp.'

'What did you do when her body showed these symptoms?' counsel went on.

'I immediately got off the bed,' the witness answered. 'She was completely relaxed as though she was in a dead faint. One eye was just slightly open. Her mouth was a little open too. There was a faint line of bubbles which I assumed to be froth, just on the edges of the lips. It was a muddy colour and appeared to be slightly blood-flecked.'

According to his story, the prisoner then tried to revive her and when she remained senseless he lost his head and put her out of the porthole. When Steer had tapped on the door, he admitted saying, 'All right.' But he could not account for the pressing of the bells. Nor would he admit that he had received any injuries from Miss Gibson. He also denied having made the statement to the police about her struggling and the body going into the water with 'the hell of a splash'.

'Would you describe yourself as a truthful man?' was the first question put to him in cross-examination by Mr Roberts. It was a deadly one.

'I think so, sir.'

'You do,' counsel went on. 'You were the last person to see Miss Gibson alive?'

'Yes.'

'You put her through the porthole at three o'clock on the morning of 18 October?'

'Yes.'

'Did you for the next eight days make untrue statements with regard to that, on at least six occasions?'

'I did that, yes,' Camb admitted. 'I was thinking only of myself.'

'Self-preservation,' commented the prosecutor. 'Did you intend to persist in that untrue denial on your part?'

'I think I did.'

'Did you intend to take that secret with you to your grave?'

'I would say yes.'

'No matter what unhappiness or misery was caused to her relations or anyone else?'

'By that time I had already entangled myself into lies.'

'When did you decide to alter your story?'

'In the police headquarters.'

'Why?' counsel rapped out the word sharply.

'I realised by then that I was definitely incriminated by the witness Steer,' replied Camb. He went on to agree with the prosecutor that he had told an untrue story until he felt that that story would not serve its purpose of saving him.

'Don't you call that curious conduct for a truthful person?'

'I should say it was beastly conduct,' was the witness's candid if callous reply. His behaviour in the witness box did not impress either the judge or the jury in his favour.

The defence called a number of witnesses from South Africa, including Henry Gilbert, the actor-producer, and his wife Ina, who was a medical doctor, and also another actor named Mike Abel, who had played with Gay Gibson in the theatre there, to show that she suffered from a variety of complaints, including asthma, which might have caused or contributed to her death. Abel swore that she had five fainting fits and on one occasion her lips went blue. She was also said to be hysterical and neurotic. Dr Ina Schoub, Gilbert's wife, had not examined her professionally, she said, but she stated in evidence that Gay Gibson had discussed sex with her rather intimately. 'She told me that she had had sexual experience and that she was expecting a period within the next week.' Later, when her period was overdue, Dr Schoub said she had asked her whether she had used a contraceptive during her sexual experience. 'She looked very blankly at me,' the witness went on. 'She didn't seem to know anything about it, and asked me to explain things to her. I told her about it, and advised that she should be fitted with a Dutch cap.' Dr Schoub did not know whether Gay Gibson had taken her advice. She added that the contraceptive appliance found in her belongings was 'not quite the same thing' as a Dutch cap which 'should be fitted by a doctor'.

The last two defence witnesses were pathologists, Dr Frederick Hocking and Professor James Webster. Their testimony was to the effect that in their opinion Gay Gibson's death might have occurred in the way Camb had described. However, the former doctor also testified that he had examined the top sheet on the bed in Gay Gibson's cabin and that this examination, which had not been noticed by the government pathologists, revealed the presence of dried urine, in which were some cells of the type which line the external female sex organs. He agreed as did Professor Webster that in cases of strangulation it was a common feature for the bladder to discharge its contents.

These admissions, though made by defence witnesses, in fact greatly strengthened the case for the prosecution, since the presence of urine contradicted Camb's story that at the moment of the girl's death his body was on top of hers, as obviously in that event the urine would have been ejected over him. The virtually irresistible inference was that he was not in contact with that part of the girl's body at all but was at the head of the bed, gripping her throat to prevent any further attempt on her part to summon aid.

At all events, that was what the jury came to the conclusion had happened, since it took them only three-quarters of an hour, after a fair but unfavourable summing-up by Mr Justice Hilbery, to find the prisoner guilty. Asked by the Clerk of the Court whether he had anything to say why judgment of death should not be passed upon him, he repeated that he was not guilty. The judge then put on the black cap and sentenced James Camb to be hanged by the neck until he was dead.

The Court of Criminal Appeal held that there was no ground for interfering in the case and dismissed Camb's appeal. Nevertheless he escaped the gallows as the result of a fortunate accident for him. While the appeal was pending, the House of Commons on a free vote added a new clause to the Criminal Justice Bill then before Parliament, suspending the death penalty for five years and substituting life imprisonment for murder. Although the House of Lords subsequently rejected it, the Home Secretary decided that during the interval while the issue remained in doubt all pending capital sentences should be commuted to life imprisonment. Camb was one of those to benefit in this way.

It subsequently transpired—and this could not be put in evidence at the trial—that Camb had assaulted other women passengers on three different occasions on the *Durban Castle*. Once he entered a woman's cabin and made advances to her, which she had only been able to repel after a struggle. He did this again without success in the case of another female passenger. Finally he tried to strangle a woman passenger in a shelter on deck where tools were kept, she lost consciousness and eventually recovered to find Camb standing over her. Again, fortunately for Camb, none of these women had dared to report the matter for fear of the publicity which was bound to result.

James Camb was released from prison on licence in September 1959. He changed his surname to Clarke and got a job as a head waiter. In May 1967 he was convicted of indecently assaulting a girl of thirteen and somewhat surprisingly was put on probation for two years. Some time after that he went to Scotland where he again obtained employment as head waiter in a hotel. Here he was charged with sexual misbehaviour with three schoolgirls, as a result of which his licence was revoked and he was returned to jail to continue his life sentence. An obvious sexual psychopath, he should never have been set at liberty in the first place.

# 20

# The Atom Bomb Spies

The trial which began on 5 March 1951 in the Federal Court House in Foley Square, New York City, may well prove to be the most celebrated espionage trial in American history. Certainly no case of its kind in the United States has had wider ramifications and repercussions, both nationally and internationally. There were three defendants, Julius Rosenberg, his wife Ethel, and their confederate Morton Sobell, who had fled to Mexico but had subsequently been extradited. They were jointly charged with conspiring together with others including Ethel Rosenberg's brother David Greenglass; Harry Gold, a Swiss-born Russian whose real name was Goldnitsky; and Anatoli Yakovlev, a Soviet agent who was ostensibly a clerk in the Soviet Consulate-General in New York. The object of the alleged conspiracy was a plan to deliver information, documents, sketches and material vital to the national defence of the United States to a foreign power, namely Soviet Russia, in violation of the Espionage Act of 1917. All these individuals had originally been charged in the same Grand Jury indictment. However, Gold pleaded guilty and was sentenced to thirty years. Greenglass and Yakovlev were ordered to be tried separately, but Greenglass who had also pleaded guilty had not yet been sentenced. Yakovlev was not apprehended, since he managed to make good his escape to the Soviet Union before the FBI agents could catch up with him.

The Hon. Irving R. Kaufman, one of the district judges for the Southern District of New York, presided on the bench. The prosecution was led by US District Attorney Irving H. Saypol, who had three assistants. The Rosenbergs were defended by

Emanuel H. Bloch, a well-known criminal lawyer, and his father Alexander Bloch. O. John Rogge held a watching brief for Greenglass who was expected to testify for the prosecution.

After the three defendants on trial had pleaded not guilty, the District Attorney opened the case for the prosecution. 'The significance of a conspiracy to commit espionage,' he said, speaking in deadly earnest tones, 'takes on an added meaning here where the defendants are charged with having participated in a conspiracy against our country at the most critical hour in its history, in a time of war. . . .

'The evidence will reveal to you how the Rosenbergs persuaded David Greenglass . . . to plot the treacherous role of a modern Benedict Arnold while wearing the uniform of the United States Army. . . . We will prove that the Rosenbergs devised and put into operation with the aid of Soviet nationals and Soviet agents in this country an elaborate scheme which enabled them, through Greenglass, to steal the one weapon which might well hold the key to the survival of this nation and the peace of the world—the atomic bomb.'

The prosecutor gave due credit to the FBI for breaking the spy ring. At the same time he made it clear that this could not have been done had it not been for the information revealed by a German-born naturalised British subject named Klaus Fuchs, who had pleaded guilty in England to spying for the Soviet Union and received the maximum sentence of fourteen years under the relevant British statute. Fuchs, who was one of the senior scientific officers at the British Atomic Research Establishment at Harwell, had been sent to the United States during the war to co-operate in the development and production of the atomic bomb at Los Alamos and he had witnessed the explosion of the first test bomb in New Mexico. Nothing was hidden from him, said J. Edgar Hoover, Director of the FBI. 'Dr Fuchs had all our greatest secrets.' After Fuchs began to serve his sentence in England, FBI agents were allowed to question him, and it was as a result that the Bureau got on to the trail of the Soviet spy ring in America. Fuchs was able to identify Harry Gold, a biochemist whom the FBI had previously suspected of being active in Soviet espionage but whom it had hitherto been impossible to incriminate. The British in their turn had picked up Fuchs through the revelations of a Russian cypher clerk named Igor Gouzenko, who was employed in the Military Attaché's office in the Soviet Embassy in Ottawa.

The first of the star witnesses to be called to the stand was Max Elitcher, an electronics engineer who had worked in the US Navy Bureau of Ordnance between 1938 and 1948. Elitcher admitted to being a Communist and to have become a member of a 'cell' at Sobell's solicitation. It was also through Sobell that the witness had met the Rosenbergs and learned that they were active party members and secret Soviet agents. Julius Rosenberg, Elitcher went on, invited him to participate in the transmission of secret information from the ordnance office files. Elitcher swore that he pretended to do so, but in fact he had never given Rosenberg any information classified as secret. Under cross-examination, Elitcher admitted that he lied when he took a loyalty oath, but he firmly insisted that 'ever since the FBI got hold of him he had told the entire truth'. Finally Elitcher admitted that he had regularly acted as a courier between Sobell and Rosenberg.

Ruth Greenglass then testified that her husband had been a Communist and described how in the autumn of 1944 Julius Rosenberg had asked her to go to Los Alamos and obtain classified information from her husband David, who was a member of the US armed forces and was working on an atomic bomb project there. At first she demurred, but Julius assured her that her husband would want to help. Russia was an ally of the US, argued Julius, and as such deserved information about the bomb, but she was not getting the information which she should. Eventually, said the witness, she agreed to make the trip as her second wedding anniversary was coming up and she wanted to spend it with her husband. Julius gave her $150 for her trip, saying the money came from 'his friends the Russians'.

At first David Greenglass was reluctant to co-operate, but next morning he agreed to give his wife 'the general layout of the Los Alamos project', together with the number of employees, the experiments being conducted and the names of the scientists working there. The witness carefully memorised this information, she said, and duly passed it on to Julius Rosenberg on her return to New York.

In January 1945, the witness continued, her husband came to New York on leave, and they both met the Rosenbergs by appointment at the latter's apartment. They were introduced to a Mrs

Sidorovich. First they discussed the kind of information David Greenglass should look out for when he returned to Los Alamos. Rosenberg then explained that Mrs Sidorovich might be sent to New Mexico to get this information from Greenglass, and he produced two torn halves of a Jello box top. It was arranged that the witness, who planned to return to New Mexico with her husband, should keep one part, and whoever was sent to get into touch with her and her husband would establish his or her identity by producing the other half. Ruth Greenglass remembered that when her husband commented on the simplicity and cleverness of this device, Julius Rosenberg remarked, 'The simplest things are always the cleverest.'

In the event contact was made in June 1945 when the witness and her husband were living in Albuquerque, New Mexico. Early one morning a man called. 'I come from Julius,' he said and produced the matching piece of the Jello box top. Ruth Greenglass identified him as Harry Gold, who gave her husband $500 which David Greenglass handed over to her.

By May 1950, the witness said, she and her husband, who had been discharged from the army, were back in New York, and their relations with the Rosenbergs were closer than ever. On 24 May, according to Ruth, Julius Rosenberg burst into their apartment brandishing a copy of the New York *Herald Tribune*, which carried a picture of Harry Gold on the front page accompanied by the news of his arrest as a Soviet spy. 'You will be next,' said Julius, and urged them to escape at once to Mexico. Ruth did not think their ten-month-old baby could stand the trip, but Rosenberg brushed aside her objection and left $1,000 with them to cover preliminary expenses, telling her to have passport photographs taken and get inoculated against smallpox. But in spite of these warnings the Greenglasses stayed in New York and on 15 June David was arrested.

In cross-examination, Alexander Bloch tried to bring out that the witness knew she had committed a crime and that her direct testimony had been influenced by fear of the FBI. 'Weren't you frightened of the FBI?'

'Everyone is frightened by the FBI,' Ruth Greenglass replied, 'but it was not because I realised it was a crime that I was frightened. I didn't think the FBI wanted my husband. I thought they wanted someone my husband would lead them to, someone much more important than he and much more deeply involved.'

David Greenglass generally corroborated his wife's testimony when he followed her on the witness stand. However, he denied that he had known of the atomic bomb until he had learned about it from Julius Rosenberg. As a machinist at Los Alamos, he knew only that he was working on 'a secret device of some kind'. The details he insisted he had first learned from Rosenberg in January 1945—'fissionable material at one end of a tube and on the other end a sliding mechanism with fissionable material, and when the two were brought together under tremendous pressure nuclear reaction was accomplished'. As far as it went, this description fitted the uranium bomb which was dropped on Hiroshima eight months later.

In the following September, the witness and his wife, he said, made a trip to New York where he met the Rosenbergs and handed over a sketch of the atom bomb and a ten-page analysis, which Ethel later typed out. 'This is *very* good,' said Julius when he read it. These particulars, said David Greenglass, related to the plutonium bomb which was dropped on Nagasaki. The witness's testimony in this regard revealed such an expert knowledge that Judge Kaufman ordered the court to be cleared and cautioned the newspaper reporters present 'to exercise discretion in what they printed'. Whether or not the witness's technical evidence was understood by the jury, it clearly established that David Greenglass had been an effective spy, and had passed a mass of scientific information relating to the atomic bomb to the Rosenbergs who had in turn passed it on to the Soviet Union.

The tension created in the court-room by the witness's long recital of treachery was relieved by a small touch of humour at its close. Asked in cross-examination if, when looking at the Jello box top, he noticed the flavour, 'Yes, raspberry,' he promptly replied. This answer raised the only laugh in these sombre proceedings.

Harry Gold was the next prosecution witness. He told how he had been working for the Russians as far back as 1935, and how in 1944 he acted as a go-between for Russian agents and persons who procured information for them. At that time his Soviet superior was Anatoli Yakovlev, but Gold only knew him as 'John'. It was at Yakovlev's instruction that in June 1944 the witness first met Fuchs who promised to give him information 'relating to the application of nuclear fission to the production of a military weapon'. At a subsequent meeting in Cambridge, Mass., in January 1945 Fuchs told the witness that he was working on the atomic bomb with other scientists in Los Alamos, which he described, particularly mentioning a lens which was one of its essential parts. It was agreed between them that Gold should visit Los Alamos in June when Fuchs hoped to have more information about the bomb and its lens.

When Gold told Yakovlev of this, the Soviet master spy intimated that he had another very 'vital' job for him in New Mexico, namely to contact Greenglass in Albuquerque. At first the witness objected, he said, but when Yakovlev insisted he agreed, since he took this to be an order. After he had seen Fuchs and obtained a sealed envelope from him, Gold went on to Albuquerque where he met the Greenglasses as already described and received another envelope from them. A few days later he reported to Yakovlev in Brooklyn, handing over the two envelopes, which Yakovlev later told him contained 'extremely excellent and very valuable' information. The witness's last meeting with Yakovlev took place at the end of 1946, the day before Yakovlev sailed for Europe.

Gold was not cross-examined. This was good tactics on the part of Sobell's attorneys, since Gold's testimony had not implicated their client in any way. As for the Rosenbergs' counsel, they may well have decided not to cross-examine, because Gold had shown himself eager to help the Government in any way he could and answers elicited in cross-examination might only have made matters worse for the Rosenbergs.

Several other witnesses testified to the value of the information imparted by Greenglass as being of 'inestimable value to a nation which did not possess the secret of nuclear fission'. If Sobell and the Rosenbergs had committed the crime they were charged with, they said, their actions seriously jeopardised the security of the United States. The last material witness was a former well-known member of the American Communist Party named Elizabeth Bentley, who had gone over to the Government. While working for the Communists one of her contacts, who often telephoned her, she said, was a man who identified himself as 'Julius'.

Emanuel Bloch opened the defence by calling Julius Rosenberg to the witness stand. Answering his attorney, Rosenberg admitted that he was a first-generation American of Russian parents who had migrated to New York City. He was a Bachelor of Science, having graduated from New York City College. He told how he married Ethel Greenglass and in 1940 became a junior engineer in the US Signals Corps, from which he was dismissed five years later.

'Did you ever have any conversation with Ruth Greenglass about November 1944 with respect to getting information from David Greenglass at the place where he was working?'

'I did not.'

'Did you know in the middle of 1944 where David Greenglass was stationed?'

'I did not.'

'Did you know in the middle of 1944 that there was such a project known as the Los Alamos project?'

'I did not.'

'Did you ever give Ruth Greenglass $150, or any other sum for her to go out to visit her husband at Los Alamos for the purpose of trying to enlist him in espionage work?'

'I did not.'

Julius Rosenberg denied everything. Shown the sketch of the atomic bomb that David Greenglass had made, the witness denied that his brother-in-law had ever delivered such a sketch to him. 'I never saw this sketch before.' Apart from what he had heard in court, he could not describe the bomb. Nor had he ever taken a course in nuclear or advanced physics. He also denied all knowledge of the Jello box top; he had never introduced David Greenglass to a Mrs Sidorovich; he had never met Elizabeth Bentley and had never spoken to her on the telephone. Nor had he tried to induce the Greenglasses to leave the country and he had not provided them with money for their trip. Finally he denied that he and his wife had ever contemplated fleeing the country themselves.

Asked in cross-examination by Saypol whether he had been discharged from his job in the Signals Corps because he was suspected of being a Communist and thus belonging to an illegal organisation, he was obliged to admit that this was so.

'Were you a member of the Communist party?' the District Attorney asked bluntly.

Rosenberg paused for a few moments. Then he replied: 'I refuse to answer on the ground that it might tend to incriminate me.'

He repeated this reply when confronted with a statement he had signed on joining the Signals Corps to the effect that he was not then and never had been a member of the Communist party. The court sustained the witness's objection to incriminating questions and ruled that he was not required to answer them.

At the same time, in answer to further questions, Rosenberg protested his loyalty to the United States. 'I will fight for this country if it were engaged in a war with any other country,' he declared. On the other hand he admitted that he felt some admiration for the achievements of the Russians, particularly in improving the lot of the underdog. 'I felt and still feel,' he added, 'that they contributed a major share in destroying the Hitler beast who killed six million of my co-religionists, and I feel emotional about that thing.'

Judge Haufman intervened at this point to ask a couple of questions which the witness tried to dodge.

'Did you approve the communist system of Russia over the capitalist system of this country?'

'I am not an expert on those things, Your Honour, and I did not make any such statement.'

'Did you ever belong to any group that discussed the system of Russia?'

Again the witness took refuge behind the protective constitutional amendment. 'Well, Your Honour, I feel at this time that I refuse to answer a question that might tend to incriminate me.'

Ethel Rosenberg's testimony was along the same lines. She blandly asserted that she was a loyal citizen of the United States and had never engaged in espionage. Everything her brother and sister-in-law had testified to was false, she said. But when she was asked in cross-examination about her affiliations with the Communist party, she refused to answer as her husband had done.

No further witnesses were called for the defence, since Morton Sobell did not testify.

In rebuttal, the prosecution called a New York commercial photographer, who stated that about mid-June 1950 the Rosenbergs and their two children had three sets of passport photographs taken in his studio. Mr Rosenberg, the witness said, told him that they were going to France to look at some property Mrs Rosenberg owned there.

In the closing speech to the jury on behalf of the Rosenbergs, Emanuel Bloch concentrated on the unreliability of Ruth and David Greenglass as witnesses. 'Don't you think that the Greenglasses put it over on the Government when Ruth Greenglass was not even indicted?' he asked the jurors. 'She walked out and put Greenglass's sister in. David Greenglass was willing to bury his sister and her husband to save his life. Not only are the Greenglasses self-confessed spies, but they are mercenary spies. They'd do anything for money. . . . Any man who will testify against his own flesh and blood, his own sister, is repulsive, revolting, and is violating any code of civilisation that ever existed. He is lower than the lowest animal I have ever seen.'

'The Greenglasses have told the truth,' said District Attorney Saypol in winding up for the prosecution. 'They have tried to make amends for the hurt which has been done to our nation and to the world.' As for the other major prosecution witness, Harry Gold, said the prosecutor, he could gain nothing by testifying as he did except the inward relief of having told the truth. 'Harry Gold forged the link that points indisputably to the guilt of the Rosenbergs, and he was not even asked one question in cross-examination.' In reality, the DA continued, the unreliable testimony came from the Rosenbergs, who had denied planning to leave the country, in spite of the testimony about the passport photographs. 'The Rosenbergs have magnified their treachery by lying here.' Furthermore they were linked with Sobell in their espionage activities, since Sobell had flown to Mexico with his family in the same month that Greenglass had been paid by the Russians through Rosenberg to do likewise. 'Sobell's conduct fits the pattern of membership in this conspiracy and flight from an American jury when the day of reckoning had come.'

After the fairest and most impartial summing up of the evidence by Judge Kaufman, the jury retired at four fifty-three in the afternoon of 28 March and did not return until eleven o'clock next morning when they pronounced all three defendants guilty as charged.

'Your crime is worse than murder,' Judge Kaufman told the Rosenbergs when they came up for sentence eight days later. 'In your case I believe your conduct in putting into the hands of the Russians the A-bomb years before our best scientists predicted Russia would perfect the bomb has already caused the Communist aggression in Korea, with resulting casualties exceeding 50,000 Americans, and who knows but that millions more of innocent people may pay the price of your treason?' The judge then formally sentenced them to death.

While not doubting for a moment that Morton Sobell was also engaged in espionage activities, the judge said he was bound to recognise the lesser degree of his implication. He was consequently given thirty years, the maximum prison term provided by the statute. Next day David Greenglass was sentenced to fifteen years in the light of the considerable help he had rendered in the prosecution of the Rosenbergs.

A series of appeals and petitions followed, which in the case of the Rosenbergs had the effect of delaying the execution of the death sentence for more than two years. Their petition for executive clemency was presented to President Truman on 11 January 1953. It was supported by a flood of letters mostly in favour of the sentence being commuted, among others by Albert Einstein, the world-famous scientist, and a group of 3,000 lawyers who declared that 'the death penalty would not conform to the great pattern of Anglo-Saxon jurisprudence'. But President Truman declined to act on the petition which reached him during the last days of his term of office, and he left the decision to General Dwight D. Eisenhower, his successor in the White House.

President Eisenhower refused to interfere with the sentence on the Rosenbergs. 'The nature of the crime for which they have been found guilty and sentenced far exceeds that of taking the life of another citizen,' the new President declared. 'It involves the deliberate betrayal of the entire nation and could very well result in the death of many, many thousands of innocent citizens. By their act these two individuals have in fact betrayed the cause of freedom for which free men are fighting and dying at this very hour.'

Meanwhile the appeals and motions for stays of execution continued. At the beginning of June, the Rosenbergs' counsel announced that his clients had rejected the offer which had been made to them on behalf of the Attorney-General that their sentences would be commuted to life imprisonment if they made full confessions and exposed any other members of their spy ring who had not been brought to justice. 'By asking us to repudiate the truth of our innocence,' they said at the time, 'the Government admits its doubts concerning our guilt. We will not help to purify this foul record of a fraudulent and barbarous sentence.' Shortly afterwards the Supreme Court voted by a majority of five to four against granting a further stay of execution.

At the last moment it looked as if there would be a stay when Supreme Court Justice Douglas ordered it in response to an application for time to argue a point of law, namely that the Espionage Act of 1917 had been superseded by the Atomic Energy Act of 1946, under which a death sentence could not be imposed except on the recommendation of a jury. On 19 June Justice Douglas's decision was revoked by a majority of the Supreme Court, Justices Douglas and Black dissenting, and Frankfurter in effect doing so with a plea for more time to consider. Defence counsel submitted a final petition to the President for clemency which Eisenhower again rejected, while conceding that the execution of two human beings was a grave matter. 'But even greater,' he said, 'is the thought of the millions of dead whose death may be directly attributable to what these spies have done.'

The Rosenbergs went to the electric chair in Sing Sing the same evening and met their end bravely, protesting their innocence to the last. The time of execution was advanced from the usual hour of 11 p.m. to 8 p.m. to avoid carrying out the sentences on the Jewish Sabbath. Julius and Ethel Rosenberg were the first Americans to be sentenced to death for espionage by a non-military court, while Mrs Rosenberg was the first woman in the United States, since Mrs Surratt had been sentenced for her part in the assassination of President Lincoln, to suffer death by the judgment of a Federal tribunal.

No one can seriously question the fairness of the trial or the manner in which the various appeals were conducted. The question remains, should the Rosenbergs have been executed for furnishing secret military information to an ally in time of war against a common enemy, bearing in mind that most of the incriminating evidence came from self-confessed accomplices? Many people think that they should not. It is for the reader with the advantage of hindsight to form his or her own judgment in the matter.

# Index